AINSLIE'S ENCYCLOPEDIA *of* THOROUGHBRED HANDICAPPING

AINSLIE'S ENCYCLOPEDIA of THOROUGHBRED HANDICAPPING

by TOM AINSLIE

WILLIAM MORROW AND COMPANY, INC.
NEW YORK   1978

Library of Congress Cataloging in Publication Data

Ainslie, Tom.
  Ainslie's encyclopedia of thoroughbred
handicapping.

   Includes index.
   1. Horse race betting—Dictionaries. I. Title.
II. Title: Encyclopedia of thoroughbred
handicapping.
SF331.A49   798′.401′03   78-9755
ISBN 0-688-03345-8

BOOK DESIGN   CARL WEISS

Printed in the United States of America.

5   6   7   8   9   10

PREFACE

This encyclopedia is for persons presently or potentially interested in Thoroughbred racing, an exciting sport which includes an audience-participation game—pari-mutuel wagering. It is possible to enjoy the sport without playing the game, but hardly anyone tries. The twin interests are inseparable for an overwhelming majority of racing fans, stable owners, horse trainers, supervisory officials, and racetrack executives and employees. They bet. Some of them bet successfully.

The function of the present work is to encourage development of the handicapping skill on which lasting enjoyment of Thoroughbred racing inevitably depends. Like encyclopedias in other fields, this one explores its subject comprehensively and alphabetically. Whatever is relevant to handicapping races and betting on horses will be found here. Whatever is not will not.

I have chosen an alphabetical presentation because it offers pleasant options. It favors browsing. It facilitates the search for specific information. And it enables readers to avoid material that may strike them as too familiar or tiresome.

The reader should be forewarned that handicapping is treated here as a splendid game rather than a shortcut to wealth. Although I know scores of handicappers who live on racetrack winnings and have done so myself, I can testify that professional horse-betting is a way of life unsuited to the normal personality. But when approached as a hobby, handicapping provides endless rewards, sometimes including money.

During the ten years since my last printed attempt to deal comprehensively with Thoroughbred handicapping, racing has undergone substantial changes. Accordingly, a considerable amount of new material appears in these pages. For much of it, I am indebted to the research of Frederick S. Davis and Dr. William L. Quirin. Thanks also for generous help from Eric Astrom, James E. Bannon, Rod Blair, Jeremy Brigstocke, Raymond Calvert, Lou Cavalaris, Jr., Walter D. Coffey, Jim Cruse, John Cuddihy, H. Grant Denn, Peter Glenn, Henry Kuck, John Schipani, and, as always, my old and knowing friend, Howard A. Rowe.

Tom Ainslie
Millwood, N.Y.

NOTES

The encyclopedia concludes with a glossary and a thorough index. The index lists all topics in the book, with the page numbers where each appears.

When an article mentions a subject discussed in pertinent detail by another article, the reference appears in small capital letters: WEIGHTS.

For the reader's convenience, the minutes, seconds, and fifths of seconds of Thoroughbred running times are presented as follows: 1:13.1, with the numeral before the colon stating the number of minutes, the numeral between the colon and period the number of seconds, and the final numeral the number of fifths.

AINSLIE'S ENCYCLOPEDIA
of
THOROUGHBRED HANDICAPPING

A

AGE. The age of the horse becomes a handicapping problem when three-year-olds race against their elders. Conventional wisdom holds that the younger animals need substantial advantages in the WEIGHTS to compete successfully with older runners of comparable CLASS. This is generally true, but oversimplified.

The studies of Frederick S. Davis demonstrate that three-year-olds win less than their share of CLAIMING races against older stock. In such races, about 26 percent of the starters but fewer than 19 percent of the winners are three. On the other hand, the younger horses hold their own in non-claiming MAIDEN, ALLOWANCE, HANDICAP, and STAKES races against opponents aged four and older. About 53 percent of the starters in those races are three. They win almost 55 percent of the time and, contrary to general

belief, are at no significant disadvantage at longer distances. Moreover, when entered in these higher-grade races at sprint distances in November and December, the three-year-olds enjoy a pronounced statistical advantage.

The reasons for these apparent contradictions are biological and commercial. To understand them, it is necessary to know why Thoroughbreds begin racing as early in life as they do, and why genuinely good ones aged four or more are in short supply.

In North America and Europe, the Thoroughbred becomes an official yearling on the January 1 following its birth and adds a year on each subsequent New Year's Day of its life. South of the equator, the official birthday is July 1. Each of the two arbitrary anniversaries permits BREEDERS in the particular hemisphere to arrange late winter and early spring foalings. These give horsemen maximum time to prepare expensive animals for the rich summer and fall races in which they might run as two-year-olds.

Regardless of the date on which a 21-month-old baby becomes eligible for two-year-old competition, the biological fact is that Thoroughbreds do not achieve physical maturity until six years after birth, by which time the vast majority have departed the scene.

Two-year-old legs and vertebrae are softly vulnerable to serious damage when required to carry weight at high speed on hard surfaces. Although centuries of selective breeding have combined with improved nutrition to develop Thoroughbreds larger and faster than their ancestors, a horse is still a horse. Its skeletomuscular and nervous systems are less than fully developed at two and three. Neither breeding nor feeding has succeeded in repealing that natural law or is likely to do so. Which is why innumerable race horses fall short of their inbred potentialities. They simply are unable to withstand the repeated exertions of premature training and racing.

In 1721, when the first great Thoroughbred racer, Flying Childers, made his competitive debut at the age of six, four- and five-year-olds were beginning to appear on British race courses. A 1740 Act of Parliament made age five the legal minimum, but nobody complied. Three-year-olds were soon introduced and by 1770 two-year-olds were also racing. In that time and place, "improvement of the breed" was the inherited military responsibility of gambling nobles. They raced immature animals because it was lucrative to do so and costly not to. The modern, industrialized sport compounds those realities.

An abundance of rich purses is available to North American and European two- and three-year-olds, but not to older runners. This emphasis supplies the rapid profit, quick turnover, and minimization of cost on which successful commerce rests. During 1974 and 1975, for example, North American tracks offered 182 stakes races with purses of $100,000 or more. Of these, 45 were for two-year-olds, 52 were restricted to three-year-olds, and 74 were for three-year-olds and older. Only three were for four-year-olds exclusively, and eight were programmed for horses aged four and older. All 11 of those unusual events took place in Southern CALIFORNIA, which by then was well on the way to recognition as America's most successful racing center.

The enormous prices paid for promising livestock at yearling auctions would be drastically reduced if the purchasers could not anticipate returns on investment in the shortest possible time. The OWNER who refused to unveil a prize animal until the age of five or six would be the first such eccentric in modern racing history. That owner not only would decline the rich opportunities most likely to repay the initial investment, but would prolong the time and cost of maintaining an inactive horse. Worst, the owner would run the real risk of losing everything if the animal suffered AILMENT or INJURY while awaiting its full growth.

When a U.S. or Canadian Thoroughbred is unraced before age three, the cause is probably medical. Well-funded barns also proceed slowly with promising animals that need an extra year to outgrow infantile clumsiness. In either case, one may assume with confidence that the three-year-old racing for the first time in its life was bred well enough or behaved impressively enough to warrant the cost of patience. All other Thoroughbreds able to stand training begin their careers at two. In most places, small concessions are made to their vulnerability. During the early months of the year, their races are limited to three or four furlongs, with whipping prohibited. And states that allow so-called controlled MEDICATION usually forbid juveniles to race under the influence of pain-killers and other drugs.

By summer, the fleetest and strongest two-year-olds are already competing for large purses. Those that survive the important stakes events of fall and early winter usually rest briefly before chasing the money that rewards the owners of successful three-year-olds during the first months of the following year.

Not many of these better two- and three-year-olds are in evidence at age four. From 1936 through 1977, only ten of 42 U.S. champion two-year-olds held sufficient form to capture another championship at three. By no coincidence, the nine were outstanding: Alsab, Count Fleet, Citation, Hill Prince, Native Dancer, Nashua, Needles, Buckpasser, Secretariat, and Seattle Slew. And only four two-year-old champions ran well enough at four (if they ran at all), to earn championship honors among older horses. These were Hill Prince, Tom Fool, Native Dancer, and Riva Ridge.

Racing fans sadden when physically sound three-year-old champions such as Secretariat are withdrawn from competition and whisked off to stud service. The sentiment is understandable, but horsemen know all too well that the time to retire a champion is when its reputation is at the zenith, before defeat can dim or fatal injury extinguish the prospect of large stud fees. Majestic Prince, a great three-year-old, beat Arts and Letters convincingly in the 1969 Kentucky Derby and Preakness Stakes. Injury turned the tables. Arts and Letters beat the hurting Derby winner in the Belmont Stakes. Majestic Prince never raced again. Arts and Letters went on to become U.S. Horse of the Year and was sold to a breeding syndicate for about $3 million. Majestic Prince brought only $1.8 million.

Thoroughbred male champions older than four are usually GELDINGS—castrates that continue racing because they can produce revenue in no other way.

As the history of two- and three-year-old racing implies and as the policies and practices of the sport make inevitable, the typical Thoroughbred declines with age. This is why promising three-year-olds are at no statistical disadvantage against four- and five-year-olds in non-claiming maiden and allowance races. Their older opponents are generally less sound animals which otherwise would have won such races at three and been ineligible for them at four. No better selection is found at any major racetrack than the lightly raced, improving three-year-old entered at a suitable DISTANCE against repeatedly unsuccessful older horses in a race for non-winners of one or two allowance races. Furthermore, the outstanding three-year-old of winter, spring, summer, or fall (they seldom last all year), is frequently acknowledged as the best runner on the continent when fairly weighted and entered at the right distance. In that connection, one scarcely need mention Man O' War, Citation, Secretariat, Count Fleet, Ruffian, and other supreme three-year-olds. Indeed, of the 42 U.S. Horses of the Year from 1936 through 1977, 22 were three-year-olds. The number would have been higher but for the remarkable old geldings Kelso and Forego, who captured that honor in eight of the 42 years.

The situation of animals that run for claiming prices reverses what takes place among more valuable stock. If a random three-year-old is at a disadvantage in claiming races against older horses, the explanation again is found in the economics of the sport. The tendency among owners is to enter a three-year-old at unrealistically high claiming prices. The owner hopes that the animal might finally come into its own and knows that a lowered claiming price invites some other barn to buy the horse and take it away. The claiming prices of three-year-olds are so exaggerated that handicappers never take for granted that the winner of a claimer restricted to that age group will be able to beat older horses unless dropped in price by at least 20 percent. Claiming prices of two-year-olds are even more inflated, for the same reasons.

The running times of three-year-old races early in the year are usually two- or three-fifths of a second slower than those recorded by presumably comparable older horses at sprint distances, and as much as two seconds slower at longer distances. Later, these time differences dwindle. By November, they disappear. Aside from the difficulty of defining "comparable older horses" in terms of claiming prices or allowance conditions, the gradual reduction in time differences traces to (a) the increasing ability of healthy three-year-olds as the year passes, (b) the natural reordering of claiming prices as owners abandon lofty hopes and try to win purses, and (c) the accelerated deterioration of older horses.

Of all approaches to the age factor, full-dress SPEED HANDICAPPING is most effective. Persons without the time for such computation do well enough. They demand a drop in claiming price for a three-year-old attempting to compete for the first time with older horses. And they bear in mind that an improving three-year-old is at no disadvantage against the stock it encounters in non-claiming maiden and lesser allowance races.

AILMENTS. Respiratory infections, blood disorders, intestinal parasites, digestive disturbances, skin afflictions, and adverse reactions to MEDICATION may affect the Thoroughbred's ability to race or train. A severe bout of "cough" (catchall term for respiratory problems ranging from mild colds and allergic irritations to influenza) may permanently damage the breathing apparatus and even make the animal a BLEEDER. A low blood count undetected or inadequately treated can transform a useful horse into a chronic loser and hasten the end of its career. A competent TRAINER is vigilant about all such possibilities, noticing the slightest change in a racer's behavior at the feed tub, in its stall, or outdoors. However, physical INJURIES and the disabilities to which they may lead are more often the reason for a Thoroughbred's deterioration.

In the final quarter of the 20th century, when the North American racing season was a year-round affair and a shortage of racing-sound horses a major problem, an absence from competition—whether caused by illness or not—became, paradoxically, a hopeful sign. Handicappers found that horses returning to the wars after layoffs of more than a month often benefited greatly from those vacations. Some trainers were able to win with such an animal in its first attempt, although strenuous effort frequently had an adverse effect, causing subsequent losses. More patient trainers instructed their riders to let returnees run on their own courage without undue pressure. In such circumstances, EARLY SPEED or a finish in the first half of the field was often a sign that the horse would be able to win its next start. Considering how few horses were able to run well after layoffs over the preceding 50 years, this phenomenon gave evidence that what most Thoroughbreds needed during the 1970's was a rest.

ALLOWANCE RACES appear in endless variety on North American programs. An allowance race among the better horses at a track of high quality is likely to be superior in PURSE value and overall CLASS to all but the topmost STAKES at a lesser track. By the same token, successful allowance runners at a minor track can seldom win uppergrade CLAIMING RACES on a major circuit. At most tracks, the class distinctions are blurred between middling allowance races and the higher-priced claimers, but the quality of top-allowance events equals that of some stakes. Indeed, stakes runners often appear in featured allowance races.

Except that allowance runners are not for sale, the CONDITIONS of eligibility for their races resemble those of claiming races. They specify the previous accomplishments that render a horse ineligible for entry, the maximum WEIGHTS to be carried, and the weight allowances (reductions) to be granted horses with inferior records.

Having defeated some of the track's best non-winners in a non-claiming MAIDEN race, a two- or three-year-old's next start is customarily an allowance affair open, as the conditions say it, to "non-winners of a race other than maiden or claiming." On some circuits, the conditions for a comparable race specify "non-winners of two races." In the first case, the field may be invaded by a more experienced animal that has already won several high-priced claimers. In the second, a horse would be ineligible after having won two races of any kind.

Two-year-olds often run in stakes after their first or second allowance efforts. Three-year-olds attempt to win their way through allowance races for non-winners of two, three, and perhaps four races, at which stage they compete under more demanding conditions. In allowance races for horses of high class, the conditions usually limit entry to animals that have not won a race or two or three of a stated purse value since a certain date. A minimum distance for these previous victories may also be specified. Weight allowances go to horses that have won fewer than the maximum permissible number of races of the stated purse value or higher, or have not won at all since a more remote date. In setting a maximum purse value for previous winning races, the conditions state the amount earned by a winner, rather than the amount of the entire purse. Thus, at a track where the winner of a race gets 65 percent of the total purse, conditions for an allowance race might refer to "four-year-olds that have not won $6,500 since December 4"—meaning that the race is open to any horse of that age that has not taken the winner's share of a $10,000 purse since that date.

The horse unable to pay its way at the lowest allowance level for which it is eligible is said to have "run out of conditions" and must eventually ship to a different circuit or run in claiming races.

Some handicappers who go to the track every day know the local horse population so well and remember each race so clearly that they can tell at a glance whether any entrant in an allowance race is likely to be outclassed and whether another might have an advantage in that respect. The figures produced by means of advanced SPEED HANDICAPPING are a great help in that kind of appraisal, but demand more time, effort, and experience than most recreational handicappers can give. A good alternative is to collect official RESULTS CHARTS from DAILY RACING FORM. These include the purses and other conditions of past races, plus important details about individual performances therein. Except after mid-season reductions or increases in the local purse schedule, it is safe to assume that the class of allowance and claiming races at any track increases with their purses.

To handle allowance races with consistent success, the handicapper must make the necessary class distinctions between past performances in allowance and claimer, allowance and allowance, or allowance and stakes. A thorough knowledge of the class factor and mastery of one or another analytic technique are essential. Otherwise, the FUNDAMENTALS of handicapping apply straightforwardly.

AMERICAN RACING MANUAL. Published each summer by DAILY RACING FORM, this enormous work tabulates and reviews the events of the previous year and updates essential long-term statistics. Contents include the record of every active horse, owner, trainer, and rider; RESULTS CHARTS of the most lucrative STAKES; descriptions of notable accomplishments by horses and persons; a goodly amount of historical material; diagrams and measurements of all tracks; Thoroughbred auction-sales records; names and addresses of breeding establishments and racing organizations; plus an endless miscellany of information useful to the industry and its fans.

AMERICAN STUD BOOK. In 1896, THE JOCKEY CLUB began registering North American foals identifiable as Thoroughbreds. Until then, that work had been done with good will and poor accuracy by various promoters of the breed. Like other registries, including Great Britain's venerable General Stud Book, this one acccpts animals whose sires and dams are already registered in an approved stud book. In effect, therefore, a horse is a Thoroughbred if its ancestry is that of a Thoroughbred, which means that it descends from one of three Arab stallions that founded the breed in the 18th century. It also means that if you pursue a horse's lineage to within three or four generations of the founding sires, you almost certainly land in muddy waters. In those days, the practice was to accept as Thoroughbred any horse that ran like one and for which a plausible pedigree was claimed. Nowadays, the main problem is one of IDENTIFICATION. Is the foal actually by the named sire and dam, or was there a mix-up? The Jockey Club hopes that blood typing will reduce the incidence of such problems.

ANGLES are subsidiary aspects of the past-performance record from which inferences may be drawn about the intentions of the stable or the readiness of the horse. After every race, happy bettors praise the angles that inspired them to "love that horse." And losers often find the angle which, they are sure, would have drawn them to the horse if they had not overlooked it the first time around: "I should've had it. Horse worked out yesterday and was dropping two pounds off last week." Or, "Look. Horse ran good for sixty-five hundred, then ran bad for eight thousand and now he was in for only six grand. Today was the day. I should've had it."

Because they are easily explained and can be concocted in endless variety, angles are the mainstay of the SELECTION SYSTEMS with which promoters make millions in direct-mail sales to gullible horseplayers. The systems do not work. The reason they do not work is that angles signify little when removed from a context of properly comprehensive handicapping. Most angle systems make a selection of any horse whose record contains a particular feature, entirely regardless of the rest of its record and usually without consideration of the other horses in the race. But handicapping—whatever style or technique may be employed—requires comparison of horses, using criteria more basic than angles. This book includes relevant angles in its discussion of FORM and the other FUNDAMENTALS of handicapping.

APPRENTICE. Race riders of outstanding talent being scarce, promising newcomers are warmly welcomed. To encourage their development, the RULES OF RACING allow the trainer who uses an apprentice jockey to subtract pounds from the weight that the horse would carry if a journeyman rode. In most jurisdictions, an apprentice is allowed ten pounds off before riding five winners, and seven pounds until winning 35. If less than a year elapses between the fifth and 35th winner, the allowance is five pounds for the remainder of that year. And for an additional year, the apprentice gets three pounds when riding a horse owned or trained by the original holder of his/her contract, provided that the contract is still in force. No apprentice allowances are given in STAKES or HANDICAPS.

The typical track PROGRAM's daily list of leading jockeys usually includes the name of at least one "bug" rider (so called because of asterisks printed next to the WEIGHTS to be carried by horses for which apprentice allowances have been claimed: One asterisk indicates five pounds off, two means seven, and three stands for ten). If the listed youngster's winning percentage is 15 or higher, his/her agent has been obtaining live mounts. This does not necessarily prove that the apprentice is superior to all riders with lower winning percentages, but it does indicate that a weight allowance and a fit horse often overcome the defects of inexperience.

The usual apprentice is best situated on front-running horses in SPRINTS, wherein success often depends on a fast exit from the STARTING GATE and a minimal ability to steer. Rating a horse over longer distances and making rapid, productive decisions in congested traffic are large challenges which require experience as well as talent. Inasmuch as most North American races are sprints, and most sprints are won by horses with EARLY SPEED, and a fit horse of that type can only benefit from a weight allowance, trainers use apparently ungifted apprentices—and stampede to hire apprentices who display real ability.

Another attraction of the apprentice is youthful enthusiasm and unsophisticated daring. These qualities are less characteristic of older riders. Eagerness to risk the neck often wanes after several spills, years of rigorous dieting to prevent normal growth, and repeated defeats in the political intrigues of the trade. Moreover, the apprentice is usually too young to be troubled by the difficulties of navigating between the hazards of racing and the concerns of marriage and parenthood.

The hot apprentice who heads the list of leading riders on the local circuit, or even nationally, is seldom so successful after losing the bug. Horsemen no longer able to get five pounds off their fit runners are inclined to use shrewder, seasoned riders while waiting for the next teen-age sensation to materialize. Among riders whose success continued without interruption after the end of outstanding apprenticeships was Willie Shoemaker, as good an apprentice as anyone ever saw. A natural lightweight, he continued to develop his already considerable ability and presently became an all-time great. Others of remarkably precocious talent were Sandy Hawley, Chris McCarron, and Steve Cauthen, all of whom were good enough to win stakes races at longer distances without benefit of weight allowances long before their apprenticeships expired.

The handicapper never overlooks the presence of a hot apprentice on a horse entered at a DISTANCE suitable to both. This often means that the horse is in better form than its record might suggest—especially at tracks where languid officials permit an apprentice to be named as rider of three or more horses in a single race. The horse finally chosen by the young rider's agent is almost always one with a good chance.

On the other hand, the assignment of an unprominent apprentice invites negative interpretation. When hoping to win, horsemen naturally try to get the best available riders. Some use apprentices simply to exercise their horses in a competitive setting, and hire better jockeys when the horses are ready to perform well. These patterns become evident to handicappers.

ARIZONA racing is celebrated for the phenomenal speeds achieved at Turf Paradise, a one-mile track near Phoenix. In 1967, a three-year-old named Zip Pocket set world records at five (:55.2) and five and a half furlongs (1:01.3), which were still unsurpassed ten years later. In December of 1966, the same colt set a world record of 1:07.2 for six furlongs, broken in 1972 at Longacres—the Renton, Washington, oval which is

Turf Paradise's chief rival as fastest racing strip on earth. Unfortunately, the quality of the Thoroughbreds that race in Arizona is not high. Speeds decline sharply as distances increase. Turf Paradise's purses for CLAIMING and ALLOWANCE races are comparable to those of Finger Lakes, Cahokia Downs, Charles Town, Latonia, and Florida Downs—minor tracks all. More minor than that are the other Arizona tracks, Prescott Downs, a half-miler near Prescott, and Rillito Downs, a five-eighths-miler at Tucson. Visitors to Turf Paradise enjoy the racing, which is uncomplicated by the fitful weather of more northerly regions. Surprisingly, the Turf Paradise winner's circle is by no means a monopoly of horses with extreme EARLY SPEED. Horses that run slightly behind the leaders in the early stages can be counted on to win about 45 percent of the races. Which means, of course, that the other 55 percent go to horses fast enough to be first, second, or third at the first CALL.

ARKANSAS offers 50 days of excellent racing from early February to early April each year at Oaklawn Park in the resort city of Hot Springs. As the only track in the state, and easily accessible to race-starved punters from Texas, Oklahoma, Tennessee, Mississippi, Missouri, Kansas, and other nearby principalities where PARI-MUTUEL BETTING is outlawed, Oaklawn is spared the cannibalistic competition that has disabled the sport in other places. But the real secret of its success is expert management. Like flourishing tracks in CAL-IFORNIA and CANADA, Oaklawn adheres to a principle widely ignored in racing: Inasmuch as the customers foot the bills, it pays to treat them with consideration and respect.

Oaklawn's clientele has a good time. The food is decent. The help is courteous. In the matter of extracting funds from fans, the watchword is restraint. Aside from a DAILY DOUBLE, no MULTI-PLE BETTING occurs. Fostering the valid notion that winning is more fun than losing, the management encourages show betting. About 25 percent of all the money bet at Oaklawn is to show—a phenomenon unheard of elsewhere. Nobody can win much that way, but more fans leave as winners and fewer lose their shirts.

Best of all, the quality of the racing is high. Purses for bread-and-butter CLAIMING and ALLOWANCE races are surpassed only at the major tracks of Southern California and NEW YORK. Accordingly, good stables flock to Oaklawn, making life more pleasant for the serious handicapper. The one-mile racing strip is not especially fast but allows the best horse a reasonable chance to win, even if he may be somewhat short of EARLY SPEED.

AUCTION POOL. A forerunner of head-on wagering with BOOKMAKERS. The auctioneer, a kind of bookie, "sold" each starter in the race to the highest bidder. The proceeds went to the "purchaser" of the winning horse after the auctioneer deducted about 5 percent for

himself and, if operating at a track, skimmed off a fee for its management. The main disadvantage of auctions was that no bidder could guess at the odds on a horse until all bidding had ended. After the Civil War, bookmakers invented more attractive propositions and auction pools lost favor.

AVERAGE EARNINGS INDEX is a useful means of evaluating the worth of a sire or broodmare. Devised by the late Joseph A. Estes, distinguished editor of THE BLOOD-HORSE, the AEI divides the average earnings of a stud's or mare's offspring by the average earnings of all other Thoroughbred runners during a given year or period of years. In a year when the average earnings of all racers are $4,000 and the progeny of a particular sire win an average of $8,000, the sire's AEI is 2.00. Such a figure would place the animal in the top 5 percent of North American studs. The concept has been elaborated in several ways. For example, the average earnings of the racers produced by an individual mare from her matings with one stallion can be compared with the average earnings of her other produce. The calculation might show that a fashionable sire's good AEI benefited as much from the quality of his mares as from any genetic contribution of his own.

In 1976, Bloodstock Research, a computerized statistical project in Lexington, Kentucky, presented a useful refinement called Standard Starts Index, which compared each runner's average earnings per start with those of all others of the same sex and age rather than with all others regardless of sex and age. Among other things, the research indicated that a colt with an SSI of 15.00 or higher was a far better stud prospect than one with an SSI below that level.

See also, BREEDING.

AVERAGES, LAW OF. This superstition has no place in handicapping. To begin with, an average is a mere arithmetical convenience. The only "law" associated with it is the certainty that it is trickier than other statistics. Even the highly useful AVERAGE EARNINGS INDEX is flawed by the inclusion of two-year-old fillies with four-year-old colts. Apples and pears are forever being lumped as "average" fruit, which is no way to investigate apples or pears.

The mail-order hustler sells a SELECTION SYSTEM with a paper workout that yields an average mutuel payoff of $12. But if you remove the accidental $128 winner from the list, you discover that the average mutuel has become $5.20. Or the racetrack proclaims that it is a high-class operation which pays out an average purse of $7,600 and is worth the loyalty of every handicapper and horseman in the hemisphere. But after you deduct the $200,000 bundles awarded to two-year-old stakes races and the like, you realize that the PURSES for day-in-day-out CLAIMING and ALLOWANCE races are no higher—and the horses no better—than at Golden Gate Fields where, at least, the weather is good and the speed stands up.

What is normal running time for three-year-old colts and geldings going six furlongs in $7,500 claiming races at the local track? By no means is it the average time recorded in such races. Too many apples and pears. To make an average even remotely useful, a homogeneous sample is necessary. The realistic search for a six-furlong par time for three-year-old, $7,500 males begins with elimination of all races for MAIDENS of that age and gender, because maiden races have a slower par time of their own. Furthermore, the researcher discards times run when the track was not dry and fast. To average the times of the remaining 16 races might suffice, because the sample is sound. But a more sensible procedure would be to seek the median. Striking out the three fastest and three slowest of the times, the worker does well to pick the time around which the others seem to cluster—the time midway between the faster and slower halves of the sample.

The limited usefulness of averages becomes painfully noticeable when innocent horseplayers decide to take advantage of the so-called law. FAVORITES win about 32 percent of races, year after year. That is, one race in every three, when calculated on an annual basis. But this guarantees nothing about the winning percentage of favorites during the few days on which the horseplayer decides that profits will be obtained by betting all favorites, doubling the bet after each loss. For favorites to lose 15 races in succession is perfectly compatible with a year-long winning expectation of .32. Starting with a $2 bet, the follower of the law of averages would need $32,768 for the fifteenth bet, if still playing the horses.

By the same token, no jockey is ever statistically "due" to win the fifth ride after four successive losses, even with a seasonal winning average of .20. Every jockey from Willie Shoemaker down has experienced numerous streaks of 30 or more consecutive losses.

None of this is intended to promote disdain for statistics. On the contrary, handicappers need them. For example, when Frederick S. Davis published careful past-performance statistics covering a range of study unprecedented in the history of racing, he upgraded the handicapping of every attentive reader and sent dozens of emulators stampeding to computers. And when William L. Quirin demonstrated through statistics that enormous profits resulted from backing appropriately bred horses in their first and second races on grass, another milestone was passed. The problem with statistics is merely one of making sure what they mean and to what limits they can be applied.

B

BANDAGES. Leg wrappings may or may not improve the chances of the individual horse but can be depended on to perplex racegoers. Some handicappers refuse to back a bandaged horse, yet bandaged horses win races. Indeed, certain stables bandage all their runners, ailing or not. Other stables use bandages in hopes of discouraging rival outfits from claiming fit animals. Here is a guide to the various bandages and what they signify:

1. Stall (or standing or shipping) bandages are large, padded cylinders which encase the legs of some horses *en route* to the PADDOCK before the race. They protect against injurious contact with the horse's own hooves, or the hooves of another, or fence posts. The GROOM removes them on arrival at the paddock stall.

2. Cold-water bandages of flannel or felt sometimes adorn the forelegs from ankle to knee, making the animal look like an accident case. Before going to the paddock, many horses stand in tubs of ice, which numbs sore legs against the discomfort of racing. Bandages, having been soaked in the ice water, prolong that effect. They are removed at the paddock.

3. Short racing bandages protect horses that tend to scrape their hind heels when running on a sandy track. The difficulty is known as "running down" and is seen less often at California's hard-surfaced tracks than at the deeper ones of the East. Rear bandages also may be used for muscular support or for horses whose abnormal racing gaits cause them to "interfere"—striking a leg with a hoof.

4. Large bandages on the forelegs, if not removed before the race, indicate

real or incipient tendon trouble. A seriously bowed tendon (a rupture of the tendon sheath), prevents a horse from racing. The best treatment for a bow of any degree is rest, but numerous Thoroughbreds race on minor bows until they break down altogether.

For the handicapper, the main questions about the horse with front racing bandages are whether it has been successful in them or not and whether they are newly added to its regalia. If the horse has been performing well with foreleg wraps, seems best in its race, and shows no signs of distress in the paddock or post parade, the handicapper then decides whether the odds are generous enough to compensate for the possibility that the legs may finally give out. If the horse has not worn front running bandages before and has not been racing or working at frequent intervals, caution is advised. If the animal is also being dropped in CLASS or if it displays nervousness or reluctance before the race, it should be avoided. Such horses do not win often enough to repay the handicapper what can be lost on them.

BEATING THE RACES is the supremely gratifying accomplishment of the rare bird who cashes enough winning tickets to produce surplus capital after payment for the season's travel, parking, track admission, DAILY RACING FORM, PROGRAMS, food, drink, and bets. For astute handicappers adept at MONEY MANAGEMENT and alert to the game's constant evolutionary changes, beating the races is a realistic goal. The effort demands single-minded concentration and monastic self-control. These are not everybody's idea of fun, nor need they be. The great majority of recreational handicappers enjoy themselves immensely, lose comfortable amounts, and can say with truthful conviction that their days at the races are inexpensive entertainment. This is as it should be. Fun, not money, is the prime objective of any recreation. Indeed, fun, not money, is the primary incentive of most winning handicappers. To end the two-week vacation or the entire race meeting or the whole year with more capital than was in hand at the beginning is to enjoy the prize known nowadays as an ego trip. The beater of the game deploys unusual skills, wins enough to prove that much, and returns to the disorder of the real world with a deep sense of self-validation. A grand feeling.

None of this should be mistaken for the grim business of making a living at the track. Those who try full-time betting and fail pay a price. Those who try it and succeed pay a greater price. They have transformed a game into a matter of life and death. So long as their prosperity—or even their room, board, and walking-around money—depends on racetrack winnings, their days and nights allow time for little else. Not many professional horseplayers can endure such stress with digestion, blood pressure, and domestic tranquility unimpaired. They persist not because their lives are continual rounds of pleasure but because they can find no better alternatives.

New handicappers interested in trying to beat the game are in position to do so after they have demonstrated that: (a) they can break even or win a little on most series of 100 racing selections and (b) can find enjoyment in the constant study that refines handicapping and betting procedures. By the time that stage is reached, it surely has become evident that success is measurable only in the long range. One may be sublimely confident of annual profits without the least certainty about the outcome of the next week, the next day or, especially, the next race. To understand this thoroughly is to approach the forbearance and stamina essential in this and all other great games.

More than forty years ago, the late Robert S. Dowst stated that a good handicapper's most sensible course was to specialize in consistent horses of adequate CLASS. On animals able to win 20 percent of their starts, he said, it was possible to cash 40 percent of bets at average ODDS of 2–1, for a profit of 20 cents on each wagered dollar. He was absolutely right. I proved it for myself with real money. So did many others. But the game changed. In Dowst's time, only 10 percent was taken from PARI-MUTUEL BETTING pools for state taxes and track operations. As this is written, the deduction is usually 18.5 percent. Dowst's 2–1 shot now pays $5.00 instead of $6.00. And consistent horses are so unusual and so highly regarded that they are more likely to pay $4.00 than $5.00. Be that as it may, to hit 40 percent winners at an average price of $5.00 is to

recover $1.00 on every dollar bet. The 20 percent profit has been reduced to zero. Nowadays most of us play short-priced horses for fun, expecting only to spin our wheels, losing nothing but winning little. Our handicapping is much more elaborate than that of the Dowsts who introduced us to the game. We look for prices. For instance, if we can be right just a third of the time on selections at about 3–1, we end with a 32 percent profit. Beautiful.

See also, GAMBLING.

BETTING that one horse will beat others is the natural essence of racing and always has been. When horses hauled war chariots or carried knights, the breeding and race-testing of swifter, more durable stock were military urgencies. But betting remained a basic incentive. The winning owner welcomed the silver plate or golden cup awarded by whatever throne was tottering at the time and then collected the proceeds of bets, which made the mare go. After the internal combustion engine abolished the prancing charger, racing continued to serve the basic purpose without which it never would have achieved popularity in the first place. That purpose is sport, of which the indispensable feature is betting.

The earliest bets were person-to-person transactions. One nobleman offered to bet that his horse could beat another's. Challenge accepted, the rival families, friends, and vassals then made wagers of their own. The tradition persists in the modern STAKES race, but the person-to-person bets posted by hopeful OWNERS are now called nomination and starting fees, for later division among those whose runners finish in the money. Few owners rest there. At any track, a list of the pari-mutuel department's biggest customers would include the names of many owners. Whether inheritors of family stables or newer to the game, most owners bet. Many bet heavily, with both fists, day after day.

They have no monopoly on it. Few non-bettors are found at racetracks. Betting is what racetracks are for. In addressing the public and attempting to drum up trade, however, the tracks behave as if betting were only incidental. Their promotional messages hardly mention that allurement but emphasize the beauty and gallantry of the horse and the excitements of the race. Track managements have made few attempts to broaden these appeals, probably because earlier efforts have failed. Radio, television, and the press consistently reject racetrack advertisements in which the fun and sometime profit of betting are explicitly described. And so the tracks are generally passive, as if a low profile might deter some wowser from leveling vice charges, and as if the charges might stick. Meanwhile, society evolves. By 1977, the U.S. had embarked on a course which would lead inevitably to widespread legalization of casino gambling, OFF-TRACK BETTING, and betting on other sports. None of which would help Thoroughbred racing.

See also BETTING SYSTEMS, BOOK-MAKERS, MONEY MANAGEMENT, MULTIPLE BETTING, PARI-MUTUEL BETTING.

BETTING COUPS occur when insiders cash winning tickets on horses whose superior ability has been concealed from other bettors. It happens every day. To hide the true FORM of a horse is an obsession with TRAINERS who hope to win purses (and bets) in CLAIMING RACES without losing their horses to other barns. They do this by racing an animal at the wrong DISTANCE or in fields of excessive CLASS or with unsuitable JOCKEYS or by conducting secret WORKOUTS or by conniving to have the times of workouts reported falsely or not reported at all. Similar maneuvers precede upset victories in other kinds of races, especially those involving MAIDENS.

To fatten the ODDS, skilled operators may place large, red-herring bets on a lukewarm favorite whose chances they discount. A bet of $2,000 has a dramatic effect when deposited in the PARI-MUTUEL machinery a few minutes after the betting windows open at a major track. The horse's odds plummet. TOTE-BOARD watchers stampede to bet on the horse. Odds rise on all the other starters, including the one favored by the tricksters. Just before betting closes, and too late for many members of the crowd to follow suit, the manipulators buy, for example, $4,000 in tickets on the horse they like. This depresses its odds, but not enough to matter.

In a race at old Agua Caliente in Tijuana, Mexico, in 1932, one of the owners of the track, Baron Long, ran a two-horse entry which was 20–1 in the MORNING LINE. The favorite in the race, one Linden Tree, was odds-on in that line. Enormous sums of money were bet on Linden Tree with BOOKMAKERS throughout the United States. Shortly before post time, Long bought about $20,000 worth of mutuel tickets on his entry, dropping their odds to 2–1 and elevating Linden Tree to almost 10–1. Linden Tree won easily, paying $21.40. Since Long officially had done nothing more reprehensible than bet on his own horses, he was allowed to remain in racing.

The professional gambler Arnold Rothstein scored numerous coups before somebody finally murdered him over a grievance unconnected with the sport. Two of his biggest swindles were engineered with Max Hirsch, a trainer who later became a revered figure. Shortly after World War I, the pair won an estimated $1.25 million on Sidereal, a two-year-old maiden whose good form was so widely unknown that the morning-line odds were 30–1. After Rothstein and cohorts had wagered a small fortune, the bookies stopped taking bets but it was too late. On another occasion, Hirsch successfully concealed the form of Sailing B., a stakes-quality two-year-old. At Rothstein's insistence, the horse ran in a $1,500 selling race, and the outfit collected about $500,000 at 8–1.

BETTING SYSTEMS are lucrative for those who publish and sell them but only multiply the losses of those who buy and use them. Their sales appeal rests on claims that they enable the customer to organize a profit from a succession of bets that normally would produce a loss. This involves "progressive" betting—increasing the size of the wager after each loss, and cashing a large bet on the inevitable longshot winner. When events unfold that way, an otherwise losing series of bets might well become profitable. But no law of God or man requires the winning horse to materialize at the end of a losing series. When it comes at the beginning, while the bets are inconsequential, the comparatively small profits are dissipated by subsequent losses. No system of MONEY MANAGEMENT can make a good handicapper of a poor one. Until the handicapper is able to pick enough winners at odds high enough to show consistent profits in bets of equal amounts ("flat betting"), the best course is to study handicapping and bet minimum amounts, if any. Having become more expert, the player is ready to turn attention to money management, tailoring his bets in patterns calculated to build wagering capital more rapidly than flat bets can.

BITS are the mouthpieces, usually metal, to which the reins attach. By tightening the rein on one side or the other, the rider steers his horse through traffic and holds it on course around turns. Sound, well-schooled Thoroughbreds respond readily. After mouth injuries or heavy-handed treatment, others become tender-mouthed or unwilling to accept the bit, or both. Bold Ruler, whose tongue was almost severed in a yearling accident, did not come to hand until his trainer, Sunny Jim Fitzsimmons, switched to a rubber bit wrapped in soft gauze.

A horse is said to "grab the bit" or be "on the bit" when it clenches the implement and runs as fast as the rider allows. Tired or dispirited horses figuratively "spit out the bit," loosening their mouths and shortening stride. Not many Thoroughbreds run well without pressure on the bit. The best riders give their mounts time to settle into stride and let them grab the bit when ready. To watch Willie Shoemaker, Sandy Hawley, or Steve Cauthen manipulate the reins and coax unprecedented speed and stamina out of an inexperienced or reluctant horse is to see the bit employed as intended—for maximum communication between intelligent rider and encouraged mount.

Bits come in all shapes and sizes. The most interesting is the run-out bit, which protrudes farther from one side of the mouth than from the other. To prevent an unsound or eccentric horse from bearing in or out, the bit provides extra leverage on the protruding side, while blunt prongs reinforce the message by pressing on the other.

BLEEDER. In the stress of a race, the Thoroughbred's air passages are fiery red, the blood vessels engorged. If a capillary bursts, the horse cannot breathe

freely and slows to a walk. Some horses are chronic bleeders but usually respond well to treatment with furosemide (Lasix). In states that permit this MEDICATION on the day of a race, trainers administer it to non-bleeders, which greatly outnumber bleeders. By increasing a horse's urinary activity, Lasix masks the presence of unsanctioned drugs, frustrating the already outgunned chemists in charge of post-race urine, blood, and saliva analysis. The honesty of racing is properly suspect wherever a state racing commission adopts lenient rules governing the use of Lasix. A sport rationally aware of its dependence on public trust would ban use of the drug in non-bleeders.

BLINKERS reduce the horse's field of vision. Obstructing its view of things that might frighten or distract, they often promote cooperation between runner and rider. Depending on whether the horse's inability to maintain course or stride is actually amenable to treatment with blinkers, much experimentation may be required before a suitable style of blinker is found. Frequently, it turns out that the horse performs best without hoods of any kind.

Problems relieved by blinkers trace in most cases to equine eyesight and mentality, which differ greatly from those of man. The horse's eyes are on the sides of its head, not in front. Each eye sees independently and in virtually all directions, including the rear. Being a herd animal that feels safest when close to other horses, the normal Thoroughbred tends to slow down when it gets the lead in a race. Centuries of breeding have not obliterated this instinct, although training sometimes inhibits it. An occasional horse, descended no doubt from generations of herd leaders, feels that its natural place is at the head of the procession. Bold Forbes was such an animal. Trainer Lazaro Barrera equipped him with a blinker that provided a rearward view and capitalized on the champion's reluctance to let another horse catch him. More usual, of course, are blinkers that prevent a horse from noticing that it has left its companions behind.

Some horses fear the inside rail and bear out to avoid it. They may benefit from blinkers that block their view of it. But Whirlaway's problem in that regard ended when Ben Jones opened the left blinker so that the horse could see the rail. Apparently he had been afraid of what he could not see and had been bearing out to get as far from the rail as possible.

John Nerud, patient trainer of Dr. Fager, Gallant Man, and Ta Wee, once told Teddy Cox of *Daily Racing Form,* "I've never been much of a blinker man, because I don't believe the Thoroughbred ever cared to have his vision limited. I would say that about sixty percent of the horses racing in blinkers would do much better without them."

Because the addition or removal of blinkers, or modifications in their design can affect performance drastically, changes in the equipment require permission from the STEWARDS.

Thorough handicappers keep an eye peeled for the program notation, "Blinkers on." It often heralds improvement by a lightly raced two- or three-year-old that has been stopping on the lead, failing to run straight, or performing timidly in traffic. "Blinkers off" indicates that the equipment did not solve whatever difficulty had been blamed for the horse's failures, and suggests that the problem may have less to do with eyesight or mentality than with INJURY, poor schooling, or an AILMENT. Nevertheless, an occasional horse wins when finally restored to the unblinkered state in which it ran poorly during an earlier stage of its career.

BLOOD COUNT. Without abundant red blood cells, the Thoroughbred starves for the oxygen needed at times of full exertion. Good stables routinely take blood counts, and recognize one of less than 7 million (red cells per cubic millimeter) as bad news. A count of 10 million or higher is preferred. Among many reasons why leading trainers seem to work miracles with CLAIMING animals taken from rival barns is that they spend time and money on details of this kind.

BLOOD-HORSE, THE. A superbly edited weekly published by the Thoroughbred Owners and Breeders Association, this magazine covers all aspects of the racing industry with genuine grace and admirable objectivity. Subscriptions include annual supplements full of statistical information about the accomplishments of sires, dams, and their offspring. The fan can become a successful handicapper without this magazine but will miss the enjoyment of knowing who is who and what's on their minds. Subscriptions from Box 4038, Lexington, KY 40504.

BOOKMAKERS originated in the days of person-to-person betting, when strangers could wager most conveniently if a third party was willing to hold the money until the race was over. Performing this service as stakeholder was only a short step from charging a commission for it, and finally accepting bets from individuals. In 18th-century Britain, the bookmakers' ring had become a standard feature of all race meetings. Scandal abounded. Having discovered that maximum profit derived from fixing races so that heavily backed favorites would lose, bookmakers were diligent about fixing all the races they could. After establishment of the British Jockey Club, matters improved. Bookmaking, on and off track, remains legal in the British Isles and most other civilized countries. Its practitioners enjoy social standing commensurate with their wealth. They own well-bred horses, sponsor important races, and are the very pillars of the turf. At this writing, one of the largest British firms included a member of the peerage.

In the U.S. and Canada, off-track bookmaking has seldom been legal except in Nevada. And the establishment of PARI-MUTUEL BETTING banished the books from North American tracks. However, the profession endures covertly in all large cities and many small ones, rendering such conveniences as it can to horseplayers unable or unwilling to go to the tracks. Interestingly, the heir to a British bookmaking fortune in football pools owned a successful racing stable in California during the late 1970's, earning acclaim as a splendid sportsman. That local operators of football pools were candidates for the hoosegow was ironical but unemphasized.

See also, OFF-TRACK BETTING.

BREEDERS. The breeder of the horse is the person or group that owns the animal's dam (mother) at the time of foaling. Of about 25,000 active U.S. Thoroughbred breeders listed by THE JOCKEY CLUB in 1975, more than 17,000 owned but one or two broodmares. Small operations of that kind are essentially sporting enterprises. They exist outside the mainstream of the market-breeding industry, members of which own and/or manage the most expensive stallions and broodmares, auction the offspring for prices that stagger the mind, and constitute a decisively powerful force in the economics of Thoroughbred racing.

For example, syndication arrangements by leading market breeders allow collaborating stable OWNERS and racetrack operators to become joint proprietors of fashionable stallions, with virtual exclusivity in breeding their own mares to the jointly held studs. The amounts paid for syndicate shares in glamorous stallions like Secretariat or Wajima, and the prices fetched by their progeny demonstrate that big-time breeding is more profitable than racing. Names celebrated in both fields appear repeatedly on syndicate membership lists, signifying great good fortune and large influence but by no means insuring that the monopolized stallion will always mate with mares most likely to accelerate the improvement of the breed.

Nowadays hardly anyone says "improvement of the breed" with a straight face. To be sure, U.S. breeding establishments produce superb horses, some of which survive long enough to establish themselves as comparable to horses of any era, any place. But these are individual phenomena. The breed itself is in trouble. In 1955, slightly more than 9,000 Thoroughbred foals were registered with the Jockey Club. By 1965, the number approached 19,000. Ten years later, it exceeded 28,000. Quality could not keep pace with quantity. During the 1970's, horses won at major racetracks that would have been hard put to compete at minor ones in decades past. And horses won at minor tracks that might never have raced at all, had they even been foaled. The general deterioration of the breed was a consequence of lengthened racing seasons, nine- and ten-race daily programs, and the relationship between pari-mutuel revenues and the number of horses in each race. Small fields meant lower odds, unattractive to horseplayers. Larger fields necessitated the racing of unsound animals, many of which could not run without pain-killing drugs.

For owners of one or two mares, breeding became more than ever a sporting gamble. The services of good stallions were now less easily obtained, not only because of syndicate monopolies but because good stallions had become an even smaller minority than usual, with their stud fees out of sight. Able to employ only such stallions as were available at reasonable prices, the little breeder's expectation of getting a good race horse were small. In which connection it should be observed that the well-known march of science notwithstanding, the breeding industry's matings result in living foals barely 53 percent of the time.

Some handicappers check the name of the breeder in the DAILY RACING FORM credentials of a previously unraced or lightly raced horse. If the animal was bred by a well-known outfit and is to race for the breeder, the handicapper supposes that it may be a prize specimen, too promising for disposal at a yearling sale. And if the breeder-owner is also the trainer, the handicapper's antennae quiver. Statistics sometimes strengthen these suppositions. In 1975, Canada's foremost racing figure, E. P. Taylor, set a North American record when horses he bred earned purses of $2,369,145. Taylor-bred stock won 344 races in 2,604 starts—13.2 percent. And horses that he did not sell but raced in his own Windfields Farm silks won 49 of their 226 attempts—21.6 percent, which is more like it. In 1976, Taylor surpassed his own earnings record. Horses bred by him won $3,022,181 with 356 victories in 2,718 starts (13.1 percent). Those that he kept for himself won 39 of 202 (19.3 percent).

Interesting, but far from typical. Except for an occasional Taylor, the leading breeders of the year usually turn out horses that win about 10 percent of their total starts. Success in breeding traces, of course, to those few horses that win higher percentages and lots of money. This means that a horse from Claiborne or Spendthrift or one of the other mammoth stud farms is not *per se* a good bet. Of far more consequence is the name of the animal's TRAINER and, above all, the facts about its previous performances on the track.

BREEDING. Good breeding is no guarantee of good performance. All Thoroughbreds descend from champions, but most of them lose more often than they win—including those that number champions among their parents and grandparents. To be sure, after a horse has demonstrated that it can run, or that it can run in some circumstances but not in others, a student of blood lines can explain these talents in terms of pedigree. If conscientious, the expert would then cite contrary examples—horses of identical or closely similar ancestry that could not handle such situations or, for that matter, any other. The genetics of the Thoroughbred differs in no fundamental from the genetics of human beings. Inheritance is a lottery in which talented parents are more likely than untalented ones to produce talented offspring. But talented parents also produce untalented offspring. And

youngsters with inborn talent can be ruined by misfortune. Among Thoroughbreds, this may mean poor schooling, inexpert career management, AILMENTS, or INJURIES.

A handicapper who concentrates on actual past performances can prosper without knowledge of breeding. But study of the subject leads to winners in races that otherwise might seem unplayable. Opportunities arise when a horse from a good barn tries the kind of race for which it seems appropriately bred, facing a bunch that has already shown little ability on, for example, TURF.

The pedigree information most useful to handicappers appears weekly in THE BLOOD-HORSE and THE THOROUGHBRED RECORD, in the huge annual supplements sent to their subscribers, in DAILY RACING FORM articles and tabulations and in that paper's yearly AMERICAN RACING MANUAL. What follows should equip the reader to understand the literature:

Terminology. The Thoroughbred's father is the *sire* and the mother is the *dam.* The filly or colt is said to be *by* the sire (one of his *get), out* of the dam (one of her *produce).* The paternal grandsire, great-grandsire, etc., are simply *grandsire,* etc., without use of "paternal." But the sire's mother is the *paternal granddam.* The *maternal grandsire* is called that, or *broodmare sire.* The maternal granddam is simply *second dam* or *granddam,* who was daughter of the *third dam* and granddaughter of the *fourth,* and so on.

Foals of the same sire and dam are *full brothers* (or sisters or both). From the same dam by different sires, they are *half-sisters,* or half-brothers or both. Foals by the same sire from different mares are related as closely as half-brothers and half-sisters but no point is made of it and no term describes it. Horses with different parents but identical grandparents are *brothers-* or *sisters-in-blood.*

The paternal ancestry, from sire to grandsire to antiquity, appears on the topmost line of the pedigree diagram and is called the *male line, top line,* or *tail male.* Thus, Secretariat traces in tail male to Phalaris by way of Bold Ruler (Secretariat's sire), Nasrullah (grandsire), Nearco, and Pharos. The bottom line of the pedigree is that of the dam's *family.* Known sometimes as *tail female,* it proceeds from dam to granddam and thence from each mother to her own mother.

Every Thoroughbred traces in tail male to one of three 18th-century Arab stallions that had been imported to England. Research discloses not more than 18 distaff families. Efforts to produce fleeter, more durable runners have long since resulted in a mixture of sire lines and families which leaves each Thoroughbred a blood relative of every other. Nevertheless, when closer inbreeding is comparatively recent in a runner's genealogy, pedigree experts call attention to it. For example, if a winner's great-grandsire (the third generation back) also appears somewhere in the pedigree at the fourth generation back, it is written that the horse is inbred to that ancestor 3 × 4, or that the horse is inbred to the ancestor "with two free generations"—those being the number of generations between the horse itself and the most recent contribution of the ancestor.

Pedigree Analysis. The horse's *Daily Racing Form* past-performance record includes the name of its sire, dam, and maternal grandsire. Thus, it is Secretariat (Bold Ruler–Somethingroyal, by Princequillo), Princequillo having sired Secretariat's dam. This is all the breeding information a handicapper needs. When Secretariat came to the races, his pedigree made plain that he might be a good two-year-old and that he might eventually do well in turf racing. After his first two starts, he looked like a potential champion not because of his pedigree but because of his racing ability. Be that as it may, whoever reads the racing press soon learns the names of the most successful sires, broodmare sires, sires of two-year-olds (known as juvenile sires), and also the names of leading broodmares.

Enthusiasts of bloodlines carry their studies farther than that, although not as far as they might prefer. Practicality interferes. Secretariat's full roster of ancestors in the 22 generations that separate him from the Darley Arabian (one of the three founding fathers of the breed) includes 8,388,606 names. Some recur often. Nobody can analyze the racing and breeding accomplishments of more than the three most recent ancestral generations without dabbling in confusion.

More to the point, it is a waste of time. One of extremely few geneticists to study the Thoroughbred was Dr. Dewey G. Steele of the University of Kentucky. He wrote, "Pedigrees must be judged primarily on the basis of ancestors in the first and second generations, and individuals beyond the third generation may for all practical purposes be ignored. There is no evidence that the tail-female line or any other line exercises a hereditary influence greater than would be expected on a purely chance basis."

The late Joseph A. Estes of *The Blood-Horse* and his successor, Kent Hollingsworth, have proved repeatedly that the best race horses are most likely to produce topnotch runners. To be sure, the lore of the turf is replete with the names of champions born of unglamorous parentage, and the names of yearlings purchased for hundreds of thousands of dollars at auction and unable to run. Surprises of that kind are among the many excitements of the sport but do not negate statistical reality: The higher the racing quality of the stallion and broodmare, the larger the probability that their offspring will run well.

Handicappers really need not concern themselves with such debate. The annual lists of leading sires, leading juvenile sires, and broodmare sires, plus periodically published updates of current records help identify two- and three-year-old newcomers as promising or not. In that connection, it is important to check not only the sires whose get win the most money, but those whose offspring include a high proportion of winners.

Speed Breeding. Most two-year-old races are SPRINTS. Sires that beget a high percentage of two-year-old winners are invariably speed sires whose sons and daughters can be expected to continue sprinting well at three. Whether they can stretch out to longer distances remains moot until each has tried.

Distance Breeding. Stallions whose names appear on lists of leading sires and broodmare sires but not on the list of top juvenile sires are often those that transmit ability for racing at distances beyond a mile. Those that appear on both the juvenile-sire and other lists may, like Bold Ruler, beget animals of high speed, including some able to carry their speed at distances.

Mud Breeding. Before the advent of the well-drained, sandy modern racing strip, gooey mud was an aftermath of heavy rain. Today's "muddy" track is less forbidding and dries out rapidly. Horses whose feet are small and cuplike seem to handle mud well, but nobody has been able to establish that one or another sire gets a preponderance of good mud runners. The handicapper who finds that a certain horse runs unexpectedly well on a muddy track is advised to write down the name. The next time the condition occurs, the horse may run well again.

Grass Breeding. Mackenzie Miller and other horsemen noted for success in TURF RACING have maintained for years that it is impossible to predict whether a horse will perform well on the sod. Dr.

William L. Quirin studied the phenomenon and showed that horses of certain lineage produce the highest proportion of good grass runners. Outstanding in this respect were Princequillo, his offspring such as Round Table, Prince John, and Hill Prince, and members of succeeding generations such as Stage Door Johnny, Knightly Manner, and Advocator. Other important names were Sir Gaylord, Sir Ivor, Drone, Le Fabuleux, Tom Rolfe, Chieftain, Exclusive Native, Sea-Bird, Herbager, Hawaii, Grey Dawn II, Vaguely Noble, TV Lark, Secretariat, Mongo, Intentionally, Nijinsky II, Bolero, Ack Ack, and Vent du Nord. The appearance of any such name as a horse's sire or broodmare sire can be taken as a sign of promise in an animal making its first or second attempt on grass.

Claiming Races. A horse entered in a CLAIMING RACE is so impaired that its parentage is irrelevant to handicapping. Many claimers were bred to be champions but things did not work out. They can be handicapped only in terms of past performances, except for an occasional grass-bred animal trying a turf race under claiming conditions.

State-Breds. To encourage development of their own Thoroughbred breeding industries, states not renowned as breeding centers provide incentives by adding extra money to the PURSES of races restricted to runners bred in the particular jurisdiction. In New Jersey, New York, Washington, Illinois, and others with such programs, certain sires beget more than their share of winners.

Handicappers who keep track of such statistics have an advantage.

Sire vs. Dam. Each parent contributes equally to the genetic pool of the Thoroughbred, the human being, or the chipmunk. Handicapping and other analysis of breeding emphasizes the male line only because it is convenient to do so. A stallion mates with upward of 40 females a year. But the gestation period is 11 months, which limits the broodmare to one foaling per year. Five years after he has gone to stud, enough of the stallion's get have raced to permit informed appraisal of his breeding powers. Many more years, including occasional miscarriages or failures to become pregnant, must pass before anyone can be sure about a broodmare. However, breeding literature includes ample information about the racing records of broodmares, in case some handicapper is not content with the knowledge that a particular two-year-old represents a first-rate juvenile sire and a great broodmare sire.

BULL RINGS. Racetracks less than a mile in circumference are known as bull rings, which they resemble. Except for Sportsman's Park (the five-eighths-mile track in Cicero, ILLINOIS), and a half-miler in Pomona, CALIFORNIA, North American tracks of less than a mile offer racing of minor quality. Their sharp turns place a premium on EARLY SPEED and inner POST POSITIONS. Running times are generally slow, because the horses are unsound and can seldom stay on course around turns without disengaging the clutch. Nevertheless, the percentage of winning FAVORITES at minor tracks is usually as high as elsewhere. At many bull rings, horsemen and their friends and families seem to outnumber the paying customers. It pays to watch the TOTE BOARD for signs of betting activity by some stable and its followers.

BUTAZOLIDIN is the trade name for phenylbutazone, the anti-inflammation agent legalized in states whose authorities sanction "controlled" MEDICATION for racing purposes. Relieving the pain of damaged tissue, it enables trainers to run horses that might otherwise be rested. The practice is defended with the specious reasoning that "bute" is not really dope because it "does not make a horse run faster than he normally runs. It just helps him run his race." And in depriving the animal of the vacation that might permit it to recover from its trouble, racing under the influence of bute subjects the injured part to additional stress and possible destruction.

BUZZERS or *joints* or *gads* are battery-powered devices which startle horses into running faster. Concealed in a jockey's hand or even built into the whip, the buzzer imparts a low-voltage electric shock or simply vibrates rapidly. Although jockeys are grounded each year after being charged with carrying the forbidden instruments, it can be stated with great certainty that joints function mainly as part of the paraphernalia of TOUTS. JOCKEYS, GROOMS, and TRAINERS, fully aware of the penalties inflicted on those caught using buzzers in competition, sometimes raise money for themselves by displaying the gadgets to susceptible "clients"—suckers eager to profit from supposed FIXES.

C

CALIFORNIA. The Southern California circuit of Santa Anita (in Arcadia), Hollywood Park (near the Los Angeles airport), and Del Mar (near San Diego) consistently offers the best Thoroughbred racing in North America. Spared by geography and wise management from the cutthroat competition that undermined Eastern racing during the 1960's and 1970's, the Southern California tracks were able to persist in longstanding policies stunningly unfamiliar to Eastern visitors. Chief of these were efforts to make a day at the races a memorably pleasant experience. Customer accommodations are unsurpassed. Track employees are genial. The climate is a powerful ally. The racing is intensely competitive, featuring good horses and riders, large fields, and fast footing.

Drawing on an enormous population, which may include the highest percentage of handicapping enthusiasts in the U.S., and benefiting from detailed reportage in the Los Angeles and suburban press, Santa Anita and Hollywood card more than their share of important STAKES, paying the customary purses of $100,000 and up. Enough revenue remains for CLAIMING and ALLOWANCE purses even higher than those of NEW YORK. Del Mar's purses are not quite as large as that but are substantially higher than any except those of New York and the other two Southern California tracks.

Santa Anita's one-mile main track, although extremely fast, is a fair test of Thoroughbred ability. Horses that run behind the early leaders win about 45 percent of the races, doing better than that as distances increase beyond six furlongs. In periods of wet weather,

EARLY SPEED benefits. Inside post positions are dreadful in sprints. The spectacular turf course features a downhill run from far outside the main oval, an unusual right-hand turn, and a few yards of dirt where the horses cross the main track onto the home stretch. Inner post positions are best in the one-and-one-eighth-mile races that use only the inner grass strip. But in longer grass races and sprints involving the downhill chute, middle positions are better. Unlike most turf courses, Santa Anita's is quite favorable to horses fast enough to get the early lead.

At Hollywood, a one-miler, wire-to-wire victories on the dirt are more frequent than at Santa Anita, but the overall statistics show that horses that run third, fourth, or fifth in the early going manage to win more than 40 percent of the races and, in some seasons, do at least as well as early-speed types in races around two turns. Outside posts are generally best in sprints, inside in routes. The grass course is usually short-cropped, helping horses unable to run on other lawns. Inside post positions are preferable, and early speed seldom lasts to the finish.

Del Mar's one-mile track has a shorter stretch than the others. Horses with early speed win more than half the races. At all distances, a fast start and an inside post are hard to beat. The grass course is also hospitable to speed and the first six posts are best.

During the two-week interval between the September closing of Del Mar and the opening of Santa Anita's Oak Tree

meeting, the racing takes place at Pomona, a half-miler 30 miles from Los Angeles. Purses for rank-and-file horses match those of Monmouth Park, slightly below Arlington Park or Keeneland, and higher than Churchill Downs or Hawthorne. Early speed and inside post positions pay well: FAVORITES win the standard one of every three races.

The San Francisco area has two good one-mile tracks, Bay Meadows and Golden Gate Fields, which offer running conditions most intriguingly diverse. Bay Meadows rivals Churchill Downs, Fort Erie, Fair Grounds, Sportsman's Park, and Belmont Park among tracks where the best horse need not have great early speed to win. Horses that run on or close to the lead in the early stages win less than half the time. At Golden Gate, early speed wins as many as 70 percent of the sprints and is not to be sneezed at in longer races. The quality of the racing is inferior to that of Southern California but overnight purses compare favorably with those of Keystone and Tropical-at-Caider.

Besides the Bay Meadows and Golden Gate sessions, Northern California has Thoroughbred racing at Ferndale, Fresno, Sacramento, Santa Rosa, Solano, and Stockton. The horses could be worse and the sponsoring state and county fairs generate a happy atmosphere.

CALLS AND POLES. The colorfully striped poles on the track's inside rail tell the riders, the public-address announcer (known as the race caller), and the audience how far the horses have run and how far they are from the finish line. The poles are named in terms of their distance from the finish. Thus, at a typical one-mile track, the first pole passed in a one-mile race is the 15/16 pole, after the horses travel half a furlong and are seven and a half furlongs from the finish wire. After they run a quarter of a mile, they are at the three-quarter pole on the far end of the clubhouse turn. The half-mile pole is two-thirds of the way down the backstretch. The three-eighths pole is the first one encountered on the far turn and the quarter pole the last, just before the turn for home. Thus, the eighth pole marks the beginning of the race's final furlong, and the final drive through the stretch.

Daily Racing Form RESULTS CHARTS show each horse's running position at each of the principal points of call, which, in the standard six-furlong race, are the start, the half-mile pole (after a quarter-mile of running), the quarter pole (after a half-mile), the stretch (around the sixteenth pole), and the finish. Below the running lines appear the times for each relevant fraction—the quarter-mile (at the half-mile pole), the half (at the quarter pole), and the finish. Results-chart analysis is somewhat complicated by the fact that each horse's running position at each call is accompanied by a superior number (3^2) indicating the number of lengths, or less, by which the animal was ahead of the horse closest to it in the procession. Thus, 3^2 means that a horse was running third, two lengths ahead of the fourth horse. To find out how far it was behind the horse that happened to be leading at the time, it is necessary to find that leader on the chart, note its margin over the second horse, and then add that number of lengths to the second horse's margin over the third horse. Having done so, the handicapper can refer to the official fractional times and apply the usual one-fifth-second-per-length formula to the problem of estimating how long it took the horse to run that much of the race.

The *Form*'s PAST-PERFORMANCE TABLES are less complicated. In all races from five and a half furlongs to one mile, the first number that appears with a superior number on the past-performance line shows the horse's running position at the half-mile pole. The superior number now shows how far the horse was behind the leader or, if it was leading, its margin over the second horse. In Eastern editions of the *Form,* a longer past-performance line includes a number showing the horse's position immediately after the start (in all races up to and including seven furlongs). In longer races, that number (which is unaccompanied by a superior, lengths-behind figure) shows the horse's running position after a quarter-mile of racing. This is extremely helpful in a handicapper's appraisal of early speed at longer distances.

CANADA. The Ontario Jockey Club operates Woodbine and Greenwood, both near Toronto, and Fort Erie, just across the border from Buffalo, New York. The circuit offers interesting sport in pleasant surroundings. Woodbine usually runs for 90 days from mid-May to mid-July and during September and October. Besides a richly traditional stakes schedule which includes the classic Queen's Plate for Canadian three-year-olds and the Canadian International Championship (a turf race akin to Laurel's Washington, D.C., International), the Woodbine programs compare in purse structure and overall quality with those of Churchill Downs or Golden Gate. Fort Erie, open for 56 days before and after the first Woodbine meeting, is in the same class bracket. Greenwood has the earliest and latest dates, in March-April and November-December. Its CLAIMING and ALLOWANCE purses are comparable to those of Detroit, Fair Grounds, or Timonium.

The one-mile Woodbine track favors horses with EARLY SPEED, especially when the strip is wet. Outside posts are best at SPRINT distances, inside ones preferable at one and one-sixteenth miles. TURF RACING gets special emphasis. A seven-furlong inner course, used primarily for stakes races, features grass as heavy as that of many British tracks. Inside posts are preferable and so is a measure of early speed. The renowned Marshall turf course differs considerably. With a lengthy backstretch outside and parallel to that of the main dirt track, it includes a sweeping turn before crossing the dirt strip onto the inner course. It accommodates races from six

furlongs to two miles. Its grass is thin, its surface hard. Horses that dislike the inner oval sometimes improve dramatically on the Marshall. Post positions and early speed are meaningless at longer Marshall distances, but inside posts help in the sprints.

Fort Erie is a rarity. Like Bay Meadows, Fair Grounds, Sportsman's Park, and Belmont Park, it tires most horses that try for the early lead. To win on the head end, the speed horse must be much the best in its field. Outside posts usually prevail in sprints, inside ones at longer distances. A seven-furlong turf course lies inside the one-mile main track. Like other such strips, it rewards inside posts and a vigorous stretch run.

Greenwood is a three-quarter-mile oval. Its short stretch places a premium on early speed and inside posts.

Visiting handicappers find to their delight that Woodbine and Fort Erie horses trying grass competition for the first time usually have worked out on that footing often enough to prepare well. Both places have training tracks of grass—facilities seldom provided elsewhere. A more bothersome aspect of Ontario racing is the horse that jumps up and wins after training at one of the farms in the Toronto area. Its record offers no hint of improvement, or even of recent training, but there it stands in the winner's circle. To limit surprises of that kind and, for that matter, of all kinds, the Jockey Club sponsors publication of the continent's supreme TIP SHEET, known as the *Woodbine* (or *Fort Erie* or *Greenwood*) *Journal.* The daily pamphlet analyzes the prospects of every horse in every race. At this writing, it has for years selected a higher percentage of winners than any other public handicapping service in the Dominion. Seasoned Ontarians may survive without the *Journal,* but U.S. tourists are advised to use it.

The Province of Alberta has five BULL RINGS—Northlands Park, Marquis Downs, Lethbridge, Regina, and Victoria Park. Winnipeg, Manitoba, has Assiniboia Downs, and Vancouver, British Columbia, has Exhibition Park. At all, the watchwords are inside posts and early speed.

CLAIMING RACES. More than 70 percent of North American races are claimers. Although rich STAKES races stimulate headlines, the essential quality of a track's daily racing program is determined by the kind of livestock that compete in its claiming races.

The CONDITIONS of eligibility for a claiming race specify a price or range of prices for which any starter may be purchased by a licensed stable OWNER who enters a claim for the animal before the race. In most states, a stable must run at least one horse at the race meeting before claiming another. CALIFORNIA, LOUISIANA, WASHINGTON, and Alberta eliminate that rule. Their "open" claiming encourages the establishment of new stables by relieving them of the need to buy horses privately (and expensively) before being allowed to build their holdings with claims. Open claiming draws stout resistance from entrenched owners, who see no reason to facilitate competition from newcomers. Indeed, influential elements are so eager to discourage fresh competition that some places now compel anyone who claims a horse to refrain from selling it privately for months. This assures that nobody will enter a claim for the mere purpose of helping a friend enter the sport at a reasonable price.

Further to limit claiming activity, most states require that a newly claimed horse's claiming price be raised by at least 25 percent during its first month in the new barn, and forbid the animal to race elsewhere during that period. ILLINOIS is an exception, allowing stables to race newly claimed animals at whatever levels they please.

The purpose of claiming races is competition among horses of equal CLASS, or thereabouts. This assures owners that even the feeblest runner may win some day, if a race with a low enough claiming price is found for it. The system also penalizes barns that run horses at unrealistically high prices. A horse that loses only because it is entered in fields too good for it may develop the habit of losing. But the animal does not ordinarily stop eating. So the owner collects no purse money, continues to pay bills, and not uncommonly watches the horse persist in losing even after it has been dropped to a claiming price at which it might previously have been able to win. On the other hand, to enter a $20,000 horse in a $10,000 claimer means winning a purse and a bet, but someone else usually halters the creature and takes it away for less than its real value.

All customs and regulations notwithstanding, racing stables find ample elbow room for the maneuvering that culminates in a better horse defeating lesser ones at good odds without being claimed. The barn area is a hotbed of intrigue. Like Lisbon during World War II, it is overrun with spies and counterspies. Trainers hire informants to tell them whether the rival's horse is actually hurting or whether the bandages and iodine stains are only camouflage. A few well-spent dollars plus keen eyes and ears often make possible the claim of a horse just before it rounds into winning form. Some of the most successful claiming stables prosper in that way—winning purses with horses whose ability was developed under other auspices. Also, many larger outfits form non-aggression pacts. Neither party claims from the other, but they both gang up on someone else. The saddest sack on any backstretch is the owner-trainer of a one-horse stable after other horsemen perceive that the horse is getting its legs under it. Next time it runs, the horse is claimed and the stable is out of business until its owner can locate a new runner.

During the 1960's and 1970's, claiming price became an undependable indicator of Thoroughbred class. Year-long racing and a horse shortage pressed the owners and trainers of sore horses to run them even more often than usual, and with even less concern for their long-range welfare. The horse able to fend for itself in a $10,000 claimer last week might well be unable to win at $5,000 next week, having finally been worn to the nub.

During that period, many handicappers learned to prize DISTANCE, FORM, and SPEED as more significant than rises or drops in claiming price. Rested claiming runners repeatedly proved able to move far up the price ladder before wearing out again. During 1976 and 1977, more claimers won ALLOWANCE and stakes races in New York and other major Eastern racing centers than would have been considered possible 15 or 20 years earlier.

Another aspect of claiming price as a measure of class was found in the growing discrepancies among horses running for similar claiming prices on different circuits. During the winter of 1976–77, for example, older horses running with $8,500 claiming tags at MARYLAND and FLORIDA tracks were unmistakably superior to those fetching $10,000 in New York and New Jersey.

Large differences in claiming price continue to signify decisive differences in equine quality, but are seldom a matter of handicapping concern. If a horse moves from a victory at $5,000 to a race against $15,000 animals, the handicapper assumes with justified confidence that the trainer is cuckoo. Or if a horse drops from $15,000 to $5,000, it surely has gone bad. In all cases of drastic price rises or drops, considerations of distance, form, and speed usually help. If not, and if doubt persists, the handicapper avoids betting on the race. A race is PLAYABLE to the degree that it lacks mystery, permitting the handicapper to appraise each starter's chances in terms of reasonably predictable ability.

Pursuing the relationship between claiming price and class, it is essential to understand that horses of vastly differing talents run at the same claiming price. For the grossest example, a two-year-old MAIDEN filly entered for $25,000 is no match whatever for a five-year-old gelding that runs in a race open to any $25,000 animal on the grounds. Handicappers who save RESULTS CHARTS or log race CONDITIONS in notebooks often cash bets on horses whose apparent increases in claiming price conceal moves to less difficult levels of competition. At minor tracks, for example, it is customary to classify cheap claimers according to the number of races previously won at the particular price. Thus, a horse that wins the track's supreme $2,000 claiming race—for those that have won a few such races in the past—almost always does so in better time than the horse that wins a gallop against livestock entered for $2,500 in a race for non-winners at that level. A casual handicapper, noticing that the winner of the $2,000 race is not only nine years old but is now trying to step up 25 percent to $2,500 company, might downgrade the animal and would often be mistaken.

At major tracks, any claiming price covers a multitude of situations. The least of these, of course, are maiden races for fillies and mares. Next are maiden races open to males. Next are races for animals that have not won a

race all year, or for a period of months. Slightly better are those for horses that *have* won. As the number and recency of permissible victories increases, so does the quality of the competition. In most places, however, a race open only to horses bred in the particular state is greatly inferior to a race in which any otherwise qualified horse may run. And, of course, the best claimer at a given level is the one open to all male three-year-olds and up or four-year-olds and up, regardless of previous achievements.

Although SELECTION SYSTEMS almost invariably presume that any old allowance race is of higher class than any claimer, the fact is that top-grade claiming races at major tracks engage animals able to hold their own in allowance company, and even in lesser stakes. At what claiming price does this occur? Each season, the handicapper takes careful note of the highest-priced claiming races at the local track, the kinds of horses entered, and the purses awarded. In 1974, for example, a nice New York runner that had been doing well in $25,000 claimers was often at an advantage when entered in a typical allowance affair for non-winners of a race or two other than maiden or claiming. By the winter of 1976, the same kind of horse was running for an inflated $35,000 claiming price.

CLASS is quality as demonstrated in competition. High class is the willingness to win in fast company, plus the physique to do something about it. Lower class is a shortage of willingness, speed, or stamina, or some combination of them. As a property of living things, Thoroughbred class is anything but permanent. It changes, more often for the worse than the better. Legs go bad. Temperaments sour. Last year's classy runner is no longer the same animal. Accordingly, class is inseparably related to FORM.

When out of form, no Thoroughbred should race. It betrays its lack of fitness through loss of appetite, indifferent workouts, distressed behavior, lackluster appearance and, of course, poor performance on the track. Raced when it should be rested, it lacks its previous class and may emerge from the ordeal with class severely and permanently damaged. This happens to Triple Crown candidates, classic winners, green two-year-olds and $3,000 eight-year-olds alike.

Experts may cite CONFORMATION or BREEDING in their conjecture about the potentialities of an unraced horse, but the truth cannot be known until the horse has defined itself in actual races. It may compete many times before settling down sufficiently to beat a field or two and stand forth as (for the time being) a future stakes winner, a useful $15,000 claimer, or $1,500 worth. This holds true absolutely regardless of the price that may have been paid for the animal as a yearling.

Because class is synonymous with current ability, it is central to the deliberations of all handicappers. As we shall see, they approach the factor diversely. But after they have exercised their vari-

ous techniques, it becomes clear enough that they have (a) eliminated plainly outclassed horses as non-contenders, and (b) separated the likely contenders by means of formulas designed to ferret out significant class differences. Probed further, handicapping theory concedes that a Thoroughbred of relatively high class need not be at its absolute peak of form to defeat lesser animals and, when in exceptionally fine condition, might be able to win at other than its favorite distance, or when burdened with unusually high WEIGHTS, or with an unfavorable POST POSITION. In most races, however, class differences are not so pronounced. The final decision usually depends on careful analysis of class in its interrelationships with the other FUNDAMENTALS of handicapping.

Here are the principal means of evaluating class:

Speed. The better the horse, the faster at the distance. The median speed of races at any track and any distance for horses of a given age, sex, and class level is about a fifth of a second faster than the median in the next lower class bracket, and about a fifth slower than the median in the next higher. To determine these medians is grueling work which requires compilation of a representative series of running times in each age-sex-class-distance category at the individual track on days when the racing strip is dry and fast. When based on adequate samples, the medians compensate for the well-known and widely baffling variations in running time that so many horsemen and handicappers attribute to the unpredictability of Thoroughbreds and the undependability of time as a handicapping factor. In reality, departures from median times are due less to Thoroughbred unpredictability than to wind, dampness, jockeying, racing luck, improving or declining form and class, abnormally fast or slow early speed, and changes in the depth or resilience of the racing strip caused by track maintenance or a lack thereof.

The times of an individual Thoroughbred's recent races are a sample too small to absorb and balance the effects on running time of weather and the other variables just mentioned. To tell how well a horse actually ran, the speed handicapper modifies its official time with a speed variant (generally called "track variant")—a number intended to factor out all influences on running time except the actual quality of the race and the performance of the horse. This book's articles on SPEED HANDICAPPING present various ways of confronting that task. The best techniques enable a competent analyst not only to evaluate the recent class of contenders but, equally important, to identify those whose form and/or class may be improving or worsening. Because extremely few handicappers have the time or motivation for all that work, it should be remarked that less demanding procedures also help. For example, DAILY RACING FORM speed ratings, unmodified by a variant, often point out contenders of superior current class. Extensive computer studies have demonstrated this and have also shown that when the *Form* speed ratings are

supplemented with the paper's own simple variant (which, as of 1978, was published only in its Eastern editions), results become more satisfactory. Comparisons of *Form* speed ratings are most reliable when made entirely on the basis of races at the same distance over the same track.

Results Charts or Notebooks. Because a race described in the *Form* PAST-PERFORMANCE TABLES as an allowance or a $10,000 claimer surely differs greatly from other allowance races or $10,000 claimers, some handicappers attend to the class factor by clipping and filing results charts. These contain detailed eligibility conditions which reveal class differences unspecified in the past-performance tables. Other handicappers record each day's eligibility conditions in a notebook, along with pertinent information about the running of every race. If a study of charts or notes discloses that a horse has been performing honorably in circumstances more demanding than other contenders have faced, the horse's chances are probably better than may be apparent to horseplayers who do not know whether one previous allowance or claiming race was of higher quality than another. Thus, the odds may be attractive—the hallmark of a good bet.

Many handicappers assume that the class of a race is proportional to its PURSE. This has always been true when comparisons were confined to races at one track, and mid-season raises or reductions in the local purse schedule were carefully noted. It also is true that tracks offering higher purses attract stables of generally higher quality. Thus, it can be taken for granted that a $10,000 claiming runner from a track with a relatively modest purse schedule will be outgunned if it ships to Hollywood Park and tries to run in a $10,000 claiming race. But such generalizations can be carried too far. Year in and year out, allowance horses from Bay Meadows and Golden Gate Fields win claiming races at Santa Anita or Hollywood Park, although those Southern California races command higher purses than reward allowance winners in Northern California. Similarly, allowance runners that ship from Aqueduct to compete for smaller purses at Monmouth Park do not always win. Summing up, the question of track class can be resolved over the long haul by expecting horses that have been winning relatively large purses at one track to defeat horses that have been winning relatively small purses at another. But the handicapper is interested more in the next race than in the long haul. Lacking confident knowledge that the case at hand involves not only higher past purses but a horse of authentically higher class, the prudent handicapper passes the race, letting the SHIPPER run a race over the track to show what it can do locally.

Earnings. Responsible studies, including various computer exercises, show that horses with comparatively high previous earnings win more than their share of races, and horses with poor earnings win less. If the high earnings are of recent vintage, the horse is likely to run at short odds. It also may be on the downside of its form cycle and lose. If the

earnings were collected many months previously and the horse's recent performances have been poor, we have the phenomenon known to system peddlers as "back class," which means former class. The individual past-performance table may show previous victories in races of higher class than the one being handicapped. If the animal's gross earnings are the highest in its field, it has a somewhat better statistical chance to win than any other starter. And if the handicapper calculates average earnings by dividing each horse's number of races this year (or this year and last) into its gross earnings over the corresponding period, the highest quotient also identifies the horse that would be the likeliest winner if no other handicapping standard were applied. Finally, the earnings table can be dismantled to show the average purse for which the horse has competed most successfully in the past. In a region where the winner of each race gets 65 percent of the purse, the place horse gets 20, the third 10, and the fourth 5, the handicapper multiplies each animal's number of wins by .65, its seconds by .20, and so on, including whatever fourths may appear in the past-performance lines (they are not included in the earnings summary atop the past-performance table). Adding all the resultant products and dividing that sum into the horse's gross earnings gives the average-purse figure. In a sample of 403 allowance races, Frederick S. Davis found that horses that had competed well for purses at least 30 percent higher than the purse of the upcoming race won just about twice their share of the time. That is, they represented 10.5 percent of all the starters but won 20.9 percent of the races.

Davis and others have created effective handicapping procedures in which past earnings are a factor suggestive of present class. When such an approach remains alert to the decisive importance of current form, it deserves respect. If a horse of formerly high class has gone out of form and descended the scale but has recently begun to round into form sufficient to make it a contender in weak company, its previous accomplishments are surely relevant to the situation, even though the horse may never again run as well as it once did. The horse whose good earnings are ancient history does not win often enough, even at high odds, to qualify earnings alone as a dependable means of separating contenders.

Consistency. The late Robert S. Dowst, a justly venerated figure in the dubious field of handicapping instruction, preferred a horse that had won at least 20 percent of its starts and had, moreover, shown that it could maintain that level against fields of the quality it was now being called upon to face. To this day, consistent horses have a much better chance to win than inconsistent ones do. But fewer consistent horses are to be found and, in any event, last year's consistency seldom reveals much about this afternoon's performance. In an era when current form and ability at the distance are the decisive handicapping factors in most races, consistency assumes significance only if recent. Fred Davis found that a horse unable to win as many as two of its latest six starts

needed strong attributes in other departments to be worth a bet in an allowance race. Horses that had won two or more of their latest six were by no means certainties in their next outings, but deserved close attention.

Direct Comparison. At a handicapping seminar in 1975, I was greeted by a young man who said he was making a living through bets on horses pointed out by a classification technique which I had once described in print as "The Golden Notebook." Anyone capable of maintaining so involved a set of records deserves rewards beyond a mere living. The procedure resembles speed handicapping of the highest order but concerns itself only with class-form comparisons of horses, without reference to running times.

Like advanced speed handicapping, this approach requires careful analysis of each race after it is run. To miss a single race can undermine the entire effort. And, if the handicapper operates on the East Coast, with its constant equine traffic from track to track, best results necessitate analysis of every race at as many as five tracks a day. The equipment for this, besides extreme self-interest and an abiding love of handicapping, are *Daily Racing Form* results charts and past-performance pages, plus a notebook.

Here is a sample from such a notebook:

4. 12.5, 35/40, 3up. 360

The notation means that the fourth race of the day entailed a $12,500 purse for three-year-olds and up entered to be claimed for $35,000 to $40,000 and that the winner emerged with a rating of 360, a shorthand figure signifying that the handicapper believes it is a $36,000 horse and should run like one, defeating $35,000 horses or losing to $37,000 horses in its next race.

Wherefrom the arbitrary rating of 360? And what about ratings for the horses that ran behind the winner? And why no notation of the race distance?

Answering the last question first, when the handicapper makes selections in future races, the notebook functions in tandem with the past-performance tables of the horses entered in those races. The past-performance lines give the distance of each past race, and where the individual horse finished. The ratings of non-winners are calculated (in most cases) by simply subtracting formula amounts from the notebook figure assigned to the winner. And the winner's rating derives from delicate analysis of (a) the results chart of its winning race, and (b) its own rating and those of its competition immediately before that winning race. For those pre-race ratings, previous notebook pages are consulted along with the relevant past-performance lines.

If a horse won a race for animals priced as high as $40,000, one might expect its rating to be at least 400—or $40,000. In some circumstances, to be sure, its rating might be even higher than that. It all depends on how the race was run and which horses were actually in the hunt before losing, and what their own pre-race ratings happened to be.

This particular winner's rating of only 360 suggests that if any higher-rated animals were in the field, they didn't run an inch. That winner had nothing to beat but a few lower-rated horses.

The authority with which a horse wins also influences its rating. If it tow-ropes its field and draws away at the finish, signifying vigorous form and likely improvement, the handicapper probably decides that it can tolerate a substantial rise in class. He might give it a 420 or 430, especially if the horses in closest pursuit had come into the race with figures of 390 or 400.

After a victory so authoritative, the handicapper's notebook would contain an additional figure—the one assigned to the horse that finished second in what amounted to a private race among the losers. Here again, the rating would be governed by the manner in which this second horse beat the others, how the others rated before the race, and what the performance seemed to imply about the animal's class and fitness in its next start.

When horses simply get out there and run their races, and none shows special improvement, the post-race ratings closely resemble the pre-race ones. If, as happens often, one of the losers suffered bad luck, the excuse should be recorded in the notebook: "#5, 370" would mean that the fifth-place horse ran into trouble and, if unimpeded, would probably have earned a rating of 370.

To rate the horses that run behind a winner without noticeable excuse, deductions from the winner's figure are made at whatever standard rate suits the handicapper. One excellent method deducts 10 points per beaten length in rating a horse that hinted future improvement by showing more early speed than usual, or by showing a strong run in the late stages. And 20 points per length are deducted from the animal that lost without distinguishing itself in any way. These particular ratings need not be assigned until the horses run again, whereupon a glance at the past-performance lines and the relevant notebook pages tells the tale.

Another workable approach rates the winner and, if appropriate, the second and/or third horses in ways already described, but reassigns the pre-race figures to horses that lost predictably without displaying improved or deteriorating form. Horses that lost while improving or tailing off have their pre-race figures increased or lowered according to the handicapper's estimate of their immediate propsects.

One of the great advantages of the notebook is that the handicapper can correct errors as events unfold. If entire races or individual horses were inaccurately rated, and subsequent results prove it, the handicapper simply revises the inaccurate race ratings and thenceforth the ratings of all horses whose figures were distorted.

Readers may wonder why all this notation cannot be made right on the results charts, without the bother of a notebook. It can be done that way but, in the East, the handicapper is saddled with bales of results charts from various racing circuits. In whatever mode the handicapper chooses to proceed, the effort ensures extremely accurate class/form evaluation of horses, a profound advantage at the betting windows.

Past-Performance Tables. By comparison with the intricate operations reviewed above, a cursory look at class notations in the past-performance tables is less than satisfactory. But it works well enough to make winners of players who undoubtedly were losers before they began to understand the significance of the various class rises and class drops disclosed in the past performances. Some helpful rules of thumb:

1. Because runners in maiden-claiming races have not yet established anything about their class other than that their trainers have a dim view of it, differences in maiden-claiming prices mean little. A maiden that loses when entered for $20,000 is no cinch if dropped to $12,000. In these races, form, speed, and ability to run the distance are almost always the whole story.

2. The winner of a maiden-claiming race has defeated animals of unestablished or nonexistent quality. Without knowledge that it showed legitimate speed, the handicapper should not expect it to beat previous winners unless dropped in claiming price.

3. The winner of a *non-claiming* maiden race may not be a future stakes winner but at least is well-regarded enough to have been protected from claims. Moreover, it has beaten other more-or-less promising maidens. In its next start, for non-winners of an al-

lowance race, it may enjoy a real advantage. It should never be downgraded for moving from a maiden race to that kind of allowance company. It moves there because the rules require it to. If it won its maiden race nicely and now meets a field composed mainly of horses that have failed repeatedly at this low allowance level, it probably is a good bet.

4. A step to the next higher allowance level or claiming price is no problem for a lightly raced horse that has done everything asked of it in the recent past. Neither does it threaten loss to an older horse—even a cheap one—that has shown some improvement.

5. In better allowance races, a record of good performance in stakes company is a sign of class, especially if the better races were recent, the horse appears to be fit, and the distance is right. Interestingly, Fred Davis discovered that a random horse that has run in a random stakes is a prospect when entered in an allowance race, regardless of how it may have finished in the stakes. Obviously, its chances improve when it withstands closer scrutiny of its present condition and other fundamental attributes. Nevertheless, previous stakes runners were only 28 percent of all the horses in Davis' allowance-race study, but won 47.5 percent of the races.

6. When horses move in class from allowance company to claimers, or from one claiming price to a lower, the class drop may be more apparent than real. On every circuit, the horses that compete in top-level claimers are at no disadvantage against weaker allowance animals. The claiming prices and allowance conditions at which this occurs vary from place to place and year to year but are readily determined by observation of purse schedules, analyses of speed, and study of recent races in which such claimers opposed allowance stock. A horse unable to cope with $15,000 claiming animals that have not been winning many races is not likely to defeat a field of $12,000 runners in a race open to recent winners. As this suggests, if a horse has been running respectably in losing efforts against recent $15,000 winners, it will have easy pickings when dropped into a scrimmage against $12,000 ones with poor performance records. A collection of results charts comes in handy for this kind of study, as does an ability to evaluate the dropped-down entrant's recent trends in form and speed. Is the trainer trying to win a purse or merely trying to unload the horse on another barn? Or both? The answer often is apparent before the race. As a generality, large claiming-price drops almost invariably indicate physical deterioration. Moneymaking runners are in such short supply that barns do not normally try to dispose of them at cut-rate claiming prices. Sometimes these damaged animals win, but not often enough to balance the low odds that they are likely to pay. Interestingly, as late as 1977, Eastern racing audiences had not yet become adequately suspicious of horses dropped sharply in claiming price, continuing to overbet them as if a price drop were still a sign of all-out stable effort, as it had

been two decades earlier. Even more interestingly, drops in claiming price were not yet so conspicuous a sign of despair in Southern California. In a good handicapping procedure entitled *The Winning Prescription* (published by Jabno, Inc., Pasadena, California), Robert E. Becker, Ph.D., showed how successive meetings at Santa Anita, Hollywood Park, and Del Mar were roundly beaten when play was confined to horses dropping down after good recent races. In the East, the dropdown after a good recent race had become rare.

Pace. Many handicappers, including more than a few professionals, depend on detailed analyses of the fractional times of each contender's best races. Various rating procedures rank the horses numerically. For example, the official quarter-mile, half-mile, and final time of the most recent race in which a horse performed well is written down, along with the horse's own final time or *Daily Racing Form* speed rating in that race, plus a number representing the class of the race ("50" might mean a $5,000 claimer). The horse that ran in the race with the fastest quarter-mile time is awarded 10 points, and the other horses one point less for each fifth of a second slower official quarter-mile time. The same procedure rates each of the official half-mile times and each horse's own final time or speed rating. The horse that ran in the race of highest class also gets 10, and others less at the rate of one point per 5 points of class. If all rated races were at the same distance on the same track and the times are modi-

fied with a speed variant expressing the relative speed of the track when each race was run, the final figures are a good indicator of class differences. Without variants, they are less reliable. And they are even less reliable when ratings are not confined to recent races, with alert attention to improving and declining form.

Some handicappers simplify the work by eliminating the quarter-mile or half-mile time. Others overcome the absence of speed variants to some extent by rating each of the contenders' three most recent races, regardless of distance, using PAR TIMES for each fractional and final time and assigning each horse figures that represent the difference between its own performance and par at each stage of the three races. In this method, official times are used only as a basis for calculating a horse's own time. This is done conventionally, in terms of the number of lengths behind the leader at each call. One-fifth of a second is added to the official time for each length behind.

A comparable approach ignores time but rates the horses on their running positions or lengths behind at each stage of their latest three races. A horse running first gets a 10. Others get one point less for running second, two less for third, and so on. Or a point can be subtracted for each length behind a leader at each point of call. In 1976, Jayce Killaen, a Canadian handicapper, published a computer study that yielded more sophisticated and much more productive ratings of that kind.

CLOCKERS time the morning WORK-OUTS with stopwatches, reporting their findings to the DAILY RACING FORM or the office of the track's racing secretary or, in some cases, to private clients who pay well for unpublished information such as the high weight of the exercise rider, how far the horse ran from the rail on the turn (covering extra distance), how tired the animal was after the exertion and, I am afraid, the number of extra fifths of a second that found their way into the official workout report on a horse that actually ran faster and is ready to win. Exposed to temptation as some clockers are, better tracks take pains to ensure the accuracy of their reports. Stakes horses get so much attention that their published workout times are invariably accurate. Allowance and claiming runners are another matter. At most tracks, the wise handicapper pays more attention to the frequency and distances of workouts than their times.

COLOR is of no importance to the handicapper. Gray horses run as well as bays or chestnuts or roans, in case a contrary superstition has been peddled to the reader. And horses with white feet or white stockings (lower leg), such as Secretariat, manage to survive. The fact that some horsemen prefer dark feet and ankles is entirely irrelevant to the handicapping process, which depends on analysis of actual performances.

COLORADO. Centennial is a one-mile track near Denver. Its purses for day-in-day-out claiming and allowance races approximate those of Pocono Downs and Assiniboia Downs and are lower than those of other minor tracks such as Waterford Park and Charles Town. The percentage of winning FAVORITES keeps pace with the national average (32 or so), and a horse need not have high EARLY SPEED to win, although it helps.

COLORS. The racing colors of the individual stable may become part of the tradition of the turf if the stable is Calumet or Whitney and wins enough big races. The success of the stable's current TRAINER is much more important to the handicapper than are the colors of its silks. Colors are mentioned here only because surprisingly few racegoers take a hard look at them when the horses come onto the track before the race. If one knows the colors worn by the riders of the likely contenders, the race becomes easier to watch. To disregard colors and try to identify the key horses by the numbers on their saddle cloths is more difficult.

CONDITIONS. The conditions of eligibility for each race are prescribed in writing (the condition book) by the racing secretary. That functionary's first objective is to write conditions suited to optimum numbers of ready, available horses. A secondary goal is to schedule races covering a wide enough CLASS range to accommodate all ready horses during each 10- or 12-day period covered by the book. And at tracks operated or otherwise influenced by the

OWNERS of prominent stables, the secretary may contrive to write an occasional race made to order for the pet runner of one or another such outfit. Racing secretaries have no need for the numerical complications and other rarefied studies that occupy the handicapper. Because racing folk classify Thoroughbreds in terms of claiming prices and/or numbers of races won and/or number of wins at stated PURSE values and/or WEIGHTS carried, the secretary merely tries to write each race tightly enough to exclude animals too accomplished for the field. Thus, the conditions for an allowance race might restrict eligibility to non-winners of $6,500 (winner's share of a $10,000 purse) twice in the past two months. If the secretary knows the local horses, such a race makes sense, attracting the owners and trainers of eight or ten fit Thoroughbreds that might be unable to compete with horses of greater recent achievement. If the secretary has reason to expect that a superior horse might be entered (having won one $15,000 race two weeks ago after a long layoff), the conditions can be elaborated to put unbearable weight on winners of a large purse during the specified two months or, for that matter, at any time.

A careful reading of the conditions, including those governing weights, is mandatory in handicapping. Often enough, comparison of a horse's past-performance record with the conditions of the upcoming race shows that the animal is over its head or that, barely qualifying for entry, and carrying top weight in the field, it is a probable con-tender. Regardless of the handicapper's favorite approach to separating contenders (after having identified them), final selections improve when the conditions of the race being handicapped are compared with the conditions under which the horses ran their recent races. *Daily Racing Form* RESULTS CHARTS are vital. The horse narrowly beaten in a race open to any $15,000 claiming animal has performed well in competition of higher CLASS than would be found in another race programmed for three-year-olds that had never won at the distance. On the face of it, and even without reference to comparative times, it can be taken for granted that the narrow winner of the latter race will now be attempting a much larger order.

See also, FOOTING.

CONFORMATION. Buyers and sellers of young Thoroughbreds are much concerned with the physique of each animal. The closer the conformation approaches perfection, the less the likelihood that the animal will fail because of some structural defect. Yet actual perfection has not been seen. Horsemen have had serious doubts about the physical attributes of immortal runners from Eclipse (haunches too high) to Exterminator (too bony) to Morvich (knock knees) to Count Fleet (pasterns vulnerably long) to Noor (suspicious-looking ankles) to Buckpasser (fragile hooves) to any horse you care to name.

That being the case, it is pretentiously futile to go to the PADDOCK to evaluate the conformation of a horse. Mighty fine conformations finish last in $2,000 claiming races, the handsome animals being disabled by inadequate respiratory systems (invisible from the paddock rail) or flawed mentality (not always conspicuous until the race). The proper concentration of the handicapper is the horse's record. The visit to the paddock supplements the record by helping the handicapper decide whether a top selection seems ready to race. Its unpromising behavior may stem from discomfort or battle-weariness, either of which is more significant than conformation. Through diligent application and repeated practice, some handicappers learn to recognize the small, high-heeled, cuplike hoof associated with superior ability in mud, and the large, low-heeled, flat foot that often comes into its own on grass. Of all aspects of conformation, these merit most attention from handicappers who can find the time.

See also, BANDAGES, INJURIES, PADDOCK.

CONTENDERS. A horse is a legitimate contender if it seems to be in good FORM, is suited to the DISTANCE of the race, and is at no obvious disadvantage in CLASS, EARLY SPEED, or FOOTING. The effort to identify contenders and eliminate probable non-contenders is the first phase of the handicapping process. The second is separation of the contenders—the attempt to find a sensible bet. For this, the handicapper sees if distinctions can be made in terms of class, early speed, POST POSITION, WEIGHTS, FOOTING, JOCKEY, TRAINER, PADDOCK and, finally, ODDS. Certain SPEED HANDICAPPERS and other adherents of numerical rating formulas skip the first phase, accepting all starters as contenders and allowing numbers to make their selections for them. Procedures of that kind demand less thought but fall short otherwise. Too often, they confer top ratings on non-contenders, especially horses out of form or unsuited to the distances at which they are entered. When non-contenders win, they sometimes return handsome mutuel prices, elevating the bettor's morale without repaying previous losses on non-contenders that ran poorly. Much better results derive from scrutinizing each field in terms of form, distance, footing, and gross class discrepancies, eliminating the non-contenders (including a satisfactory proportion of betting FAVORITES), and finding a selection through closer study of the actual contenders.

D

DAILY DOUBLE. Among numerous MULTIPLE BETTING propositions with which track managements and their senior partners, the state legislatures, try to empty the pockets of defenseless gamblers, the daily double was the first to become a standard feature of North American racing programs. The bettor undertakes to pick the winners of two races—usually the first two on the day's program. The money goes into a separate pool. After lawful deductions of perhaps 18.5 percent of the pooled money for state taxes and track operations, the winners collect the remainder of the pool. Whoever has picked one winner and one loser is in the same boat as those who bought tickets naming two losers.

For decades, the double was sucker bait of a kind more blatant than could be found in any gambling casino. It was a pig in a poke for persons silly enough to make bets without knowing the ODDS. But in the 1970's the proposition was improved by the introduction of modern odds-display facilities at better tracks. Wherever the probable payoffs are posted during the betting period *before the first of the two races,* the double is less noxious. In OFF-TRACK BETTING and at tracks that do not reveal the various payoff possibilities until betting has ended, the double remains a snare. In the best of circumstances, it is a bet more risky than others, not only because of the difficulty of picking two winners in succession but because, odds display or not, the bet must be made before the first of the two races, preventing the player from inspecting the horse or horses selected in the second of the two races. This greatly enlarges the gamble, which already is greater than most doubles fanciers realize.

For example, the probability that the

FAVORITE will win a random race is higher than the probability that any other horse will win that race. The figure is about .32, equivalent to odds of 2–1. The probability that favorites will win both of any two races is .11, or 8–1. But favorites do not usually pay 2–1. Because of a pari-mutuel takeout which in the 1970's was skimming about 36 cents from each $2.00 bet, the median mutuel price of natural 2–1 favorites was $5.00—odds of only 3–2. When two 3–2 favorites win the daily-double races, the payoff seldom exceeds $12 (5–1), which no sane human being should accept when the actual chances against winning are closer to 8–1.

Although informed racegoers with reserved attitudes toward the doubles also give up about 18 cents of each wagered dollar and find the exorbitant house percentage severely difficult to overcome, they at least can pick their spots. The double sometimes qualifies. Where the probable payoffs are visible before the double bet is placed, a handicapper may discover that tickets on various combinations of contenders in the two races could pay enough to justify the risks. One of the more attractive opportunities of this kind arises when the handicapper likes a horse going at good odds in one of the races and believes that the other race is essentially unplayable because the present FORM and other attributes of the horses are beyond appraisal. Knowing that longshots often win such races and that even the favorites pay 2–1 or more, the handicapper "wheels" the sound selection in the one race—buying tickets that couple it with every starter in the other. If the prime selection wins, the payoff may be high. But if the winner of the unplayable half of the double turns out to be short-priced, the handicapper may notice that more money could have been made by skipping the double and buying extra win tickets on the good selection in the other race. An unwelcome variation of this arises when the winners of both ends of the double are longshots. Much too often, a combination ticket on the winning pair pays less than would be made with a parlay. That is, the proceeds of the winning tickets on the longshot winner of the first race can be bet on the selection in the second race. One reason doubles payoffs on longshot combinations may produce less profit than an ordinary parlay is that racegoers tend to overbet longshots in the doubles, thereby depressing their prices to some extent. Another reason is that betting stables occasionally concentrate their own investments in the doubles, thereby avoiding the clearly visible reduction in ordinary win odds and the popular rush toward the windows that large straight win bets might produce.

Some handicappers who keep an eye on the pre-race displays of probable payoffs manage to cash some doubles tickets when both races strike them as playable. They couple two or more selections in each of the races—whatever combinations include their top choices. And they bet only when content that each ticket will pay enough if it wins to warrant the outlay.

DAILY RACING FORM. This newspaper's copyrighted RESULTS CHARTS and PAST-PERFORMANCE TABLES are the official records of North American racing. No jockey, trainer, owner, or handicapper can function without the *Form,* and none tries. In addition to the essential information in the charts and tables, the paper reports recent WORKOUTS, keeps abreast of developments among breeders, summarizes the public proceedings of leading organizations in the field, publishes interviews with industry leaders, reports the rulings of stewards and state racing commissions, and contains daily columns about humans and horses at individual tracks. At this writing, a full newspaper-size *Form* was printed for circulation in East Coast racing centers, and tabloid editions were offered everywhere else in the U.S. and Canada.

DELAWARE. Despite financial setbacks in competition with nearby Maryland, New Jersey, and Pennsylvania tracks, Delaware Park continued its traditional summer meetings into the late 1970's. First and foremost a horsemen's track, Delaware resembled Keeneland in giving influential stables frequent opportunities to test inexperienced runners. Programs were replete with MAIDEN and TURF races, in addition to the usual main-track fare. Delaware even was a refuge for STEEPLECHASES, seldom seen in major-league environs. Purses for overnight races compared favorably with those of Bowie and Laurel, attracting enough fit Maryland horses to permit trainers from that state to dominate the winner's circle. The track had always been one of the most pleasant in the East, with reasonable prices, a woodsy paddock, and courteous help. As the crowds diminished, the place became a true paradise. With six daily EXACTAS, two TRIFECTAS, and a DAILY DOUBLE to occupy the tourists, it was no problem for a handicapper to buy a *straight* win ticket at the last minute before post time. And good seats were plentiful. The one-mile oval, though somewhat deep, was more hospitable to horses with EARLY SPEED than most handicappers realized, and became more so when sloppy. Drying out, it was tiring to front-runners, much like the main tracks at Aqueduct and Belmont Park. The seven-furlong grass course favored stretch-running ability and the six innermost post positions.

DISTANCE. Successful handicapping begins with the ability to weed out non-CONTENDERS whose records proclaim poor FORM, inadequate CLASS, or unsuitability to the specific distance of the race. Distance is the least complicated of these factors, and much the least frustrating, yet the most neglected. A handicapper gains great advantage by spending a couple of minutes trying to decide which starters may like the distance and which may not.

About 72 percent of North American races are SPRINTS at distances of less than a mile. After the age of two, American Thoroughbreds race six furlongs more often than any other distance. Having been bred and trained for that limited function, most of them prefer it. But breeding and training are imprecise and Thoroughbreds are not machines. Most fields of horses entered to run six furlongs include a few that belong at other distances.

Horse A always flies from the starting gate as if jet-propelled, but tires on the turn for home and cannot be found at the finish. That animal needs to run four-and-a-half-furlong dashes at some BULL RING. Horse B lacks EARLY SPEED and is seldom in the front half of its field in the first quarter-mile, but usually gains ground in the final stages. It occasionally wins on days when TRACK CONDITIONS and/or duels for the early lead and/or RACING LUCK conspire to pickle horses that are quicker from the gate. If the track programmed races at six and a half or seven furlongs, B might have the extra territory it needs to reach the front more frequently. Properly trained, it might also be a candidate for races at a mile or more around two turns. In those circumstances it would have more early speed than many of its opponents, and might win more often.

For reasons invalidated by reality, some handicappers assume that every TRAINER can be depended on to enter a fit horse at comfortable distances. But no track offers races at enough distances to suit every horse. Moreover, some trainers seem oblivious to the distance factor—or behave as if they were, which amounts to the same thing. Even in California and New York, the capitals of

the sport, trainers repeatedly send horses into sprints that they cannot possibly handle, or into ROUTES beyond their capacities. Competence is not more widespread among trainers than among plumbers or authors. This becomes inescapably evident when a really expert trainer finally gets hold of an habitually misplaced animal, corrects its SHOES, improves its nutrition, grants it a needed rest, enters it at proper distances, and moves it up the class ladder.

Trainers who understand the distance factor use it cleverly, deliberately running horses too long or too short, trying to improve their form while concealing the improvement from other trainers and, of course, from bettors. Handicappers attentive to distance can usually tell when a horse has been misplaced for conditioning purposes. Or when a supremely astute operative such as H. Allen Jerkens enters a sprinter in a long race, or a miler in a sprint, observant handicappers know that here, at last, is a situation in which it might pay to assume that a previously typecast animal is ready for something new.

For purposes of identifying contenders, one can accept the individual horse as suited to the distance of the race if it has already demonstrated its ability by winning at that distance, or at least finishing in the money after running in the first half of the field most of the way. The more recent the victory or in-the-money finish, the more convincing the evidence. But if the good performance was followed by a succession of failures, a second look may disclose that the animal's running style has changed. Injury-connected recesses from racing and training sometimes alter a horse's gait or weaken or strengthen its wind. The fact that a horse led from wire to wire at today's distance six months ago is not persuasive if its recent efforts have found it devoid of early speed, running like a race horse only in the home stretch, too late to win.

The relevance of a horse's latest performances cannot be overemphasized. The handicapper must compare today's distance with the distances of the horse's latest race or two or three, and with the manner in which the horse ran. Did it perform like a horse that wants more distance? Less distance? Might today's lower class enable it to carry its early speed closer to the finish or enable it to overcome its lack of early speed and catch cheaper opponents?

The handicapper should always regard as a contender any horse entered at a longer distance after performing in shorter races as if it needed longer. Equally welcome is a horse entered at a shorter distance after showing early speed and tiring. This holds true even if the animal has failed in the past to handle today's distance. If races or WORKOUTS have been recent and frequent enough to suggest physical fitness, and if a preliminary glance reveals no severe class disadvantage, the horse is a contender worth examining more closely in comparison with the other contenders.

When the recent record seems unclear as to a particular Thoroughbred's liking for the distance of its race, Frederick S. Davis supplies helpful criteria. His research shows that 80 percent of all winners go to the post with past-performance records that include occasions on which they finished first or second—or less than three lengths behind the winner—at a distance not more than one-sixteenth of a mile different from the distance of the upcoming race. Equally qualified are horses that may not meet the standard but have performed that well in races *both* longer and shorter. To clarify, when today's race is at six furlongs, a horse is acceptable that has won or finished second or less than three lengths behind at five and a half, six, or six and a half furlongs. So would a horse that finished so well at *both* five and seven furlongs, even if not at six.

Among horses attempting to stretch out an extra sixteenth or eighth of a mile, the style of recent performances is an accurate indicator. A horse can be accepted at face value if it won its recent shorter race while drawing away or with apparent speed in reserve. So can a horse that ran well in the late stages, failing to win only because the race ended too soon. A less likely candidate is the type that barely hangs on to win at the shorter distance, or repeatedly loses while tiring. Facing essentially the same quality of opposition at a slightly longer distance, such a horse is even less likely to survive the stretch run. The exception would be one that tired in the first race of its career or in its first race after a lengthy absence. Assuming that it comes from a good barn, the one race may well have been the conditioner it needed, and the extra distance may be no problem.

Much has been written about Thoroughbreds that win at long distances after tiring at short. This happens most often when sprinters try materially longer distances, such as a mile or beyond. In these circumstances, the handicapper examines the distance question more elaborately. Will the sprinter have an easy time getting the early lead and saving ground by loping comfortably along the rail on the first turn? Does it have an inside post position to help in that respect? Is it lightly weighted? Might it be facing horses of lower class than the sprinters with which it has been competing? When the answers are affirmative, the horse is a contender, and will remain so if it seems to be in form.

Horses whose best performances have been at one and one-sixteenth or one and one-eighth miles or farther are less likely to be contenders in sprints than is the fit sprinter in a middle-distance race. If the horse has been showing good early speed in longer races but fading in the stretch, a handicapper may reasonably suppose that it might be more successful in a sprint—but should not expect that it will have enough speed to run with the early leaders. Early speed in sprints is considerably more rapid than in routes. So the horse switching from a long to a short race is at a disadvantage and cannot be regarded as a contender except in situations where (a) the horses with early speed look as if they might defeat each other, (b) the others are no

great shakes, (c) the track is kindly to come-from-behind types, (d) the horse may have a class advantage and, by no means least, (e) the ODDS are attractive.

Let me emphasize that the identification of contenders on grounds of distance is inseparable from the factors of form and class. With experience, this first phase of the handicapping process occupies but a minute or two and ends when horses least likely to run well have been eliminated for one or another patently obvious reason. This frees the handicapper for the more delicately detailed job of seeking differences among the actual contenders.

A final note should begin with acknowledgment that careful attention to the distance factor does not immunize the handicapper against loss, but guarantees fewer errors. Having presided over thousands of highly personal postmortems in which I attempted to explain why my horse lost, I have most often decided that it lost because its form was not as sharp as anticipated, or because some other horse was in unexpectedly good form. Somewhat less often, I have been able to blame RACING LUCK. Least often, the horse has lost because I overestimated its ability at the distance or underestimated the distance ability of another. But scarcely a day has passed on which a horse of mine has not finished ahead of some overbet animal unable to get the distance of the race.

See also, TURF RACING.

DUTCHING. Before PARI-MUTUEL BETTING expelled the BOOKMAKERS from the racetrack lawns, handicappers could actually shop for favorable ODDS. Each winning bet paid whatever price the bookmaker quoted when the deal was made. A wager on a winning horse might pay 6–1 to an early bettor, with latecomers collecting only 9–5 on the same winner after a hot tip drove down the price. Nowadays, of course, the winning horse pays everybody the same odds, which are computed after betting ends.

Taking bets at fixed odds imposed great demands on the bookmakers' mathematical powers and made it impossible for them to maintain a stable rate of profit from one race to the next. In all other respects, their odds complied with the principles that now govern the pari-mutuel system. The higher the percentage of the total betting pool accounted for by bets on a given horse, the lower its odds. Assuming the unheard of—a nonprofit pool which paid winning bettors every penny wagered by the losing bettors—a horse on which 33 percent of the money had been bet would pay off at 2–1, and a horse that had attracted half the money would pay even money. No odds layer functioned with a 100-percent book, however. Depending on the pressures of competition and the leniency of track management, the bookmaker would skim as much money from the pool as the traffic would bear. If he tried to pocket 12 percent for himself, he operated what was known as a 112-percent book, calculating his odds to assure that profit margin. When betting on an unexpectedly hot contender threatened to narrow the margin, the bookmaker lowered the horse's odds sharply and, if

necessary to restore balance to his book, "laid off" the extra money—betting it with a cooperative colleague.

It is said that a character called Dutch learned how to exploit the system by creating what came to be known, in his memory, as a dutch book. A shrewd shopper, he specialized in betting on every horse in a race in such a way that the odds percentages added to less than 100. Scaling all bets in proportion to the percentages, he and his followers were guaranteed a percentage of profit representing the difference between their "book" and 100. Dutch sweetened the kitty considerably whenever he could refrain from betting on a low-odds horse in expectation that it would lose. If the forecast was correct, proportioned bets on the other runners enlarged the profits by the percentage of the eliminated horse's odds.

All this is enough to paralyze a nonmathematical mind, but it becomes clearer. Let us try. A dutching handicapper who foresaw a favorite's defeat might decide that the winner would be any of three horses offered at 3–1, 5–1, and 9–1. Working, as dutchers did, in terms of a 100-percent book, the player knew that bets on the 3–1 shot represented about 25 percent of all the money that would remain in the pool after the bookmaker had taken his share. The 5–1 shot represented 16.7 percent and the 9–1 shot 10 percent. Betting $10 per percentage point, the total outlay was $517. If one of the three horses won, the dutcher collected not less than $1,000. Alert shopping increased the profits. The 9–1 shot might be obtained for a less expensive 12–1. Those were the days.

Under the pari-mutuel system, there is no such thing as an old-fashioned dutch book in which profit can be assured by betting proportioned amounts on every starter in a race. That is because the pari-mutuel book is always in perfect balance. There can be no shopping for advantageous odds on two or three horses. Everybody with a winning ticket collects the same odds. But the old-fashioned elimination of short-priced horses, with proportioned betting on the others, is still possible, though dreadfully difficult. To compensate for late odds changes, the dutcher must recalculate the amounts of the bets while standing on line to buy the tickets—and must strive to place the bets in the last possible seconds before the windows close. Yet nobody can queue up before the $2 and $5 windows at the same time. Accurately proportioned bets are possible at one window only by (a) risking hundreds if not thousands on $5 or $10 tickets, or (b) tinkering with the percentage figures to produce rounded bets that may seriously alter the rate of profit.

To minimize the effects of late odds changes and avoid being shut out before all necessary bets have been placed, the dutcher needs at least one partner capable of cool, rapid computation. Having collaborated on their handicapping decisions, the partners must then coordinate their arithmetical activities while standing on separate mutuel lines. Furthermore, they must be resigned to betting comparatively large sums of money in hope of earning comparatively small ones. When they guess wrong and a dutched-out horse wins the race, they have lost a good amount of money on an odds-on bet and, if still game, must try to recoup by winning subsequent odds-on bets. No easy task.

Nevertheless, hope dies hard. For readers who might like to experiment with a dutching partnership, a table of odds percentages accompanies this article. Dry runs will demonstrate that the approach fails—even on paper—unless rooted in extremely competent handicapping. The team must be right more often than wrong about the poor prospects of horses whose odds represent a good percentage of the money that will be available to winning bettors after the deduction of take and breakage. Having scaled their bets to comfortable amounts by multiplying each odds percentage by the same whole number or fraction, and having made sure that each amount is fully negotiable at the windows (no $3 bets at tracks that accept only $2 or $5), and having been able to adjust to last-minute odds changes, and having seen one of their horses actually win, the partners will profit.

To make things easier, the accompanying table assumes that a horse posted at 2–1 on the infield odds board will pay exactly $6.00, representing 33 percent of the pool after take and breakage. The fact is that such a horse might actually account for as little as 28.6 percent of the pool, paying $6.80. When the horse is bet by the dutchers and wins at

$6.80, their profits rise. But in no circumstance, except a late drop in odds, will it pay less than $6.00. Now an example:

The partners have decided that a certain 3–1 shot will lose and that proportioned bets on four other starters will repay them nicely. The four are listed on the infield odds board and the track's video displays at 5–2, 4–1, 6–1, and 8–1. The respective percentages are 29, 20, 14, and 11. Betting $1 per point, the partners rush off in separate directions. One of them goes to a $5 window to buy five tickets on the 5–2 horse, four on the 4–1, two on the 6–1, and one on the 8–1. The other lines up at the $2 window for two tickets on the 5–2, two on the 6–1, and three on the 8–1. If they have chosen their windows wisely and get their bets down in the merest nick of time, minimizing the possibility of odds change and reducing the need for recomputation, and if the dutched-out horse loses, they will collect $101.50 if the 5–2 shot pays only $7.00, more if he pays $7.20, $7.40, $7.60, or $7.80. They will get $100 if the 4–1 shot pays only $10.00, but more if the payoff approaches its upper limit of $10.80. They draw $98 if the 6–1 shot pays $14, more if more. And $99 or more on the 8–1 horse. Their profit on the $74 investment will be not less than $25, and probably more than that. A 34 percent profit, at least.

See also, EXACTA.

ODDS	PERCENT-AGE	ODDS	PERCENT-AGE
1–9	90	9–2	18
1–5	83	5–1	17
2–5	71	6–1	14
1–2	67	7–1	12
3–5	62	8–1	11
4–5	56	9–1	10
1–1	50	10–1	9
6–5	45	11–1	8
7–5	42	12–1	8
3–2	40	13–1	7
8–5	38	14–1	7
9–5	36	15–1	6
2–1	33	18–1	5
5–2	29	25–1	4
3–1	25	30–1	3
7–2	22	40–1	2
4–1	20	70–1	1

Note: If the posted odds do not appear here, use the nearest odds. For example, 20–1 odds call for a percentage of 5.

EARLY SPEED. Regardless of DIS-TANCE, about 60 percent of all races on North American dirt tracks are won by horses that contend for the lead in the first quarter-mile of the running. Few racing surfaces are so deeply cushioned that they consistently favor more leisurely types that break slowly from the STARTING GATE and come along in the late stages. Such atypical tracks are identified in this book's articles about the racing in various states. At all other places, handicappers expect most races (on normal days) to be won by horses whose PAST-PERFORMANCE TABLES include numerous 1's, 2's, and 3's at the first call (see CALLS AND POLES). The advantage of early speed usually increases when tracks are wet or, in the Northeast, when strong winds blow behind the early leaders during their run down the backstretch.

When a Thoroughbred in good FORM not only has early speed but is clearly superior in that respect to the other starters in its race, it often overcomes defects of CLASS or distance preference. It gets loose on the front end and builds an unbeatable lead. For reasons far beyond present knowledge of equine mentality, most early speedsters produce their fastest times if unopposed in that way. When elevated in class or claiming price or otherwise more likely to experience early challenge, they often run neither as fast nor as far. Before deciding that a horse is the speed of its race, it therefore is essential to check the circumstances in which it has finished well after showing good early foot. If it has beaten off other horses after running a close second or third or holding a slender lead at the first call, it is more reliable than the kind of animal that keeps going only when far in front at that point. Paradoxically, a sprinter that does not persevere when hooked by other horses in the first stages of races at its best distance may be a better prospect when entered at a longer distance against slower beginners from which it can flee. WEIGHTS, POST POSITION, and JOCKEY help determine whether such a horse has every possible advantage in that kind of situation.

The importance of early speed is a unique aspect of the kind of racing that takes place on dirt ovals. In European racing on heavy grass over courses that run up and down hills with abrupt turns and straightaways of irregular length, jockeys leave the gate more slowly and attempt to expend their mounts' energies evenly. The hardest running comes at the end. But virtually all North American dirt races, including the most important STAKES at classic distances, are marked by deceleration: The fastest quarter-mile is the first, and the slowest is the last. To a considerable extent, North American races are won or lost in the first quarter-mile. Which is to say that what happens at the finish is often incomprehensible without analysis of what happened in the beginning.

All this being true, a racegoing handicapper's emphasis during the early stages of the afternoon or evening program is to see whether the early speed is holding up or whether wind, moisture, or track-maintenance activities have shifted the advantage to horses that do not necessarily contend for the early lead. The handicapper notes the horses running first, second, and third at the half-mile pole in sprints and after the first quarter- and half-mile of running in races at a mile or beyond. If they finish better than expected, the speed is at an advantage. If they finish worse than expected, come-from-behinders may be due for a decent day. And, of course, if they finish pretty much as forecast, the situation is normal.

ENTRIES. Customer preference for races with large fields and big mutuel payoffs led during the 1970's to the end of an old, reassuring tradition which governed the betting on two or more horses that raced against each other but had the same OWNER or TRAINER or both. Such horses formerly appeared in the track program as 1 and 1A, or even 1, 1A, and 1X. Bets on the entry, as it was called, paid off if only one of the horses finished as bet. But with the horse shortage and a wish to provide maximum alternative bets in every race, tradition was suspended. In CALIFORNIA, NEW YORK, and NEW JERSEY, when a trainer entered horses of separate ownership, the entry rule no longer applied. What might have been a race with only five betting interests now offered six. Just as the lesser horse in an old-fashioned entry occasionally had run better than the one whose reputation accounted for the entry's short odds, the trainer's longshot (owned by Mr. A) might now defeat the favorite (same trainer, but owned by Mrs. B). The supposition that the betting trainer and both betting owners were astonished by the result was not unanimous among racegoers, a cynical lot. Among horsemen themselves, the old tradition of stable entries was missed. Although entries invariably produced lower mutuel prices, they tended to shield trainers from charges of favoring one owner over another. Also, they permitted cooperative racing tactics by riders of the coupled horses—one rider sacrificing his horse with high early speed so that the stouter, slower-starting stablemate might come on in the end. Such tactics would be scandalous if employed by riders of horses listed in the program as opponents. As of this writing, no scandal of the kind has arisen and it seems probable that the old entry rule will be phased out in most major racing centers.

ENTRY BOX. An innovation helpful to recreational handicappers and newspaper selectors became universal in big-time racing during the 1970's. Horsemen were now required to enter their horses 48 hours before the race. This permitted DAILY RACING FORM to issue advance editions of its PAST-PERFORMANCE TABLES on the afternoon before each program, giving press and public extra time for handicapping. The old rule had deferred the close of the entry box until 24 hours before the program.

EXACTA. Known in some places as perfecta or exactor, this immensely popular form of MULTIPLE BETTING invites the player to pick the winner and second-place horse in exact order of finish. It originated as a pitiless exploitation of uninformed gamblers whom it enticed

with visions of huge payoffs on longshot combinations. It remains an out-and-out lottery in OFF-TRACK BETTING and at any track that does not display the probable payoffs throughout the pre-race wagering period. To pick a winner is difficult enough. To pick a winning exacta combination is far more difficult. Betting on exactas is a waste of money unless the bettor is a good handicapper who knows in advance what his chosen combinations of horses will pay, and can compare those prices to what might be made with bets on one horse at a time at the conventional win and place windows.

A handicapper who knows how to make such appraisals enjoys a substantial advantage at certain tracks. These not only display probable payoffs during the exacta-betting period but (a) offer exacta races with fields of eight or more horses, and (b) do not take a higher percentage of money from exacta pools than from straight win pools. In circumstances of that kind, a handicapper who likes the chances of a short-priced favorite may find that the animal is being underbet in the exactas—meaning that higher odds are obtainable on the horse through exacta bets. It happens because the wishful gamblers most involved in exacta wagering tend to overbet longshot combinations, thereby making them into underlays while converting short-priced horses into overlays. Where exacta races field only five or six horses, odds distortions of this magnitude occur less often. And where the legal takeout from exacta pools is higher than from win-bet pools, the extra deduction often reduces exacta payoffs sufficiently to eliminate whatever extra profit might otherwise have been obtained by betting one's short-priced choice in that pool.

When circumstances justify the effort, smart handicappers check the probable exacta payoffs nine or ten minutes before post time to see whether a large disbursement on exacta tickets might be more productive than the same outlay on win tickets. It should be emphasized again that the exacta is more likely to be an overlay if the handicapper's choice is the favorite.

Exacta vs. Win Pool. Jot down the probable payoffs on all combinations calling for your choice to win. Calculate how much money will be required to purchase a ticket on each combination. Some of the combinations (involving longshots) will undoubtedly return higher odds than can be had by betting all the money on the top choice to win. Others will pay less. If one of the probable payoffs is only $10 or $12 on a $2 ticket, check to see whether purchase of extra tickets will raise the net return to a profitable level higher than can be realized in straight win betting of the same total amount. All this presupposes a bet on every possible combination—a wheel—so that extra profits may be had in case a longshot runs second. An alternative approach is to eliminate those combinations involving horses to which the handicapper concedes little chance of running second. This reduces the expenditure, raises the profit margin (if a winning ticket materializes), and, of course, tempts fate. Longshots do run

second and sometimes win. In doing the arithmetic nine or ten minutes before the race, the player should recognize that a horse then favored by the crowd at odds of 2–1 or less will usually go off at odds even lower.

Acceptable Minimum Payoffs. If the handicapper can narrow contention to two horses and contemplates buying exacta tickets on them to run first and second with each other, each of the possible payoffs should be high enough to repay the risk. To evaluate the possibilities of a two-horse exacta bet, note the odds quoted on each of the horses in conventional win betting. Assume for example that horse A is 3–1 and horse B 4–1 in the win pool. The following arithmetic shows whether the posted-as-probable exacta payoff on the combination is worth the expense.

1. Add 1 to the $1 odds of horse A: 3 + 1 = 4. If the horse were quoted at 5–2, 7–2, or 9–2, the $1 odds would be 2.5, 3.5, or 4.5.

2. Determine horse A's odds percentage by dividing 4 into 100 (representing the total amount of money in the win pool after takeout). The odds percentage is 25.

3. Now calculate horse B's odds percentage: 100 divided by 5 ($1 odds + 1). It is 20.

4. The minimum acceptable exacta payoff on the A-B combination (A to win, B to run second) is calculated by determining the proper minimum odds percentage of the A-B exacta combination and converting that percentage into the monetary payoff it represents. The

arithmetic is not as complicated as it looks:

$$\frac{A \text{ odds } \% \times B \text{ odds } \%}{100 - A \text{ odds } \%}$$

$$= A\text{-}B \text{ odds } \%$$

Translation: To establish the proper odds percentage of the A-B combination, multiply the individual odds percentages and divide their product by 100 less the odds percentage of the horse selected to win the race. In this case 500 (which is 25 × 20) is divided by 75 (100 less 25). The appropriate A-B exacta-odds percentage is 6.67.

To convert 6.67 to its corresponding mutuel payoff price, multiply 100 (the total pool to be distributed to holders of winning tickets) by the cost of an exacta ticket, and divide by 6.67. Assuming that the local exacta ticket costs $2, 200 (100 × 2) is divided by 6.67. The quotient, 29.98, indicates that the A-B exacta should pay at least $29.80 (18 cents being lost to breakage).

To ascertain the smallest acceptable payoff on a B-A ticket (B to win, A to run second), the product of the two individual odds percentages is divided by 100 less B's odds percentage, and the rest of the procedure is unchanged. A B-A exacta would not be worth playing unless the payoff were at least $32.

Boxing. When unable to separate three horses among which the shortest exacta payoff would meet the minimum standards just discussed, it is likely that an exacta box would be more remunera-tive than purchase of ordinary win and place tickets on all three horses (provided, of course, that two of the three finished first and second). To box three horses in all possible win-place ex-acta combinations requires the purchase of six tickets. If the handicapper has been able to narrow contention to two horses and the probable payoffs on both meet minimum standards, the exacta should be played both ways—A-B and B-A, in case the wrong one of the two beats the other. Let me stress that situa-tions of this kind are infrequent. It is a sorrowful experience to see one of the two horses win at fine odds with some horse other than one's second choice finishing second. The chances of long-term survival are increased by betting two high- or medium-odds horses to win and place rather than coupling them in an exacta.

Place Wheels. When a favorite finishes second and pays $2.80 to hold-ers of conventional place tickets, some-one is sure to wave an exacta ticket representing the winning combination, paying $32 for $2. There can be no doubt that when the favorite runs sec-ond in an exacta race, the combination ticket pays generously. But the risks are high. For example, someone who wheels the favorite to finish second loses the entire investment if the horse wins. Or runs third. Whereas someone who bet the favorite to place wins if the horse wins. And also if it finishes second.

Exacta vs. Quinella. High exacta payoffs stimulated gambling so reward-ingly that most tracks abolished the older, less provocative quinella. To win money if two chosen horses finish first and second in either order, the exacta player must purchase two tickets, where one quinella ticket would have sufficed. To wheel a horse to run first and second in a nine-horse field now requires 16 tickets instead of eight. Not many gamblers play two-way exacta wheels. Instead, they tend to combine their top choices with longshots, seeking the pot at the end of the rainbow in return for a minimum outlay. The percentage of losing exacta tickets far exceeds the corresponding percentage in quinella betting. This results in exacta payoffs three or four times as large as standard quinella prices used to be. With simultaneous rises in the pari-mutuel take, this means that more people are losing more money on exactas than was lost on quinellas, and that winners not only are collecting less frequently but are getting a lower rate of profit. In 1977, when the major New York tracks found themselves in head-on competition with New Jersey's Meadowlands, New Yorkers concerned with local racing's future began advocating not only a reduction in the pari-mutuel take but establishment of the quinella as one means of helping gamblers to win an occasional bet. With the six- and seven-horse fields that had become standard in Northeastern racing, the quinella was not a guaranteed solution to anything. Payoffs of $8 would be unavoidable when favorites ran first or second.

EXCUSES. The handicapper's trek through the PAST-PERFORMANCE TABLES is not only a careful reading of the lines but an attempt to see between and behind them. The traditions of the sport and the pressures of its economics oblige horsemen to pull as much wool as possible over the prying eyes of those who compete with them on the track, at the claiming box, or at the mutuel windows. To prevail in these circumstances, a handicapper must learn to differentiate what is real about a horse and what is only apparent. Some losing performances are downright poor. Others are fully excusable. Failure to recognize these differences leads only to loss. To miss playable winners is bad enough. It is even worse to miss the superior prices they pay after a few misleading losses.

For recreational handicappers who do not go to the races every day, the footnote comments in RESULTS CHARTS help build a list of horses that lost through no great fault of their own. The "trouble lines" in the past-performance tables of the Eastern edition of DAILY RACING FORM are useful for that purpose and would be a welcome innovation in other editions, but are briefer and less detailed than chart comments. For that reason, they do not always tell an illuminating story. At tracks where the *Form*'s chart-caller knows the business and is given adequate space for comments, the footnotes are tremendously valuable.

In a properly comprehensive handicapping procedure, excuses come into play twice. When trying to identify likely CONTENDERS while eliminating others on grounds of DISTANCE, FORM, or CLASS, alertness to excuses prevents elimination of a horse whose last race was not as poor as it looks. Later, when separating the contenders, the handicapper may well give extra credit to a horse with an excuse, simply to upgrade a forgivably poor rating to a level more representative of the animal's current ability.

Excuses come in two varieties. One concerns the unsuitability of the race to the character of the particular horse and to the state of its form at the time a master-minding TRAINER entered it in a competition it could hardly win. The second kind of excuse has to do with misfortunes—strokes of bad RACING LUCK or weak riding—during a race in which the horse reasonably might have been expected to run better than it did. Here are reviews of the two types of excuse:

Unsuitable Race:

1. The horse was entered at the wrong distance but is at a more favorable distance today. If the horse showed good energy at some stage of the race and is entered at a realistic class or claiming price, it must be regarded as a contender able to run approximately as well as it has under comparable conditions in the past.

2. The horse ran in a class substantially higher than it can handle, but is now back where it belongs.

3. The horse faded in the late stages under four or five more pounds than it has ever carried successfully at the distance. If today's weight is more reasonable, prospects brighten. Associated drops in class and switches in distance are extra reassurance.

4. The horse started from an unfavorable post position. For example, the rail position in a sprint during a period when nothing has been able to win on the rail. Another example, a fast beginner that drew an outside post in a race at a mile and one-sixteenth and used up its run trying to reach the rail on the first turn.

5. The horse is a confirmed grass runner but was raced on the dirt, or is a dirt runner that was entered on grass for exercise.

6. The race was in slop or mud, in which the animal has never been able to run well.

7. The race was the horse's first after an absence of at least one month but it showed some run before losing.

8. The race was the horse's first after shipping from another circuit.

9. The rider was a green APPRENTICE or a full-fledged JOCKEY of no distinction but will be replaced today by a local or national leader or some lesser chauffeur who has already won with the horse.

Bad Racing Luck:

1. The jockey lost the whip, a stirrup broke, a bandage unraveled, the saddle slipped, or the horse stumbled.

2. Either the rider or other horses prevented the animal from running as well as it might have. The following words recur in trouble lines and chart comments: "Blocked," "Impeded," "Roughed," "Rough trip," "Checked," "Steadied," "Forced to check," "Squeezed," "Brushed," "Bumped," "In close," "Close quarters," "Shuffled back," "Forced out," "Forced wide." "Ran wide" and "Wide" refer as often

to inability to stay on course as to a miscalculated ride or traffic problems. If either term seems frequent in the horse's record, it may signify a physical or mental disability and should not be regarded as a legitimate excuse.

3. The horse got off to a slow start—perhaps was left at the gate—but ordinarily starts promptly.

With experience, application, and willing ability to go to the races every day, some handicappers become talented race-watchers, observing the flow of the entire field from start to finish (rather than concentrating only on the horses they have backed at the windows). They see things that do not always appear in results-chart commentary, such as rider errors or repeated traffic jams that prevent a horse from doing its best. These observers capitalize on the excuse factor. In fact, some of them do their handicapping entirely in terms of what they have seen through their binoculars, reserving their bets for horses that not only have displayed competitive eagerness but have been frustrated by bad luck or bad handling.

When no excuse can be found for a poor performance, one assumes that the horse has gone off form—the more so if its form already had been declining or the animal had engaged in successive hard stretch drives immediately prior to the bad performance. But if the supposedly inexcusable loss came without prior warning and found the horse finishing in the middle of its field, it often pays to give it the benefit of the doubt. Like humans, Thoroughbreds are entitled to an occasional off day.

F

FAVORITES win a third of all North American Thoroughbred races. Despite monthly and even seasonal deviations, the statistic stands firm in the long run. It applies to all tracks in races of every class and at every distance. Periods of erratic weather tend to lower the percentage. It also falls significantly below par in the abominations known as TRI-FECTA, trizacta or triple races. Higher-than-average percentages of winning favorites sometimes occur in better MAIDEN races but not consistently enough to mark those as an abiding exception to the rule.

The established fact that favorites lose two races of every three inflames the imaginations of GAMBLING types and hastens their downfall. To avoid the favorite only because it is a favorite is a loser's game. Winning handicappers follow a different path. They try to find the likeliest contender in each PLAYABLE race, betting only if they believe that the ODDS are suitable. Favorites often qualify as overlays. More to the point, they often are the best horses in their fields, even when not worth a bet at the prevailing low odds.

Of all random bets undertaken without benefit of handicapping judgment, bets on favorites are the least costly. In the era of 18.5 percent take and break-age, bets on all favorites at a meeting rarely produced a net loss of more than 13 cents per wagered dollar. Comparably uncritical bets on non-favorites in any given odds range meant significantly greater losses, despite the higher payoffs. Therefore, although favorites win only one race in three, they win considerably more often than do second favorites, third favorites, or outright longshots. Indeed, the winning chances of random non-favorites diminish in inverse ratio to their odds. The higher the odds, the lower the winning percentage.

This is not meant to encourage indiscriminate betting on short-priced horses. Quite the contrary. They lose often enough to drain most of the profits that accrue from their victories. A handicapper who ends the year ahead of the game can invariably trace most of the profit to solid selections that won at good prices. Profit from betting on 9–5 shots is more recreational than financial. Which must provoke questions: Should favorites usually be avoided? Is there not some way of identifying false favorites? When is a favorite an actual overlay?

As remarked earlier, the first priority of the handicapper is to see whether the race is playable and whether one of the contenders seems likelier to win than the rest. If the top selection's odds are reasonable, the handicapper bets. If the only noticeable difference between the two leading contenders is price, the handicapper bets on the one at the higher price or, if favorable odds suggest it and the individual personality can stand it, the handicapper bets on both. All this may take place without regard to whether the top selection happens to be the favorite. If the animal's odds are low, the handicapper need only decide whether they are lower than they should be. For even the best players, this is an inexact process. If they regard a horse's chances as overwhelmingly good, they may accept 6–5 as a generous overlay.

Many years ago, Burton P. Fabricand developed a means of unearthing overlaid favorites in races with two or more popular contenders. He reasoned that if the records of obvious contenders were sufficiently similar, the crowd would become confused, betting more than usual on the eventual second or third choices and less than usual on the favorite. Fabricand was able to document several seasons of profitable betting on slightly overlaid public choices.

As to so-called false favorites, they run every day. Without setting out to look for them, the handicapper simply checks to see if the race is playable and who the contenders may be. Favorites are eliminated because they are not yet in FORM, or are going out of form, or are over their heads in CLASS, or are entered at the wrong DISTANCE, or are saddled with excessive WEIGHTS, or are at disadvantages in EARLY SPEED. Such favorites account largely for the 67 percent of races won by non-favorites.

FILLIES AND MARES. The question of a female Thoroughbred's ability to defeat males seldom confronts handicappers at major tracks now that horsemen have adequate opportunities to run fillies (age four or less) and mares (age five or more) in races restricted to that sex. The abundance of female races is a byproduct of year-long seasons and head-on competition among tracks for all the horseflesh they can get to fill nine- and ten-race programs. Another contributing factor is the breeding industry's need for useful broodmares in quantities that would have been unimaginable as recently as the 1960's. An active stallion services as many as 40 mares a year, and more stallions than ever stand at our breeding establishments. A filly need no longer win STAKES races to qualify as a broodmare prospect. Given even a remotely impressive parent or grandparent plus a fair record in ALLOWANCE races—even in CLAIMING races—a female's breeding potentialities elevate her market value considerably above her worth as a runner.

From Kincsem, Miss Woodford, Beldame and Artful to Twilight Tear, Busher, Shuvee, Allez France and Dahlia, racing history is replete with the names of great fillies and mares who defeated the best males of their years. But contemporary American horsemen usually prefer to avoid such confrontations. They believe that, as a group, male Thoroughbreds are superior to females. Males tend to be larger, more robust, somewhat less skittish and, of course, they are unaffected by ovarian cycles. Moreover, the running times of male races are usually faster than those logged by females at every class level, from stakes to the cheapest claimers. Finally, many breeders share the baseless fear that a filly or mare that beats colts may be too masculine for motherhood. To race females only against their own kind is, therefore, an understandable preference. But the topic should not be abandoned without observing that a decent $10,000 female trounces any field of $5,000 males and can win her fair share in $7,500 male company. This means that her problem on the racetrack is not

sex or class but market value. She is a commodity of higher market value than is the mediocre colt (age four or less), entire horse (age five or more), or gelding of equal racing class. If she is worth $15,000, she can compete successfully with other females of the same value, but is outgunned by males whose own $15,000 claiming prices only reflect racing ability, not breeding potential. The same discrepancies exist in the allowance ranks, simply because a female too good to run for a claiming tag and entered in middling allowance fields is not quite the performer that a male must be to run in the same races. In topmost stakes company the situation changes. Being a bright stud prospect, a champion colt is worth millions of dollars—far more than any female.

When a female entered against males seems to be in FORM and suited to the DISTANCE, many handicappers dismiss her simply because of her sex. That is sloppy handicapping. Others refuse to touch her unless she has already demonstrated that she can beat males, which is quite sensible. Like male runners that hate to be in front because their herd instinct makes them more comfortable among other horses, many females seek their own instinctive place in the very middle of the pack, freely conceding the lead to males. Until a filly or mare has demonstrated her willingness to flout that natural rule, it is reasonable to presume that she may run poorly against males. If her previous running times have been equal to or superior to those of male contenders, it is a good idea to avoid betting on the race and let the female show how she behaves in mixed company. But if she has already defeated males, the race should be handicapped as if she belonged in it.

Not at all surprisingly, numerous females run on equal terms with males in cheap claiming races at minor tracks. It is only when the price tags get higher that differences in racing quality prevent females from competing successfully against males of the same claiming price.

Weight Concessions. Under the RULES OF RACING, females get weight allowances when racing against males, except in HANDICAPS. Aged three or more in a race before September 1, they carry five pounds less than the CONDITIONS may prescribe for males. During the final three months of each year, they get only three pounds off. Two-year-old fillies, universally accepted as quicker studies than their male contemporaries, get only three pounds throughout the year. I should point out that, in a ROUTE race open to high-class animals, a three- or five-pound concession occasionally enables one Thoroughbred to defeat a superior one, but not very often. In SPRINTS, three or five pounds is even less significant. When a filly beats colts, the weight concession undoubtedly facilitates her success, but cannot always be the only explanation.

Claiming Levels. In previous writings, I have suggested that claiming prices in female races should be discounted by 20 percent for accurate class comparisons with male claimers. The rule of thumb worked satisfactorily for years, when

females opposed males more often than they now do and such comparisons were more frequently necessary. It now appears that 25 percent would be more like it in races at the $10,000 level or below, and 33 percent in races with higher claiming prices. However, in any kind of male-female race with a filly or mare that has already beaten the stronger sex, her chances are most accurately evaluated by analysis of running styles and SPEED, as well as the kind of company in which she has been able to do her best.

FIXES. Homer claimed that the goddess Athena fixed a horse race outside the walls of Troy. It was a straight, old-fashioned chariot gallop without TRIFECTA wagering and could not possibly have been the first barney of all time. Man had been conspiring to arrange sure things ever since he dropped out of the trees and became imaginative. A conscientious review of race-fixing could fill this book but need not. Most readers already know that the problem has always been with us and still is. They should also know that its dimensions are larger than generally realized, and its effects more destructive.

The most familiar type of fix elicits occasional news headlines about jockeys and others arrested on charges of conspiring to stiff a favorite so that a betting syndicate can collect thousands in trifecta winnings. And then there are suspensions of trainers and/or grooms accused of trying to improve a horse's chances with illegal MEDICATION, which is dope. Less often, one reads that drugs may have been employed to make a fast horse run slowly. Or that some larcenist outsmarted the officials in charge of horse IDENTIFICATION and ran a ringer— a comparatively good Thoroughbred running under the name of a comparatively bad one and winning at a big price. Individual tracks are vigilant. So are their national organization, the Thoroughbred Racing Associations, and its investigative appendage, the Thoroughbred Racing Protective Bureau. Gumshoes prowl every barn area. And favorites continue to win a third of the races, indicating that extremely few are fixed. Everyone agrees that the problem is nothing to sneeze at and that vigilance is warranted, but matters are by no means out of hand. That is, matters with which tracks and their organizations choose to concern themselves are not out of hand. Others are.

More profoundly harmful than intermittently doped horses and a few corrupted riders is something that occurs without the least objection from the sport's custodians. Every day, the tracks accept bets on horses whose stables have neither the hope of winning nor the intention of trying. When one or more of the starters in a race is sent out for no purpose other than educational experience, healthful exercise, or a wish to please a racing secretary worried about short fields, that race is at least partially fixed. Whoever bets on such horses is swindled. Seasoned handicappers usually know when to steer clear. They can tell when a horse is entered at an impossible DISTANCE or on the wrong FOOTING. They know which trainers generally try to win with previously unraced

horses and which generally do not. But the rest of the crowd is defenseless. It is on that large majority of its audience that the track inflicts its most grievous cruelties, producing a customer turnover unequaled in any other branch of the entertainment industry.

Entry of a horse for schooling or exercise in an official race would be grounds for expulsion from a betting sport governed by elements that not only understood the correlation between consumer confidence and industrial stability, but cared. Too many tracks are owned and/ or administered as if contemporary North America were medieval England, where Lord A's horse ran against Lord B's on the downs behind the castle, and the weavers, millers, and tinkers were allowed to bet among themselves, observing the event from a respectful distance. The industrialization of racing, with the construction of enclosed tracks and the sale of admission tickets, modified that tradition to the extent that the respectful observer was now permitted to become a customer and provide the purse money. When PARI-MUTUEL BETTING arose, the horse-owning track operators willingly made deals which converted their playgrounds into agencies for the collection of state revenue from the customers. In return, the states allowed the tracks to continue as sanctuaries in which the horse owners could race their livestock, write the rules, set the standards, and otherwise pursue their ancient traditions.

Pari-mutuel betting has succeeded because racing is exciting to watch, inflames the appetites of gamblers, rewards handicappers and, above all, has been the only game in many a town. To survive in competition with legal casinos and open wagering on other sports, it cannot remain an owner's-insider's game. Tradition regardless, the bettor is entitled to an irrevocable warranty that the horse has a real chance to win and will be allowed to try. Horses out of form or insufficiently schooled should be confined to non-betting races in the morning. To admit them to betting races as unbet entrants is be a mistake. Their mere physical presence often affects the results. And if betless training races severely intensified the horse shortage, the bargains between tracks and legislatures should simply be modified to abolish year-long seasons and head-on competition among tracks.

FLORIDA was the capital of winter racing until CALIFORNIA earned half of that distinction. The quality of the competition at Hialeah, near Miami, was first class. Gulfstream Park, not much farther away, was only a slight cut below. Gulfstream was highly attractive in its own right and Hialeah was a racing showplace of comfort and beauty unrivaled on the continent. A third Miami track, Tropical Park, was more humdrum but gave the vacationers decent racing with good Northern horses and riders. After a hungry state government legalized other forms of PARI-MUTUEL BETTING and awarded licenses to greyhound tracks and jai alai frontons throughout the resort area, Thoroughbred racing suffered. Hialeah al-

most went out of business. In squabbles with Gulfstream for the precious "middle dates" at the height of the tourist season, Hialeah had to settle in alternate years for late, off-season dates, with fewer good stables and not enough revenue to perpetuate past glories. At the time this is written, it is impossible to foresee Florida racing as it will be when the reader finds this page.

The Hialeah main track is a mile and one-eighth long, resilient enough to make EARLY SPEED an advantage at all distances. Inside post positions are desirable in longer races, but of no importance in sprints. Early foot gets an extra boost in the slop. The turf course, like most others, favors horses able to come along in the final stages.

Gulfstream, a one-miler, is even friendlier to early speed—so favorable, in fact, that it resembles Del Mar as a setting for wire-to-wire victories. Its turf course favors late runners from the six inside post positions. The inside also helps in routes on the main track.

Calder Race Course, successor to the defunct Tropical Park, has a one-mile main track of a plastic material cushioned with sand. Slower than conventional surfaces, it gives an edge to horses that run in the first flight during the early going, but not necessarily on the lead. Inside posts are bad news at six furlongs, less so at seven, and mean nothing in longer races. They are extremely helpful to late-kicking horses on the turf course.

Florida Downs, a one-miler in the Tampa-St. Petersburg area, offers minor-league racing on a strip hospitable to the best horse, regardless of early speed. Front-runners do better when the track is wet.

FOOTING. Some Thoroughbreds can run on dirt but not on grass. Others can run on grass but not on dirt. A few can run on both, especially at tracks like Hollywood Park where the grass is short and the ground firm. In 1977, all editions of DAILY RACING FORM began summarizing each horse's turf-racing record, as well as its overall record of starts, wins, places, shows, and earnings. These summaries, as well as the detailed past-performance running lines, must be scrutinized to make sure that a confirmed grass horse has not been entered in a dirt race, or a confirmed dirt runner in a race on grass. The question answers itself in those summaries and the past-performance running lines. If the horse wins or runs close on the one footing and always fails on the other, the picture is clear. When a horse tries grass for the first time after racing unimpressively on the main track, a knowledge of turf BREEDING is helpful. Lacking such knowledge, but noticing that the animal comes from a successful barn, the conservative player passes the race entirely, rather than be stung.

A second aspect of footing is contained in the ancient racetrack phrase, "horses for courses." Some Thoroughbreds can handle the hard racing strips of California but flounder in the deeper cushions of Louisiana and Kentucky. Some run their best on the sandy surfaces of New York but need a few races before adapting to Santa Anita. The failure of some newly arrived animals to match their previous records may be attributable to the strangeness of the racing strip or, even more likely, the unfamiliarity of the environment. Handicappers who demand evidence that a SHIPPER can handle the local track miss some nice winners but avoid numerous losers.

The footing problem most often accountable for unsuccessful handicapping is that of TRACK CONDITIONS. Some horses go to pieces on a wet track, others come into their own. When a racing strip is sloppy, muddy, or heavy, no horse can be dismissed as a non-contender if its otherwise dismal record includes good performances on that kind of footing. Attention to that detail and a clear notion of how EARLY SPEED is doing are essential safeguards on wet days.

FORM is current condition, fitness, racing readiness. A Thoroughbred is identifiable as a CONTENDER when apparently in good form, entered at a comfortable DISTANCE, and not obviously over its head in CLASS. After close comparison with other contenders in light of the interrelated FUNDAMENTALS of handicapping, the contender may become a bet. The final decision generally is made on grounds of superior current class, but not without thorough study of form, which is inseparable from current class. For example, if the contenders are of approximately equal ability (as they often are), the one in the best form is for all practical purposes the class of the field. When an $8,000 runner in top form beats a $10,000 one in mediocre form, it does so because, on that day at least, it is the horse of superior class. This kind of thing happens so frequently that it should abolish confusion about the relationship between form and current, operational class. Last season's class is as irrelevant as last season's form in the record of any Thoroughbred that has displayed no recent sign of its old ability. Accordingly, the handicapper should evaluate current or potential class in terms of recent form and recent class, expecting a return to previously high levels of performance only if recent signs of improvement support that possibility.

The PAST-PERFORMANCE TABLES in *Daily Racing Form* contain patterns of good form or bad and, happily for handicappers able to recognize them, signs of improving or declining form. We begin with indicators of good or improving form:

1. *Recent Activity.* Until the mid-1970's, it could be assumed that a claimer or middling allowance runner without a race in two or three weeks was probably out of condition. In those days, when more horses were comparatively sound, handicappers extended themselves to find the ones that could be eliminated on grounds of probably inadequate form. But the game has changed. Nowadays, the effort is to locate an animal that might be included as a contender on suspicion of possible fitness.

Horses returning from layoffs of a month or two should no longer be rejected out of hand. In an era of sore, overworked Thoroughbreds, a freshening vacation often works wonders. If the absentee comes from a winning barn and is entered in a SPRINT against opponents it could beat, even if somewhat short of its pre-vacation class and form, it is not only a contender but a prospective selection. In most cases, the returning horse does not bear such strong credentials and is eliminated in expectation that more recently active opponents will get there first. In the horse's second start after its absence, it becomes more interesting. If it managed to beat at least half its field in its first outing, and especially if it did so with no great effort—finishing third or fourth or fifth without ever getting into an exhausting neck-and-neck battle for the lead—improvement is likely. Unfortunately, overoptimistic trainers or riders sometimes shoot the works with an unready horse in its first race after a layoff. Win or lose, the exertion may ruin the animal's form for weeks.

Paying due respect to freshened horses, a winning handicapper finds more selections among the recently active. A race in 30 days is acceptable at all class levels. Except in localities where WORKOUT information is scanty, a claiming horse should show a work or two during that period, and allowance runners should have at least two. By this logic, a horse that has raced in the last two weeks and has worked since then must be regarded as clearly fit, unless its record contains some of the negative signs discussed below. And how frequent should workouts be? Under normal conditions, which become less prevalent with each passing year, a horse works seven or eight days after a race and continues to work at intervals of five or six days. Other things being equal, a record of four workouts in three weeks is a strong factor.

Unsound sprinters of any class that do not tolerate frequent racing and training are acceptable as contenders after layoffs of two or three months if the record shows at least one previous victory after a comparably long rest. To be convincing, the previous occasion should have been in a race of today's class or higher, and not in a MAIDEN race. And the horse, despite its fragility, should be a consistent winner (at least two of its latest six starts) from a top-notch stable.

As a final note about recent activity, the reader is encouraged to watch for the beginning of a trend which seems likely but had not yet begun to manifest itself when this was written. If the shortage of racing-sound Thoroughbreds persists, it is probable that not only sprinters but horses entered at a mile or more will be able to win after prolonged absences from competition. As of now, Thoroughbreds generally need a preparatory race or two before recovering the form needed to win long races.

2. *A Race over the Track.* In its first race on a new circuit, the typical SHIPPER is not at its best. Which is just as well, its form being a mystery to the local handicappers. A New York or California player cannot usually interpret Illinois or Arkansas past performances and prefers to wait for the newcomer to show its worth in the flesh before betting on or against it. However, if the shipper's first effort in the new environment brings it under the wire in the first half of its field, it should improve significantly next time. Note that this applies to horses that arrive from a considerable distance. In the overcrowded East, where animals shuttle readily and successfully among the New York, New Jersey, Pennsylvania, Delaware, and Maryland tracks, a handicapper who follows events on all those circuits can often spot shippers able to win at first asking. To be sure, California horses sometimes win their first New York races, as do New York horses in California. But I know of no way to foresee these incidents without remaining in touch with the racing on both coasts all year long. One helpful practice is to expect the best from a transcontinental shipper if its stablemates have been winning or running close in their own debuts at the new track. Some barns arrive loaded to the gunwales at the start of one season, but the following year they change tactics, preferring to race their stock into shape if they can.

3. *A Good Performance.* A win described in the RESULTS CHARTS or the Eastern *Form*'s past-performance trouble line as "easily," "handily," "ridden out," or "drawing away" represents authoritative form, if it happened lately. Whether the horse will repeat in its next

race is determined by other factors, but the good victory establishes its form as that of a live contender. The same may be said for a race in which a horse finishes second, third, or fourth or within two or three lengths of the winner after one or more (even many more) less impressive efforts. This sign of improvement becomes most promising if the horse now gets extra help from a better rider, a switch in distance, a more favorable PACE, an easier class, a break in the WEIGHTS, or an improved POST POSITION. Frederick S. Davis found that a horse that finishes second has a statistically better chance of winning its next race than does a horse that wins. This discovery has since been confirmed in large-scale computer studies. The reason must be that winners usually are penalized with tougher competition or higher weights in their next starts, but runners-up seldom are.

4. *Early Speed.* After an absence from racing or a succession of indifferent performances, a display of early speed is a promising sign. If the horse is not normally a quick starter, so much the better. If it invariably shows good early speed, the sign of improvement would be found in a sudden ability to carry that speed farther than in other recent races. Among maidens, a show of early energy is a most dependable indication of better things to come.

5. *Gaining Ground.* After lackluster performances, or even a loss in which it showed improved early speed, a horse demonstrates meaningful improvement by passing other horses during a race

that it loses. Improvement of running position between stretch call and finish, and/or reduction of the distance between the horse and the eventual winner during the final stages of the race is particularly impressive, especially if the horse is not a chronic late runner that always runs that way and seldom arrives in time. But to improve running position and gain on the leader between any two calls in the past-performance running line is also significant. And to show such energy from the first to second and then from the second to third calls is even better.

6. *Speed.* An advantage of SPEED HANDICAPPING is that it expresses class and form numerically. If a horse's speed figures have increased in each of its last two or three starts, and it has not been involved in a succession of close, taxing stretch drives, more improvement is quite possible and sudden deterioration of form not at all likely. Similar indications may sometimes be noticed in the raw *Daily Racing Form* speed ratings, or through addition of those ratings and the speed variants published by the *Form*'s Eastern edition.

7. *Hidden Form.* Laden as it is with implications of conspiracy, this term has sold many a rotten SELECTION SYSTEM over the years. It refers most often to phenomena such as improved early speed or improvements of running position early or midway in losing races. We have already touched on those. Another useful example is the performance that looks terrible only because the horse was entered at a hopeless distance, in an

overly high class, or on the wrong foot-. ing (especially in a race on grass before returning to the main track for a legitimate effort or vice versa, a race on dirt before returning to grass). Many years ago, I did extremely well with small bets on horses that had run "even" or better races and were then dropped in class. An even race is one in which the horse simply lopes around the track, never threatening the leaders but never falling too far into the rearward half of its field. The drop in class may be all it needs to demonstrate better form than might be deduced from such a past-performance line.

Now for signs of poor or deteriorating form:

1. *Bad Performances.* If a horse has been running at its own distance and has neither been able to reach the first half of its field nor had an excuse for the failure in each of its last two races, it is either grossly out of form or needs a considerable drop in class. In many such cases, INJURY, AILMENT, or overwork is the problem and the horse is too badly out of form to benefit from a class reduction. The same may be said for a horse that lost running position and/or fell farther behind the leader between the first two calls in its latest race, did not recover the lost ground or running position at a later stage, and had no excuse such as footing, distance, or class. To appreciate the importance of this it is necessary to understand that the first and second calls in the past-performance running line of sprint races represent the horse's position at the half-

mile pole (after a quarter-mile or three-eighths mile of racing) and the quarter pole (after a half-mile, with two furlongs to go). This is the part of the race that includes the turn for home, where horses that are going to contend for the victory are not losing ground but gaining it or at least holding their places in the procession. In most races around two turns (at one-mile tracks and longer ones), the first two calls cover part of the first turn and part of the run down the backstretch. The second call shows the horse's running position with a half to three-eighths of a mile to go, at which point it should at least be holding its position.

2. *Poor Finish.* A horse is probably out of form if it lost two or three or more lengths in the stretch during its latest race without having demonstrated early speed and without any excuse.

3. *Poor Start.* If a horse is an habitual slow starter and again left the gate tardily, its problem has not been solved and it can seldom be accepted as a contender.

4. *Physical Problems.* Eliminate any horse that ran sore or finished lame. Also eliminate any horse that lugged in or bore out, if its record betrays previous tendencies to stray off course. And in states that forbid the use of furosemide (Lasix) for racing purposes, throw out a horse that bled. Physical problems should also be suspected if a horse of claiming or allowance grade does not return to action within two weeks after an authoritative victory. When a horse of that kind is sharp, the stable does not

dawdle about sending it after another purse. The exception, of course, is the kind of animal that requires rest between races, gets it, and wins after protracted absences from competition.

5. *Overwork*. Not much can be expected from a horse that attempts to move up in class after a race that it won while losing ground in a hard drive through the homestretch. If it had that much trouble with cheaper horses, it will have more with better horses. Furthermore, the effort may have taken enough out of the animal to make it a poor bet even if it does not move up in class. The pessimistic view may be uncalled for if the horse had not been too active or successful in recent weeks, lost its latest race in a driving finish, and may be improving.

The same principle applies with particular emphasis to many fillies and older males (age four or more), after two or more close, driving finishes in succession. Hard-knocking runners able to maintain contentious form after repeated exertion of that kind are a small minority. Most of them come from the better barns on the circuit and owe their extra stamina to the superior feed and care that successful outfits provide.

6. *Declining Speed*. If the horse's speed figures have been declining in its latest two or three races and it has not been shelved for a needed rest, expect further deterioration today.

FUNDAMENTALS. The fundamental factors in handicapping are those employed to identify and compare the likely CONTENDERS in a race. A contender is a horse that belongs in the race because it seems to be in FORM, suited to the DISTANCE, comfortable on the FOOTING, and not impossibly out of its CLASS. To subject an obvious non-contender to further examination is a waste of time. The study of actual contenders is largely a comparative analysis of (a) class, which can be approached in several ways, including SPEED, PACE, earnings, and consistency, and (b) EARLY SPEED, which is inseparable from pace. If horses seem closely matched in class and at no disadvantage connected with early speed or pace, other distinctions may be possible because of WEIGHTS, POST POSITION, JOCKEY, TRAINER, or suspicions that one of the contenders is in especially sharp form. If a single starter emerges as the likeliest winner, behaves like a winner in the PADDOCK and post parade, and goes at reasonable ODDS, a bet can be made in full confidence that the fundamentals of handicapping have been attended to. If two or more starters seem closely matched, the paddock and odds board often indicate the handicapper's proper course—which may be a bet on one's second or third choice, or a decision to make no bet at all.

See also, HANDICAPPING PROCEDURES.

G

GAMBLING mimics the awful uncertainties of life but eliminates prolonged suspense, demands no skill, and imposes only such penalties as the gambler may prescribe. It therefore satisfies profound desires. Its purest and most legitimate setting—its temple—is the casino, in which the gambler bets on random and essentially unpredictable events like the roll of dice or the turn of a wheel.

A racetrack is not a casino, even though most losers behave as if it were. Horse races are athletic contests among animals and humans of unequal ability whose records are matters of extremely detailed public record. Chance affects the results of races but does not dominate. This makes handicapping—the attempt to pick winners—a game of skill. It also makes the racetrack a bad place for an innocent gambler. Playing TRIFECTA numbers instead of horses, the gambler bucks a house percentage of more than 25 percent. Not even a skilled handicapper can overcome such odds. Gamblers therefore belong in casinos. As such facilities become more widely available, gamblers will decamp from the tracks in droves. Perhaps tracks will defend themselves by finally promoting the game of handicapping, their main appeal to the kinds of persons most likely to become enduringly loyal customers.

GELDINGS. Thoroughbred colts are sometimes so unmanageably high strung that they cannot be trained. Castration pacifies them. It also lightens the musculature in their forequarters, relieving the weight that often is more than the front legs of a colt or entire horse (age five or more) can bear at high speed.

105

Thus, geldings tend to be more rugged than unaltered males.

Some of the best racers of all time have been geldings. Parole, Roseben, Roamer, Exterminator, Billy Kelly, Sarazen, Old Rosebud, Phar Lap, Armed, Kelso, Native Diver, and Forego only begin a list that could be prolonged for pages. Earlier in the century, when fillies and mares entered more races with entire males and geldings during the springtime of the year, geldings were given extra points by handicappers. When the female was "horsing" (in heat), the entire males became more interested in romance than in running, but the gelding stuck to business. Situations of that sort seldom arise nowadays. Gelding, colt, or entire horse, the handicapper can concentrate on the PAST-PERFORMANCE TABLES without concern about an animal's breeding prospects.

GROOM. In better stables, a groom is responsible for the care and comfort of two or three horses. Horses lucky enough to fall into the hands of devoted grooms working under intelligent stable foremen and competent trainers invariably perform more successfully than do less fortunate opponents. The handicapper's pre-race visit to the PADDOCK should include a close look at the goings-on between horse and groom on their way to the saddling area and during the stroll around the walking ring. Some grooms who do not like their work or think little of their horses can be relied on to demonstrate these feelings with rough or contemptuous handling. None of this helps a horse. Much of it can be interpreted as evidence that the horse has little chance in its race. Grooms bet. With a chance to cash a bet, they behave more humanely.

HANDICAPPER. I am certain that many of the world's best handicappers treat the game as a hobby and would not dream of trying to make a living at it. Among those who practice handicapping as a profession, the range of competence is as broad as in any other field. At this writing, many excellent handicappers were employed at tracks, mostly in the critically responsible job of racing secretary. An excellent handicapper was preparing the MORNING LINE for racing programs at the major tracks of Southern CALIFORNIA, and mediocre handicappers were doing that chore elsewhere.

In every clubhouse and grandstand are handicappers who support themselves by betting on their own selections. These individualists must be good at what they do, or they could not survive. Their methods cover the entire gamut of handicapping theory and practice. Some bet huge amounts on eight or ten horses a season. Some bet just as heavily but more often—to show. At the other extreme are those who bet on as many as three or four races a day. I have never heard of a professional who bet on every race. The emphasis is always on spot play and, among the most successful, on horses whose ODDS are not smaller than their chances to win or run second or third.

Handicapping "secrets" are peddled through the mails every day. Is there such a thing as a real secret of success in this game? I doubt it. One husband-and-wife team tours the world. She prepares the statistics according to a private formula good enough to keep them in comfort while playing the horses on five continents. How they do it is their secret. Whether it includes matters of substance unknown to other handicappers is unlikely. Every winner's own method bears the imprint of the individual's personality but, so far as I have ever been able to ascertain, no method is unique except in what might be called its shape or sequence. The content is compounded of well-known fact, elaborated by individual insight and, of course, arranged to the tastes of the practitioner.

Some of the best and very worst professional handicappers earn their bread as public selectors of one kind or another. Those who prepare the handicapping forecasts for newspapers, including racing publications, work under impossible conditions, making their choices before SCRATCHES, without knowing what the weather will be, and how the EARLY SPEED will fare, and who will ride, and whose horse will pitch a wingding and lose its race in the PADDOCK. That some of them are able to finish entire seasons with records of having picked 28 or 29 percent of the winners is evidence of profound ability. Among those whose selections I have had occasion to read for extended periods, one of the best is Russ Harris, who distinguished himself on Miami and Philadelphia newspapers before emigrating to the New York *Daily News.* Other remarkably expert public selectors include Dave Feldman of Chicago, who doubles as a trainer; Clem Florio of Baltimore, whose winning percentage has often surpassed that of all other newspaper forecasters; Bion Abbott, Gordon Jones, and Jerry Antonucci of Los Angeles, and the keen handicappers whose selections appear under the by-line, "Sweep" in the California and New York editions of DAILY RACING FORM. *Form* handicappers are the real heroes of the profession. In addition to the customary disadvantage of trying to pick winners a day ahead of time, each *Form* selector handicaps several tracks per day. Some never get to the races except on days off. Indeed, the former Editor of the *Form,* Saul D. Rosen, was widely recognized as America's foremost public selector before he had seen his first horse race.

Not all public selections appear in newspapers. Some are prepared in the morning, after scratches, for tip sheets sold at tracks. Of these, the two best in North America are the *Journal,* published at Ontario tracks, and the orange *Clocker Lawton* sheet available at tracks in the East. James E. Bannon, handicapper for the *Journal,* customarily leads all public selectors in Canada. In addition to naming his top choices in each race, he analyzes the prospects of every starter. It is handicapping of the purest and most fundamental kind, based mainly on close observation of every race. The *Lawton* sheet, which depends on excellent SPEED HANDICAPPING, is so popular that it affects the odds at Aqueduct, Belmont, and Saratoga. As to handicappers who sell their selections over the telephone to clients for fixed fees or the proceeds of winning $10 bets, not much can be said. I have known some who were good handicappers and some who could not read a *Form.* Obliged by the tradition of their calling to name not more than two or three horses a day, and needing to do this in an office on the morning of the races, they suffer terrible problems, including the abuse they take after giving out losers. In the morning, it is much more difficult to pick the winners of a race or two or three than to make selections in all nine or ten races. Even when the handicapper on the telephone is an expert in his own right, his selections can hardly be preferable to those of a knowledgeable party who defers final decisions until the afternoon, when more can be known than in the morning. All of which means that the real secret of this game is to do your own handicapping.

HANDICAPPING. After World War II, professional football transformed itself from a minor sport to a national mania. It used network television to convert dial-twirlers into instant experts. Persons to whom football had been a mystery were suddenly aficionados of the buck-lateral sequence, the belly series, and the onside kick. Previously anonymous linemen became public idols. Attendance zoomed. And bookies began handling more bets on football than on racing.

Racing lacks a weekly network-television outlet and is not likely to get one. It also lacks desire to smarten up the paying customers. From the days of Henry VIII, stable OWNERS and their employees, from TRAINERS to swipes, have regarded the FORM of the individual Thoroughbred as a private matter about which the less said the better. The no-

tion that all horseplayers die broke is an article of faith among horse-owning track operators and other authorities in the industry. To the degree that they refrain from equipping horseplayers with the knowledge that might promote success at the mutuel windows, that article of faith becomes a self-fulfilling prophecy. Horseplayers may not all die broke, but some of them leave the track broke and never return. And most horseplayers, being unacquainted with handicapping, are nothing but common gamblers, a lowly state which the tracks have long been content to exploit.

I have been writing for almost two decades that education of the racegoer in the theory and practice of handicapping is urgently necessary if racing is to develop the committed clientele on which its future growth and stability will inevitably depend. Normal human beings tend to play the games that they understand, avoiding those that penalize ignorance. With the spread of other forms of PARI-MUTUEL BETTING, from jai alai to quarter-horse racing to OFF-TRACK BETTING, and with the occasional mention of handicapping at Thoroughbred racing's annual management conventions, some tracks finally have begun halfhearted efforts to extend a helping hand to the needful customer. Experts now conduct handicapping "seminars" at paddocks or beneath grandstands. These sessions emphasize pre-race analyses or attempts to pick winners. But little effort is expended on the essential business of teaching a customer how to pick his/her own winners.

The steady customer of the local track is neither the tourist on an annual binge, the business person entertaining customers for a day, nor the degenerate gambler. The steady customer is the handicapper whose ability to pick winners is a source of personal gratification. Racing needs all the handicappers it can get.

HANDICAPPING LITERATURE.
Among books intended to equip racing fans with the theory and technique of profitable handicapping, some of the best are long out of print but occasionally may be obtained from secondhand dealers. The most comprehensive is *Win, Place and Show* by the late Robert S. Dowst, published in 1948 by Pocket Books in New York. A summation of principles that Dowst had been expounding for at least twenty years, this paperback remains a superb introduction to the game, full of advice that remains practical to this day. Its largest lack is an explanation of SPEED HANDICAPPING, which in Dowst's time was a rarefied and mysterious activity. Interestingly, the most advanced work yet published on that increasingly popular subject was by an anonymous contemporary of Dowst. It was entitled *How To Select Winning Horses*, issued before World War II in an undated volume. The publisher was Montee Publishing Company of Baltimore, which also operated TURF & SPORT DIGEST in those days. The book may have been written in the 1920's. In any event, its author must have been practicing the speed hand-

icapper's trade for many years before he broke into print. His presentation is considerably more detailed than anything offered since. Another excellent book is a paperback, *How To Make Money in One Day at the Track,* by Charles S. Romanelli. It was published in 1965 by Dolphin Books, a subsidiary of Doubleday in New York. The author, a schoolteacher, was an extraordinarily creative handicapper who packaged his considerable knowledge of the game in just about the neatest, simplest, and most logical selection procedure ever offered to new racegoers. Like many other books in its field, the Romanelli work got no publicity. I did not come across it until long after it was out of print.

Among the hundred or more how-to-handicap texts that have drifted through the marketplace since the early 1960's, my own have circulated widely enough to need no special attention here. I have read all but three or four of the others and can testify that they each contain something worth a handicapper's time. Among those that offer more than that is *Bob Hebert's Secrets of Handicapping,* published in 1963 by Prentice-Hall in Englewood Cliffs, New Jersey. Robert Hebert was racing writer and daily handicapper for the *Los Angeles Times* and more recently has been California correspondent of THE BLOOD-HORSE. His book is worth hunting for. It is a nononsense explanation of a first-class selector's version of speed handicapping. As with any other handicapping book, a few technical questions are susceptible to debate, but Hebert is refreshingly generous with the details of his method. In 1975, Houghton Mifflin Company of Boston published *Picking Winners* by Andrew Beyer, the talented and enterprising racing columnist of the *Washington Star.* This entertaining book describes the author's progress from Harvard underachiever to successful speed handicapper. En route, he presents numerous facts sure to help any student of the pastime, including those who might not be ready to adopt the entire Beyer method. One of the handicappers whom Beyer credits with hastening the development of his own expertise is Steven Davidowitz, former editor of *Turf & Sport Digest.* Steve followed Andy into the bookstores in 1977 with *Betting Thoroughbreds,* published by E. P. Dutton of New York. As public selector on a Baltimore radio station, Davidowitz picked an extraordinarily high percentage of winners. His informative book emphasizes careful analysis of the fluctuating importance of EARLY SPEED and POST POSITION. He also shows how to capitalize on the patterned tactics of individual TRAINERS and, of course, how to cope with FUNDAMENTALS.

Some instructional literature is published by mail-order houses and is more readily obtainable from them than from retail outlets. The most familiar of these is the late Ray Taulbot's *Thoroughbred Horse Racing,* which Amerpub in New York has issued in numerous printings since 1950. Taulbot's pace-handicapping doctrines won him a tremendous following and are propounded at length. His

discussions of FORM and other fundamentals are even more useful. In recent years, the book has appeared in a few stores. A more recent mail-order item is *Gordon Jones To Win!*, published in 1976 by Karman Communications, Huntington Beach, California. Jones, a sometime college professor, is racing columnist-handicapper of the Los Angeles *Herald-Examiner,* for which he picks a respectable percentage of winners, including longshots. Although one gets the impression from his text that Professor Jones would rather pick a loser than risk accusations of modesty, the book contains some excellent advice. Its theme is Jones' own speed-handicapping method. It is most unusual, employing a single set of PAR TIMES for all tracks and bypassing daily calculation of speed variants—an omission that has raised eyebrows among opinionated critics. Regardless, the book offers much subsidiary wisdom and is worth reading.

Another interesting work is *Killaen's Formula Handicapping, A Professional Career* by Jayce Killaen and published by Munado Publications, Oshawa, Ontario. The Canadian handicapper's computer-calculated pace-handicapping procedure is one of the most original in years. As such, it has provoked tempests in its field. Some authorities have pronounced it drivel. Others hail it. I originally considered it interesting and thoroughly plausible. After reading several dozen letters from persons who were making money with the formula, I decided that it not only was plausible but worked. The volume includes large helpings of information about handicapping theory and technique, aside from the computer formula and examples of its application.

Of all mail-order instruction I have seen, the work of Frederick S. Davis most closely approaches universal usefulness. After devoting years to highly original study of Thoroughbred performance statistics, Fred wrote *Thoroughbred Racing: Percentages and Probabilities,* published in 1974 by Millwood Publications, Millwood, New York. The material consists of statistical findings applicable to every kind of handicapping. Included is a supporting booklet, *Probability Computation,* in which Davis sets forth specific arithmetical procedures for handicapping various types of races. Although I own Millwood Publications and edited the Davis work, I do not believe that the coincidence should disqualify Davis from mention here. I might add that before undertaking to publish the material, I tested it for 18 months at tracks from New York to Florida to California. It had only a few widely scattered losing weeks and finished well ahead of the game.

Another Millwood booklet, *Turf Racing in North America,* by Dr. William L. Quirin, appeared in 1975. Quirin, a mathematics professor at Adelphi University in Garden City, New York, offers a computer-validated list of Thoroughbred sire lines that has revolutionized the handicapping of first- and second-time starters in TURF RACING. By 1977, his revelations had spread far enough to lower the mutuel payoffs on

the recommended types of horses, but the theory continued profitable. His study is updated as a chapter in *Winning at the Races: Computer Discoveries in Thoroughbred Handicapping* (William Morrow & Company, 1979).

If I have neglected any exceptionally meritorious handicapping literature here, I apologize. And I repeat that, no matter how pompous or badly written some of these books may be, they invariably contain a thing or two worth knowing about.

HANDICAPPING PROCEDURES.

Having published a few handicapping methods myself and having seen how persons most enthusiastic about them invariably (and often unconsciously) modify them to their own tastes, I can testify that handicapping procedures are as various as the persons who design and apply them. But they can be described broadly:

1. Handicapping requires use of the PAST-PERFORMANCE TABLES published in DAILY RACING FORM, preferably supplemented by the *Form*'s RESULTS CHARTS. Persons raised among horses may sometimes be able to pick winners by looking at the animals in the PADDOCK, but their results improve dramatically if they fortify these judgments with evidence contained in the records. Daily racegoers also develop opinions from observation, believing that one horse is finally ready to win and another has been to the wars too often. But the past-performance tables refresh and enlarge recollections of that kind. Also, most handicappers do

not get to the track every day and cannot function at all without the *Form.* Some profess to do nicely by ignoring the horses and basing their selections on ODDS patterns displayed by the TOTE BOARD. It works sometimes, but I would hate to rely on it for my next meal.

2. Handicapping is either an orderly process or a waste of time. There is no middle ground. Whoever tries to handicap without the use of a pencil or pen is sure to end in hopeless confusion, whether realizing it or not. Some competent handicappers who detest paperwork minimize use of the pen by reading the race CONDITIONS carefully and then marking their programs to eliminate those starters whose *Form* records seem unsuited to the race. They then review the records of the horses they have left in contention and, after making additional eliminations, base their final decisions on the odds. Players able to survive in this way are constant racegoers with keen eyes, good memories, a feel for the factors of FORM, DISTANCE, and CLASS, and considerable knowledge of local TRAINERS and JOCKEYS. Everybody else is best off employing the pen more extensively. Its uses may be limited to the mere circling and underlining of significant material in the record, the crossing out of non-contenders, and finally the addition of plus signs and subtraction of minuses. At the other extreme, horses may be rated in accordance with one or another of a multitude of formulas, either private or published, ranging from simple form ANGLES to the most sophisticated SPEED HANDICAPPING figures. If the method honors each of the FUNDAMENTALS of handicapping and associates them with each other in a fashion both orderly and realistic, the handicapper wins.

3. Handicapping requires closer attention to contenders than to non-contenders. Old-fashioned speed handicappers apply their formulas to every horse, starting with the coded numbers on time-distance charts and modifying them according to WEIGHTS and beaten lengths. If the charts are any good, which is rarely the case, and if the handicapper has the slightest respect for form and distance, and if a decent speed variant smooths the effects of weather on running times, results can be good. However, one must mistrust any numerical or similar procedure that makes a contender of a non-contender. The way to deal with off-form, outdistanced, or outclassed horses is to eliminate them as soon as possible, sparing time and energy for comparative study of the real contention.

4. Good handicapping emphasizes recent not ancient history. Certain PACE handicappers rate each horse off the best race visible in its record, often without regard to the present form of the animal or its suitability to the class and distance of the upcoming race. Some class handicappers choose the contender with the highest career earnings, even though the horse may be a far trip from the days when it earned the money. It is preferable to compare contenders in light of recent activity and such upward or downward trends as may be discerni-

ble in the top lines of the past-performance table. Digging beyond the fourth or fifth race back may be warranted when an occasional horse shows signs of such dramatic improvement that the handicapper needs to know what its previous class ceiling may have been. In other cases, three or four of the most recent races may have been on the wrong footing or at the wrong distance, necessitating exploration of the more remote past. As to procedures that concentrate exclusively on a horse's latest race, beware. They are too easy. One cannot evaluate the latest race without placing it in the context of an animal's previous outing or two.

5. Good handicapping includes a close pre-race look at the top selections in the paddock. Most horseplayers do not bother, and neither do many successful handicappers. Anyone good enough to win without making that extra effort would win even more by going to the paddock, where losers can be avoided and winners discovered.

6. The true indicator of handicapping skill is what happens at the mutuel windows. It is possible to cash half of one's bets and end the season in red ink. It is possible to cash only one bet in four and emerge with a substantial profit. Winning players make no move unless the odds are attractive.

HANDICAP RACES originated in England at the end of the 18th century as a means of stimulating popular interest in races among Thoroughbreds not good enough for championship competition under traditional WEIGHTS which, in important races, were assigned exclusively on the basis of sex and AGE. In North America, STAKES handicaps bring together each year's best older runners and draw huge PURSES but do not arouse quite the tumult that attends the biggest races for three-year-olds. One reason for this is the retirement at three or four of most colts that have performed well enough to earn large fees as sires. The so-called handicap division of horses aged four or more is often dominated by GELDINGS and rarely includes more than two or three animals of first quality.

The interest in handicaps lies in pre-race conjecture as to whether an inferior horse under relatively low weight might be able to defeat a better one that has been assigned relatively high weight. The weights are prescribed by the track's racing secretary in his capacity as HANDICAPPER. In most years and most places, pressure from OWNERS and TRAINERS imposes a ceiling on weights. The best horse might be asked to carry 128 or 130 pounds at most, with lesser competitors scaled downward from the top. In 1976, when Forego won the rich Marlboro Cup at a mile and a quarter under 137 pounds, conceding 18 pounds to the runner-up, Honest Pleasure, the victory was properly celebrated as a great feat by a magnificent gelding.

Because the most important stakes handicaps usually involve two or three highly reputed runners that have been racing elsewhere than at the track where the race will take place, most handicappers are unable to make the detailed, comparative analyses on which confident selections depend. And the diverse weights complicate the problem. Although these events stimulate large pari-mutuel handles, they often are more gratifying to watch than to bet on. However, it can be said with certainty that the top-weighted horse always deserves the same respect from the recreational handicapper as from the functionary who saddled it with its large burden. Top-weights win far more than their share of all handicaps. And when the top-weight happens also to be a horse with a recently demonstrated liking for the particular track, prospects are even brighter. And ODDS are even punier.

Considerably below the level of the big stakes and invitational handicaps are overnight handicaps, usually for horses of top ALLOWANCE grade. STARTER handicaps, written for animals that have started for a specific claiming price dur-ing a given period, often are dominated by horses that far outclass their opponents. Where this kind of race appears with any frequency in condition books, shrewd stables sometimes go out of their way to qualify, say, a $20,000 horse by entering it in a $10,000 claimer on the first day of a new season, before anyone can claim it. The horse is then eligible for starter handicaps restricted to horses that have started for $10,000. Animals superior to their fields often win several starter races in succession under steadily increasing weights.

For some years, optional claiming handicaps were a standard feature of West Coast racing. Horses could be entered either with or without a claiming tag. Having won an optional claimer when not entered to be claimed, a horse could not again be entered at the same level unless to be claimed. Where these races still occur, research in RESULTS CHARTS is needed to make class comparisons in terms of previous purses.

I
&
J

IDENTIFICATION. Emphasizing the past-performance records as they do, handicappers are unaffected by revelations of stud farm and transportation mix-ups that end with one horse coming to the races under the name of another and being added to the breeding record of the wrong sire and dam. Errors of that kind are by no means unusual. Occasionally, horses that have already raced and won are mistaken for other horses that have already raced but poorly. If the transfer is deliberate, and the better horse runs under the name of the lesser, it is a "ringer" and all hell breaks loose. To minimize such problems, most Thoroughbreds wear lip tattoos at which a track official peers in the PADDOCK. Almost all the time, the functionary does this with eyes fully open. If the tattoo is legible, the horse has been identified and the race proceeds. During the 1970's THE JOCKEY CLUB embarked on a program of blood-typing newborn foals, which will help when doubt arises as to which foal was sired by which stallion or dropped by which broodmare. Experts agree that the most effective way to combat confusion and chicanery in horse identification would be to forbid the sale or import or export or breeding or racing of Thoroughbreds that were unaccompanied by certified descriptions of their night-eyes (known also as chestnuts). These horny growths on the inner legs identify the individual horse as positively as fingerprints identify a human being. Meanwhile, ringer incidents and more excusable substitutions of one horse for another continue, but not frequently enough to spoil a handicapper's game.

ILLINOIS was one of the great centers of North American racing until mismanagement, political corruption, and a horse shortage combined to undermine its quality. In the Chicago area, Sportsman's Park, a five-eighths-mile oval with tight turns, features the humdrum, but its purses for hard-core claiming and allowance races are superior to those of major Florida, Maryland, and New Jersey tracks, and only slightly below those at Del Mar. Arlington Park, a mile and one-eighth track operated (as of now) by the corporate ownership of Madison Square Garden, was once the scene of record performances by immortal Thoroughbreds like Dr. Fager, Buckpasser, Fort Marcy, and Tom Rolfe. It continues to spend lots of money on stakes purses, which leaves an insufficiency for the lesser races that predominate on its programs. Its purse schedule for such races is slightly superior to that of Monmouth Park and slightly inferior to those of Ak-Sar-Ben and Keeneland's spring meeting. Hawthorne, the venerable one-miler near Sportsman's Park in Cicero, pays claiming and allowance winners about as much as they get at Bowie or Laurel or at Calder's Tropical Park meeting. Less, that is, than at Monmouth or Pimlico. About equal to Gulfstream.

Arlington is kindly to EARLY SPEED in sprints, but favors come-from-behinders in longer races. One-mile races come out of a backstretch chute, as at Aqueduct, and involve only one turn. Wet weather does not always mean a better break for front-runners. Here, as at any other track, the wise handicapper watches a few races to find out how the speed is doing. Turf racing is emphasized, offering the customary advantage to stretch-runners with an established liking for grass. Outside post positions are no great disadvantage on either of Arlington's turf courses.

At Hawthorne, horses with early speed usually have an edge, but the best horse can win regardless of running style. This seems true in wet going as well as dry. Grass races go mainly to animals with good finishing kicks, regardless of post position.

Sportsman's Park has the tight turns of a bull ring but the homestretch is long enough to give off-pace horses a positive advantage on most dry days. In slop and mud, early speed tends to win more than its share. Post positions seem unimportant.

As this was written in January 1978, Thoroughbred racing resumed at Balmoral (formerly Lincoln Fields), at Crete, about 38 miles from the Chicago Loop. The horses were not great.

East St. Louis, across the Mississippi River from St. Louis, has two minor-league operations. Cahokia Downs, a six-furlong oval, favors early speed from an inside post at all distances except five furlongs, when middle and outer posts are better. Fairmount Park, a one-mile track, also seems hospitable to early speed on the inside.

INFORMATION of no practical value rains on the ears of racegoers at every track. Whether offered by TOUTS or well-wishers or simply overheard, statements abound to the effect that some TRAINER "likes his horse" or that an OWNER has just bet $4,000. Having sometimes been privy to the handicapping forecasts and betting activities of trainers and owners, I can assure the reader that as many as four stables may bet heavily and with high confidence in a single race. Four stables can never be right at the same time. Neither can two. Trainers and owners are not often expert handicappers. Trainers have too many other things on their minds, and owners typically depend on trainers for wagering advice. No winning bettor wastes time eavesdropping for rumors or plucking sleeves for opinions.

Information more nourishing than who-likes-what-horse should be disseminated at all tracks but is not. Depending on local regulations, which vary with the power wielded by stable owners, a handicapper may be unable to find out which horses have had WORKOUTS—and when, where, and how—and which have not; or which are wearing special SHOES or BITS for the first time or are newly adorned with BANDAGES; or which are on "controlled" MEDICATION; or which are in BLINKERS after racing without them. That information should be stan-dard. So should disclosure of the reasons for SCRATCHES. So should the posting of probable DAILY DOUBLE and EXACTA payoffs during the pre-race betting period. And so forth. Handicappers need more information than they get.

INJURIES. Cuts, bruises, pulled ligaments, damaged hooves, and broken bones may disable a Thoroughbred during a race or workout or even while it is cooped up in its stall. A larger category of injuries develops more slowly, through constant wear and tear. For years, it has been thought that hard racing surfaces and the stress of breaking rapidly from a standing start are most to blame for the arthritic deterioration and other skeletomuscular damage that usually precede full breakdown. Premature training and racing under WEIGHTS are also implicated. And evidence now suggests that track geometry may also account for the failure of Thoroughbreds to last longer than they do. Scandinavian research shows that if turns were properly banked, centrifugal force would inflict less strain on fragile legs. Meanwhile, some North American veterinarians have been making progress in surgical and medical treatment of acute injuries, and larger numbers of vets have been lending authority to the adoption and implementation of "controlled" MEDICATION programs which enable tracks, OWNERS, and TRAINERS to race injured horses that would otherwise be resting. With all that professional help in the masking of equine pain, the industry has not hastened to reduce injury by improving the design of racing strips.

A handicapper who takes the trouble to visit the PADDOCK before making a bet may be unable to diagnose a Thoroughbred's physical problem but at least will be able to avoid wasting money on horses whose obvious reluctance to race indicates that something is wrong.

JOCKEY CLUB, THE. In 1894, potentates of American finance and industry undertook to steer Thoroughbred racing through a critical stage of its evolution. With the growth of commercially operated, enclosed racetracks, an aristocratic sport had fallen into disrepute. At least 300 tracks held race meetings, many of them governed by highly flexible rules. Corrupted riders stiffed horses at the direction of hoodlums. Pickpockets made hay. Suckers gambled away the milk money. Moral indignation reverberated in press and pulpit. But the best and biggest tracks were run by the wealthiest stable OWNERS in the Eastern United States. These moguls perceived that racing not only was slipping out of their hands but, like whiskey, had become a candidate for national prohibition. To restore control, they formed The Jockey Club, named and patterned after the private authority established by their titled British counterparts more than a century earlier. Led by personages such as August Belmont II, who tolerated disagreement from nobody, the new organization assumed responsibility for the conduct of the sport.

The club members had the money, the power, and the best horses. They loved the sport for itself and as a status symbol, an emblem of arrival at society's apex either by birth, as in England, or through acquisition, as in America. They now defended their dominance of racing with the vigor ordinarily reserved for the administration of their banks, mills, and streetcar lines. They wrote and enforced harsh rules; issued licenses to tracks, trainers, and riders; appointed racing officials; decided which horses could race and which could not, and where; outlawed the deviant and even the disrespectful; imposed standards on the naming and registration of Thoroughbreds. They purged the infant industry and brought it firmly under their own command. They saved the game.

With the strategic retreat of private privilege during the first half of the 20th century, The Jockey Club was constrained to modify some of its dictatorial practices. It could no longer serve as racing's legislature, prosecutor, judge, jury, and court of last appeal. State racing commissions became, at least nominally, the fountainheads of racing authority, charged with the democratic chore of applying rules fairly to all comers. Yet few state governments, then or now, were eager to estrange themselves from persons as important in the nation's political and economic life as those who ran The Jockey Club. Club members had the racing commissions in their pockets and even became commission members themselves without sensing the slightest conflict of interest. To this day, club members have ready access to the hearts and minds of the political hacks so often entrusted with governmental patrol of racing.

Come war, come peace, come boom, come bust, come PARI-MUTUEL BETTING and punitive taxation of the racegoer, the club bends but does not break. Ever mindful of its original purpose, it propounds rules, registers foals, keeps records, supports equine research, improves standards of equine IDENTIFICATION, and renders other services vital to the orderly processes of the sport. Above all, it cultivates and defends the conditions under which its members race their own prize Thoroughbreds. By its very nature, the club can do no less. But the record also suggests that the club can do little more, although more is urgently needed by racing and its clientele. Without straining the imagination, one can foresee the evolution of racing to its next stage, with the influence of owner and breeder limited to normal spheres of interest—the racing stable, the stud farm, and the organizations that represent such establishments. In modern society, racetracks do not function well as adjuncts to groups of private stables and stud farms. Racetracks are unmistakably branches of the entertainment industry, most likely to thrive if operated by persons gifted in dealing with the public. Show-oriented promoters will understand that successful customer relations,

higher purses, and larger state revenues depend on what happens after the admission ticket is sold and the horseplayer enters the gate. Tracks will present their excitements in an atmosphere rendered hospitable by the elimination of shortchanging mutuel clerks, surly headwaiters, overpriced and barely palatable food, irrationally organized parking, unpleasant security guards, and inadequate seating arrangements. None of these widespread customer repellents could have become standardized without the sublime indifference of track operators from whose own cozy accommodations such discomforts are entirely absent.

The racegoer is entitled to more than most tracks know how to provide. Customer turnover will diminish and revenues increase when the bettor is treated not as a necessary evil, not as the modern counterpart of the serf who used to climb the tree to watch His Lordship's horses run, but as the welcome guest who just happens to pay the bills. Enlightened managements will extend themselves to make racing comprehensible to the uninitiated. Experienced players will warm to the sport when handicapping INFORMATION now withheld for the traditional convenience of racing stables is finally made public as part of a new effort to build a devoted constituency of fans. It will not happen soon, but happen it will.

JOCKEYS. Winning riders get the best mounts. At a typical race meeting, fewer than 20 percent of the active riders win more than half of the races. The presence of a leading jockey on a handicapper's top contender helps to confirm the selection, indicating all-out effort to get the purse. By the same reasoning, when a winning rider turns up on a horse about which the handicapper has been doubtful, it is wise to take another look at the record. The horse may be sharper than supposed. And when a top jockey switches from one contender to another in the same race, the decision is usually based on handicapping evaluations by rider or booking agent. Not that anyone can make consistent profits through remote psychoanalysis of riders and their agents. At best, the rider's record is a useful supplement to handicapping horses, but no substitute for it.

That is, persons who play jockeys instead of horses end as losers. Better mounts or not, a leading jockey opposes from two to four other leaders in race after race. One rider cannot win them all. To win as many as 20 races in 100 attempts is the mark of a hot rider. To win that many year after year is the rare accomplishment of an outstanding rider. But a 20 percent winning average is not good enough for a handicapper, especially when mutuel prices are lowered by all the folks who bet blindly on leading riders. This being the case, handicapping remains a process of trying to locate the horse with the best chance to win, after which it is helpful to check out the rider to make sure that the animal is in capable hands.

Riders can be divided into three categories:

A. Locally hot jockeys whose names appear at or near the top of the jockey standings published in newspapers and track programs. After each meeting is well under way, their winning percentages stand at 15 or higher. Also in this class are nationally celebrated riders who happen to be visiting the local track, perhaps to compete in STAKES.

B. Any rider, regardless of winning percentage, who has won with the horse in the past.

C. Any other rider.

Concerned as the handicapper must be with the significance of a switch from one rider to another, the following should help:

RIDES TODAY	SWITCHED FROM	MEANING
A	A, B, or C	Good
B	A or B	OK
B	C	Good
C	A, B, or C	Bad

Should a handicapper's top choice be tossed out simply because a Class C rider has the assignment? No pat answer will do. Some horses are so superior to their fields that they can win with any rider—especially when gifted with enough EARLY SPEED to run free of traffic. The great New York TRAINER, H. Allen Jerkens, has won innumerable races with riders unable to find employment at any other good barn. So the handicapping decision about the rider must stem from knowledge of the trainer's ways, and from careful appraisal of the horse's chances. Naturally, when a race seems likely to be close (as most do), a switch from Laffit Pincay, Jr., Willie Shoemaker, or Sandy Hawley to a rider with a poor record is often reason enough to back the second choice, now graced with Pincay, Shoemaker, or Hawley.

Racegoers sometimes become raucously critical of jockeys whom they blame for the defeat of heavily backed horses. Having seen the horse hemmed in on the rail or wide on the turn, they berate the rider without regard to the possibility that the horse may have come up empty after exertions earlier in the race or earlier in the week. Riders of tired horses cannot easily avoid trouble. The jockey may not have steered the animal into the situation, which may have formed as other horses overtook and surrounded it or, running more vigorously, hung it up on the outside.

It can be said with certainty that the very best jockeys encounter the least trouble. Their talent consists in large measure of horse sense, which translates into the ability to spare a Thoroughbred's racing energy so that some will be left for the final run down the homestretch. They break promptly from the gate and they finish strongly, patiently awaiting opportunity and remaining cool in the meantime. Lesser jockeys, operating under instructions from misguided trainers, sometimes exhaust a quick-starting horse by choking it down—reining it tightly—during the early going. This effort to save a horse for the stretch has a melancholy effect on the type of Thoroughbred that can only relax when permitted to run freely. The battle with its rider drains more from the animal than would be lost if it were allowed to settle into its natural stride, capturing the lead under a light hold. Eddie Arcaro, a great rider, and Sunny Jim Fitzsimmons, a justly renowned trainer, learned that lesson after Arcaro half-strangled Bold Ruler in the early stages of several losing races. Braulio Baeza, who knew better, restrained the extraordinarily promising Honest Pleasure so vigorously that the horse apparently became confused about its duties and responsibilities. The grandson of Bold Ruler turned neurotic and ran scarcely an inch in later races that he should have been able to win. The need to induce relaxation in a Thoroughbred is best attended to through prolonged and patient training and, so far as I know, has never been accomplished by choking it in a $100,000 race. On other mounts, Baeza shared with all other great riders the talent to let a horse—front-runner or not—settle easily into stride and fire when ready.

The mirror image of riders who smother speed horses are those who force their mounts to top speed before achieving full stride. Whooping and hollering, they whip out of the gate, open huge leads and cannot be found in the last furlong. A rider with a mechanical, inflexible style of any kind is an impossible burden to a vast majority of horses and cuts the mustard only when the mount happens to like, for example, rushing up on the outside in the last yards, or hugging the rail all the way. The stereotyped tactics of losing riders become familiar to the experienced handicapper, who bets accordingly. So do patterns that relate less to riding ability than to the individual rider's choice of the situations in which to exercise that ability to its utmost. Some riders are dependable in stakes races and appear on each year's list of leading money-winning jockeys, but behave like sacks of flour when riding in cheap sprints. Which is yet another reason why a high winning percentage or a previous good race aboard the individual horse is the handicapper's most dependable basis for deciding that the jockey suits the mount.

K

KENTUCKY is the heartland of American Thoroughbred racing. In the storied Blue Grass region around Lexington are the world's foremost BREEDING farms and Keeneland, an idyllically beautiful track which offers not only 30 or 31 days of racing divided into April and October meetings, but four separate Thoroughbred auctions that are among the liveliest and most lucrative events on each year's national sales schedule. At Louisville stands old Churchill Downs, scene of the Kentucky Derby and attendant revels. This is OWNER and BREEDER country, and the sport is tailored to that measure. A handicapper can perish from lack of INFORMATION about WORKOUTS, MEDICATION, and BLINKERS. But betting isn't everything. Kentucky racing is uniquely enjoyable, especially at Keeneland.

Along with the verdant loveliness of its setting, and the high quality of the stables that use the place as a proving ground, Keeneland offers silence. It has no public-address system, a blessing between races and a discourtesy during them. Stable owners and their employees know who their horses are and need no prompting from a squawk box. The infield TOTE BOARD tells which four horses are leading, in case you cannot see for yourself because of rain, or a poor point of vantage in the stands. The racing strip is an unusual mile and one-sixteenth in circumference. During most meetings it seems to favor inside post positions. Early speed is a help, but not overwhelmingly so when the footing is dry. In wet weather, the advantage increases. Because workout information is scant, races with first-time starters are extraordinarily hard to handicap, although the bigger barns tend to send new horses after the money and often get it. Purses for non-stakes races are second only to those of Oaklawn and Sportsman's Park as runners-up to the money paid in Southern California and New York.

Churchill Downs has long been regarded as a slow track that punishes early speed. In fact, the one-mile strip is deep and cuppy (hooves form clods), but speed horses often win the Kentucky Derby and stand up nicely in lesser races if they handicap as best. Inside posts are preferable at all distances. Bread-and-butter purses are lower than Keeneland's but roughly equal to those at Golden Gate and Woodbine.

The state also has three minor tracks: Commonwealth (formerly Miles Park), a six-furlong Louisville plant which favors early speed; James C. Ellis Park (formerly Dade Park), a nine-furlong strip at Henderson, near Evansville, Indiana (early speed had better have a class edge or is in trouble); and Latonia, a one-miler at Florence, not far from Cincinnati (speed vital when the track is dry, otherwise no bargain).

L

LATE SPEED. Although racing on dirt tracks places a premium on EARLY SPEED, about 40 percent of North American races are won by horses that do not enter contention for the lead until the final furlong or two. Those that win SPRINTS in that manner are usually fast enough to run in the middle of the pack until moving up on the home turn or shortly thereafter. Sprinters that trail their fields in the early stages win less frequently. At longer distances, inability to keep up with the first half of the field during the first half-mile is less of a handicap, probably because the laggard has another half-mile or more in which to overtake the leaders. At any distance, the horse that does its running in the final quarter-mile subjects its JOCKEY to the problem of racing room. If the rider hugs the inside rail to save ground, the horses directly ahead may hold their positions and deny the come-from-behinder the space it needs. On the other hand, if the rider guides the horse away from the rail on the turn to find room outside, the ground lost in that tactic may be more than the animal can make up in the final yards of the stretch run. Therefore, when track conditions favor early speed, a late-running horse does not handicap as a prospective winner unless its record identifies it as the CLASS of the field, and a clever rider is aboard. When the advantage of early speed is less clear-cut, a horse's chances to come off the pace and win are increased if the early leaders seem likely to discourage each other and back up in the stretch. During periods when horses with early foot seldom last to the wire, the handicapper who selects a late runner must

135

still reckon with the possibility of traffic jams, which can defeat the choice, enabling some longshot to rush from nowhere and win. Good jockeying helps, but the off-pace horse is always a candidate for bad racing luck.

In analysis of FORM, a fast-closing display of racing energy is evidence that a horse is improving. If the late speed came after a dawdling performance in the early stages, and lack of early foot is typical of the horse, a longer DISTANCE may be the prescription.

LEAD PONY. Old-timers, including this one, used to deplore the sight of horses coming onto the track in the company of lead ponies. A properly schooled Thoroughbred and its jockey should be able to find their way to the STARTING GATE without an escort. Furthermore, the pony and its rider often obstruct the handicapper's view of the horse during the post parade and pre-race warm-ups. TRAINERS and JOCKEYS generally favor the ponying, however. It tends to pacify high-strung animals, leaving them with more energy for the race. And it minimizes the possibility that a horse might pitch a tantrum dangerous to itself or others.

LEADS. When racing around a turn in the counter-clockwise pattern of the American sport, the Thoroughbred leads with its left shoulder and foreleg—the foreleg on the inside of the turn and nearest to the rail. This supports the animal and its rider with less strain than would a right lead. Coming out of the turn, the rider uses rein and leg pressure to produce a change of leads, the benefit of which is comparable to that of shifting a heavy suitcase from one hand to another while chasing a bus. The best horses change leads easily and often imperceptibly, without wasting a moment. Some younger runners have great difficulty, and even fail to change, which is one reason that they may bear out on the turn or become exhausted and lose ground in the stretch.

LOUISIANA. Fair Grounds, the old one-miler in marvelous New Orleans, offers about 100 days of racing from November through March each winter, when it rains a lot. Moreover, the track has exceptionally sharp turns and a run of 1,346 feet from the head of the stretch to the finish line—the longest in America. Some horses like the gumbo under foot, and the tight turns and the stretch, others do not. Until the PAST-PERFORMANCE TABLES show which horses can run under these conditions, the tourist's best recourse is to follow the TRAINERS and JOCKEYS with the winningest records. Certain barns that do well in summer racing elsewhere merely go through the motions here. Current winning percentages are crucial. Non-STAKES purses are not much—comparable to those of Hazel Park and Timonium. Seasonal statistics favor early speed and inside posts in fast-track races at a mile and 40 yards or a mile and one-sixteenth, but give an edge to off-pace runners and no particular posts at other distances. Early speed fares better in wet going.

Otherwise, Louisiana racing is minor. Delta Downs is a six-furlong track midway between Lake Charles and Beaumont, Texas. Evangeline Downs, another three-quarter-miler, is near Lafayette. Louisiana Downs is a one-miler near Shreveport, and Jefferson Downs is six furlongs near New Orleans. Early speed helps at the smaller tracks.

M

MAIDEN RACES. Restricted to those horses that have never won, may never have raced at all and, in some cases, may not yet have demonstrated anything in the neighborhood of CLASS, these are less frequently PLAYABLE than other races. The most expensive and presumably best-bred and most promising maidens from the best barns are found in non-claiming (straight) maiden races, billed in the East as Maidens Special Weights. Non-winners for which the barns have less hope compete in maiden claiming races.

Non-claiming Maiden Races for Two-Year-Olds. Early in the year, fledglings run in dashes covering from three to five and a half furlongs. Authentically good animals sometimes begin to turn up in early summer, at five or five and a half, but those who run in the spring are usually without real quality, except at Keeneland. Their connections hope to win a purse or two before the distances become too long. For some juveniles, anything beyond five furlongs in good company is indeed too long. Because the short sprints are run pell-mell, without RATING by the riders, the youngster that has been covering the DISTANCE faster than its rivals is a likely winner at short odds. Handicappers who calculate accurate speed variants sometimes collect better mutuels on a horse whose apparently slow time, recorded in a race against the wind or on a slow track, actually represented a better performance than that of the favorite with the faster official final time.

The complication in this and all other kinds of maiden races is the first-time starter, with or without glamorous BREEDING and impressive WORKOUTS. If the field includes a previously raced ani-

141

mal that showed good EARLY SPEED and was only narrowly beaten in better time than that of any other previously raced starter in the group, the handicapper's dilemma becomes acute. Will the barn be trying to win with the first-time starter? If so, will the debutant be ready? The reason I do not name TRAINERS who run first-timers for exercise and experience and other trainers who always try to win is that these policies are as transient as the trainers themselves. The horseman who this year is more concerned with a juvenile's long-range future than with this afternoon's race may operate on an entirely different basis by the time these words are read. New owners and new livestock alter barn policies. It happens frequently.

If a handicapper is unfamiliar with the current behavior patterns of local trainers, but understands that one of the animals making its debut was an expensive yearling sired by a recognizable name, decision is best founded on an appraisal of the other horses in the race. If one or two of them have shown ability superior to others that have already raced, it might be best to sit the race out. But when, as is at least equally possible, none of the previously raced starters has shown much, it might pay to look more closely at the newcomer's credentials. If it comes from a leading barn, has a leading rider, has been working out swiftly, and was prominently sired, it might be worth backing. A great help in these cerebrations is last year's list of leading juvenile sires, as published in the AMERICAN RACING MANUAL, plus the updated lists that appear periodically in DAILY RACING FORM, THE THOROUGHBRED RECORD, and THE BLOOD-HORSE. Another useful aid is the workout tab published daily in the *Form*. When Seattle Slew ran the first race of his career in September 1976, at Belmont Park, the audience bet him down to 5–2, knowing that he had worked like a champion at Saratoga more than a month earlier. Some knew this because they had heard about it at Saratoga. Others knew it because they heard about it that afternoon. And others knew it because they collected or noted outstanding works published in the *Form*. As to those who simply bet on Slew because his TOTE BOARD odds were dropping, let it be said that tote action is somewhat more dependable in maiden races than in other races, largely because tips are more trustworthy when they concern outstanding newcomers facing indifferent fields.

When the distances stretch out to six furlongs and beyond, and no first-time starter confuses the issue, the likeliest winner is the horse that not only showed the best speed (preferably modified with a variant) but finished second or third in its latest outing.

Maiden Claimers. After a failure or two or three in straight maiden races, a two-year-old that has displayed any run at all is always a threat when dropped into a claiming race for non-winners. If it has been harmless on the track but has recorded a sharp workout, it remains a threat, sometimes at a good price. Otherwise, maiden claimers for two-year-olds can be handicapped in much the same way as other races in that age group. Early speed plus final time is reliable.

Non-claiming Maiden Races for Three-Year-Olds and Up. Horses born late in the year or kept out of training at two because of immature clumsiness, ILLNESS, or INJURY should be examined in light of the same criteria that apply to debuting two-year-olds. A three-year-old that has performed nicely in its first or second start is almost always preferable to one that has tried and failed repeatedly, and infinitely preferable to a four-year-old that is still a maiden after conspicuous lack of success at three. Again, the policies of the barn are germane, if the handicapper has a firm idea about them. Otherwise, good breeding, good works, a successful stable and rider are most promising when the horse has already demonstrated ability by finishing in the money and earning higher speed ratings than its opponents.

Maiden Claimers. The claiming prices asked for non-winning three- and four-year-olds are not a true index of CLASS, mainly because the animals have not yet demonstrated class. To be conceded a possible edge in class, a maiden should drop about 50 percent in claiming price from its last race. And, after winning a maiden claimer, it cannot be granted much of a chance in its next race—in which it opposes other previous winners—unless it drops to a lower claiming price than it bore when breaking its maiden. Careful speed handicappers enjoy an edge in these situations, finding the occasional maiden claimer that improves so much when winning that it has a chance to win again even when its claiming price is not lowered. But such occurrences are unusual.

MARYLAND racing has become a year-round grind, attracting its audience from the huge Baltimore-Washington area and from points beyond, such as eastern Pennsylvania, Delaware, and betless Virginia. The bygone glamour is resurrected in spring, with the classic Preakness Stakes at Pimlico, and in fall, at Laurel's Washington, D.C., International, a grass race of world importance. During the 1970's, the state's non-stakes racing compared favorably with offerings in Florida, New Jersey, and Illinois. Although purses did not equal those at Aqueduct's inner (winter) track, the horses generally ran better. With liberal MEDICATION rules and an indulgent state racing commission, which for years included a prominent stable owner, the assembly-line barns of Richard Dutrow, King Leatherbury, and Grover Delp virtually monopolized the winner's circle. These outfits were good enough to win anywhere, and proved it when they chose to ship runners to other circuits.

Although one hears a good deal of grousing about the physical facilities at Maryland tracks, it should be remarked that their glass-enclosed grandstands make winter racing immensely comfortable for the clients if not for the horses and riders. Track employees are somewhat more cordial to the customer than elsewhere in the urban East.

Bowie is about 20 miles equidistant

from Baltimore, Washington, and their joint international airport. A one-miler, formerly notorious as a deep track with a long stretch kindly to come-from-behind horses, it has been transformed. EARLY SPEED often holds up extremely well, especially in severely cold weather when that running style and an inside post sometimes combine to produce selections that verge on sure things. As usual, the best approach is to read the previous day's RESULTS CHARTS carefully and, if the weather has changed, watch a race or two to see whether the strip has changed with it. Other than that, basic handicapping and respect for leading trainers and riders turn the trick.

Laurel, a nine-furlong track between Baltimore and Washington, is more consistently favorable to early speed than Bowie, although fewer races are won wire-to-wire. But, in normal conditions, a horse able to be among the first three at the half-mile pole has a good chance later. Post position is of no consequence. An inner turf course favors animals with stretch drive.

Pimlico, a one-mile track in Baltimore, varied greatly in its running characteristics during the 1960's and 1970's. For weeks at a time, speed on the inside was a monumental advantage. The best approach is to check recent results charts, bearing in mind that early speed may turn out to be more or less potent than expected in sprints but, when combined with an inside post position in races at a mile and one-sixteenth, is likely to benefit from the short run to the first turn. The famous turf course resembles others in favoring come-from-behinders, with inward posts the best.

Timonium, a five-eighths-mile oval near Baltimore, rewards early speed, especially when the footing is dry.

MASSACHUSETTS. At this writing, what remains of this state's Thoroughbred racing hangs by the fingernails. Old Suffolk Downs, near the Boston airport, is no longer numbered among the country's major tracks, paying claiming and allowance purses at the level of Longacres, Albuquerque, and Fresno. EARLY SPEED horses usually do well on the main track. A turf course favors come-from-behind types. A summer-fair circuit produces racing at Berkshire Downs, Great Barrington, Northampton, and Marshfield. The horses are on their last legs and strange things happen. Watch the TOTE BOARD.

MEDICATION. For centuries, unscrupulous TRAINERS have made winners of injured or timid Thoroughbreds by dosing them with drugs that deaden pain or stimulate the nervous system. Until the 1970's, such practices were known as doping, a grave violation of the rules. Enforcement of the rules was not merely difficult but almost impossible. The offense was always years ahead of the defense. The pharmaceutical industry produced new drugs in swift profusion. Chemists who analyzed the contents of post-race urine and saliva samples made no secret of their inability to identify new substances in time to prevent their use. Horses were running and winning under the influence of pain-killers, tranquilizers, synthetic opiates, and hormones. As soon as racing's chemists recognized a drug and added it to the list of forbidden substances, rule-violators abandoned it for something newer. This distressed the topmost leadership of the sport, which feared the effects of scandal and, more fundamentally, believed that horses unfit to race should not race. In its stately fashion, the leadership seemed to be proceeding toward the proper financing, staffing, and equipment of competent drug-detection facilities.

The horse shortage of the 1970's jeopardized track and racing-stable profits and threatened to curtail the rush of tax revenue from mutuel windows to state treasuries. Doping suddenly appeared in a new light. If usage were firmly controlled, could not certain drugs enlarge the number of race-ready Thoroughbreds without soiling the game and undermining public trust? For example, Butazolidin (phenylbutazone), was a well-accepted, effective agent against the inflammation and discomfort of injured or arthritic tissues. It shortened the recovery period and hastened the return to action of horses that otherwise might need months of rest. Why not sanction the drug for racing purposes instead of limiting it to periods of treatment between races? After all, Bute was not a stimulant. It did not enable a horse to run beyond its natural capacity. All it did was help a sore animal perform as if it were not sore.

With the exceptions of New York, New Jersey and Oaklawn, all racing circuits had by 1977 won government approval of programs permitting the supposedly controlled use of Bute for racing purposes. Definitions of "controlled" covered a wide range, were flexibly interpreted, and in many places feebly enforced. Rules limited the amounts of the drug permissible in post-race blood or urine samples and specified that horses that raced with it or without it could not be withdrawn from it or placed on it without permission. In most states, no great effort was made to keep the betting public informed of these changes. In some, information was withheld altogether. Bettors were in the dark where, as tradition insisted, they belonged. The first state candid enough to end pretense of "controls" was Florida, which finally admitted its helplessness and announced that Bute could be used or withdrawn at will.

New York and New Jersey were roundly denounced for "hypocrisy." Horses raced on forbidden drugs in those states and little was done about it, said the critics, arguing that programs of controlled medication were likely to discourage the use of illegal substances by rendering them unnecessary. Meanwhile, it became unmistakably clear that the permissive medication programs were ruining Thoroughbreds in numbers unprecedented. Bute relieves inflammation and pain but does not repair damaged tissue. Only rest and prolonged medical attention can do that. Injured horses able to race only because of Bute's effects were winning before breaking down with some of the most terribly shattered bones that some veterinarians had ever seen. Other injured horses were not winning on Bute at all. They were just breaking down.

The medication programs also permitted dosage with Lasix (furosemide), a diuretic that helps BLEEDERS. Perhaps 2 percent of racing Thoroughbreds are bleeders, but a majority of starters in Lasix-legal states run with the stuff in their systems. Racing commissions and STEWARDS who felt that the purpose of the medication programs was to control or limit the use of illegal drugs might be expected to disapprove Lasix for any horse that had not already bled in competition. Why? The only effects of Lasix on non-bleeders are as (a) a stimulant and (b) a means of frustrating chemical laboratories. By increasing a horse's urine production, the chemical flushes away the evidence of unlawful drugs. So much then for the integrity of "controlled" medication programs.

Trainers of racing-sound claiming animals use Bute and Lasix in self-defense. To refrain is to invite a claim by advertising the existence of a horse able to compete without chemical crutches. In allowance and stakes company, sound horses get Bute and Lasix because trainers hate to leave any stone unturned. Meanwhile, evidence indicates that Thoroughbreds are susceptible to profound systemic damage from long-term dosage with Bute. Wherever "controlled" medication is legal, Thoroughbreds pay the price.

For handicappers, races among medicated horses pose no problem when use of the drugs is adequately supervised. In California during 1976 and 1977, for example, medication rules were explicitly written and carefully enforced. Despite that state's refusal to inform the racing public as to which horses were on Bute, which were not, and which were being switched from one category to the other, handicappers seemed perfectly content. The racing was competitive and formful. Elsewhere, published lists of the medicated and non-medicated helped players who had the presence of mind to save all the lists and compile each animal's drug history. As a practical matter in most jurisdictions, virtually all the horses were medicated, which reduced the handicapping problem to a minimum.

At Keystone, handicappers learned to fear the horse shipped from New York or New Jersey to race on Bute. They also learned to suspect the cheap New York or New Jersey shipper that raced without Bute. Often enough, the stable was trying to unload the animal by pretending that it was physically sound. And at all tracks, including the few New Jersey and New York ones that forbade medication for racing purposes, handicapping skill included, as it always had, alertness to the curious winning patterns of various stables. Certain claiming outfits seemed almost miraculously able to win with horses that could not get out of their own way for other barns. Yet when these surprising winners were claimed from the successful stables, they once more could not run. Indeed, some of them seemed droopier and less tolerant of exercise than ever before, as if completely depleted. The side effects of illegal stimulants were suspected. Now and then a trainer was called on the carpet and warned, after which the stable's sensational winning streak ground to a halt. Other trainers, having been warned, picked up and moved to friendlier climes. Sometimes, important trainers were suspended or fined. This had been going on for decades. Handicappers coped with it by awarding extra points to any horse from a winning stable, thereby taking into proper account the ability of good trainers to improve a horse legitimately and the ability of others to win by chemical means.

MICHIGAN. Detroit Race Course and Hazel Park, both convenient to the automobile city, offer minor-league racing from early March through November. Purses for non-stakes races are a bit below those at Fair Grounds, roughly equivalent to Timonium's and better than Ohio's. Detroit is a one-miler without particular advantage to EARLY SPEED, except when wet. Hazel Park, a five-furlong strip, favors early speed on the inside, especially when wet.

MONEY MANAGEMENT. For inexperienced handicappers, for gamblers who would prefer a casino if one were available, for vacationers larking, for club members on the annual excursion, and for that majority of fans who enjoy horse racing without feeling an urge to expend effort on serious handicapping, money management begins and ends with a decision about the sum that can be lost without pain. It is a demonstration of mental hygiene. It remains so, with elaborations, among committed hobbyists whose bets invest ego as well as money and for whom seasonal profits are a realistic goal.

Employing techniques that reduce loss and increase gain, skillful money management becomes possible only after the handicapper achieves the rare ability to pick enough winners at high enough ODDS, turning a profit on most series of 50 or 100 flat $2 bets. Until that stage is reached, emphasis belongs on attempts to improve the selection procedure, with betting restricted to a thrifty minimum.

Consider these facts:

1. The sole purpose of money management is to increase dollar profits by increasing the size of bets in ratio to the growth of capital.

2. Whatever the management technique may be, it is most practical when undertaken on a seasonal or other long-term basis. It is least realistic and therefore a kind of mismanagement when it attempts to stave off daily or weekly loss. Many mail-order BETTING SYSTEMS fall into this category, purporting to rescue the player from the consequences of bad handicapping by means of PLACE AND SHOW BETTING, or by increasing the size of the bet after each losing transaction, or by using "due columns" that tell the player how much must be bet to bail out of the red on the next race, and by trying other devices that succeed only occasionally and, when successful, are

signs of transient luck rather than handicapping ability. No handicapper wins every day or every week and no sensible one expects to. If the handicapper is good enough to profit from bets of the same amount (flat bets) on almost every series of 100 selections, gimmicks like due columns, progressively higher bets after losses, and place or show bets on winning horses inevitably turn matters upside down. The bet to place or show on a winning horse materially lowers the profits that such a horse should supply. The bet increased only because a previous bet or two or six went down the drain does not improve chances that the horse will win. In sum, the most expert selector heads for calamity unless determined to adopt the long view, abandoning notions that a losing day or week is a disgrace to be avoided at all costs. In truth, the worst disgrace for a handicapper is to imitate a common gambler by depending on the individual bet rather than consistently productive selections.

3. Record-keeping is essential to money management. Without it, one has no idea where the money has gone and no possibility of refining the approach.

4. The size of each bet absolutely must conform to a long-term plan compatible with the player's own style, the kinds of risks that arouse minimum anxiety, and the winning probabilities associated with the individual handicapping procedures.

Psychology and Reality. A handicapper who generally makes 10 cents per wagered dollar on a representative series of $2 bets has made about $20 after 100 bets. Theoretically, dollar profits would be $200 if the individual bet were increased to $20 on the next series, or $2,000 if bets were $200, or $20,000 if bets were $2,000. But not everyone can increase bets with a light heart. A friend of mine, who supplements his annual income with thousands of dollars in racetrack winnings, never bets more than $5, and usually plays $2 win and $2 place on the longshots that are his stock in trade. To suppose that he could become wealthy by making $20 bets is to overlook his categorical uneasiness when risking that much money on a horse. Anxieties of that kind invariably sabotage handicapping judgment. Each individual has what might be called a threshold of discomfort and should scale all bets accordingly.

The Need for Action. Many good handicappers hate to sit in idleness waiting for the next big opportunity to arise. They crave action. Some, including a few who have broken into print, try to alleviate the problem by betting minimum amounts on most races, reserving their bigger outlays for selections they regard as prime. This conceivably works for persons genuinely able to differentiate the prime from the humdrum, but I suspect that most players afflicted with so grave a need for gambling action are never in full control and must sometimes decide to make large bets on horses that do not deserve such support—just to make the action more exciting.

Basic Minimums. The handicapper who makes 15 cents on the dollar by betting two or three times a day on horses that pay off at an average rate of 2–1 will encounter periodically fallow periods, as do we all. As many as a dozen successive losers are entirely normal. Indeed, the higher the average payoff on selections and the lower the percentage of winners, the longer and more frequent the inevitable losing streaks. One's own records prove it. In launching a money-management program, it is sensible to establish the minimum bet at a level low enough to survive a longer losing streak than the individual handicapping procedure has ever encountered. A conservative who bets to win only, never tries the DAILY DOUBLE or EXACTA, and cashes about three of every ten tickets can safely risk 5 percent of capital on each transaction. Someone who prefers to bet to win and place on horses that go at good odds would necessarily reduce long-range dollar profits by lowering the betting percentage to 2 or 3 on each ticket. To spend 5 percent of capital on a win ticket and another 5 percent to place is to challenge fate more boldly than the average temperament can stand. On the other hand, the minimum bet should remain the minimum. Thus, a player who begins with a $100 fund and a 5 percent minimum should continue to bet no less than $5, even if the first 19 selections lose. To do otherwise, reducing the size of the minimum bet as the initial bankroll shrinks, may prolong the agony but also defers the onset of profits after selections begin winning at the expected rate. As to increasing the size of bets as

capital grows, all sorts of formulas exist. Of these, the easiest is to treat each day as a unit, determining in advance that each bet will equal whatever amount is closest to the prescribed percentage of capital. To recalculate after each win or each loss is more trouble. Some successful bettors remain at the flat 2 or 4 or 5 percent of original capital day after day until the exchequer has doubled, at which point they "draw down" the profits and continue on the flat-bet basis. This lowers the seasonal profits but furnishes the steadiness that these players prefer.

Two Horses per Race. Some of the biggest winners in history have specialized in betting on two or even three or four horses per PLAYABLE race, except when able to find a single standout at good odds. With an approach of this kind, it is best to allocate a fixed percentage of capital to each bettable race rather than to the individual mutuel ticket. And it is preferable to proportion the bets so that if one of the chosen horses happens to win, the proceeds will be close to what would have been collected if any of the others had won. Let us assume that the handicapper's three top choices in a race are entering the gate at odds of 2–1, 3–1, and 8–1— potential mutuel payoffs of $6.00, $8.00, and $18.00. If the individual's minimum bet is $2, it goes on the 8–1 shot. The other bets are scaled to produce not less than $18 but to cost no more than necessary. To collect $18 on a 3–1 shot is impossible, but a $5 bet yields $20. And a $6 bet on the 2–1 shot brings the desired $18. For a total investment of $13, the handicapper makes a profit of $5 on the shortest- and longest-priced horses and a profit of $7 if the 3–1 ticket pays off. If the handicapper's betting fund is large enough, proportioned betting can be done quite conveniently by recourse to the table of odds percentages set forth in our article on DUTCHING. Using the previous example, the three horses' percentages are 33, 25, and 11. Betting $1 per point would require an outlay of $69, well within the means of someone betting 5 percent of a $1,500 bankroll. The problem, as in all other variations of dutching, is how to buy mutuel tickets of two denominations ($2 and $5) without betting too early and risking odds changes or, what may be desired even less, recruiting a partner to buy some of the tickets.

Minimizing Risk. As already observed, money bet on place tickets produces lower profits than money bet to win. On the other hand, it hedges the bet, reducing the overall risk. And, of course, it pays off more frequently. Some experts insist that short-priced horses should be bet to place only, because $2.40 to place is almost as good as $3.00 to win and can be collected more often. My own attitude is that neither $3.00 to win nor $2.40 to place is normally worth the investment. But when a horse stands out at 7–2 or better in a field of seven starters or more (3–1 with six, 5–2 with fewer), and when the FAVORITE in the race looks like a loser, a place bet is indicated—along with the win bet. I remember a week at Del Mar when I caught only two winners but cashed enough place tickets (several of the payoffs exceeded $10.00), to go home a substantial winner. Frequent racegoers make highest profits by betting to win only, but vacationers can increase the probability of a winning week by hedging with place bets. Of course, this is a far piece from betting only to place, or only to show, a practice recommended by various authorities who feel that cashing a show bet on the first race should embolden the player to try a place bet in the second and, if all goes well, a win bet in the third. On days when the first horse wins and the other two finish down the track, such a player might decide to take up Parcheesi instead of handicapping.

Maximizing Profits. Having kept detailed records for years on end and having consulted other committed handicappers who keep records, I am satisfied that most winning players make their money on horses at comparatively high odds. Bets at 2–1 or less may contribute to the profit, but not much. For most of us, the short-odds bets are a spinning of wheels, leading nowhere in particular. Somewhere about 3–1, the winning percentage declines but the returns improve enough to put us firmly in the black. Handicappers whose selections conform to that pattern need no instruction in arithmetic but may never have pursued the phenomenon to its logical conclusion. If bets at less than 3–1 are only barely profitable, reason exists to make only token bet at such odds, increasing the bets as the odds improve.

Frederick S. Davis has proposed that bets on horses at or below the handicapper's own timber line be held to one unit ($2 or $5 or $20 or whatever), and that the units increase at each interval to 7–1. One unit at 3–1 or less; two units at 4–1 or 7–2; three at 9–2 or 5–1; four at 6–1; and five at 7–1 or above. Profits are sure to multiply if the handicapper is able to tolerate the strain of applying so radical a formula. And there's the rub. If the standard betting unit is as low as 1 percent of capital and an 11–1 shot comes along, the required bet is now 5 percent of capital. Not too difficult to endure. But if the standard bet is 5 percent of capital, the longshot calls for 25 percent—an unreasonable risk. The 1 percent unit seems most sensible. There can be no doubt that some handicappers are fully capable of implementing this procedure and profiting from it.

Exactas and Such. A handicapper who has developed a healthy bankroll through win and place betting can incorporate MULTIPLE BETTING opportunities into the overall scheme of things without departing from the principles of money management. Persons with less betting capital cannot. Depending on locale, an EXACTA box costs from $12 to $30 and a wheel as much as $55. Until the player can make such bets without exceeding the percentage of bankroll normally allotted to a single race, boxes and wheels are bad business.

MONTANA. Brief summer meetings are held at half-milers near Billings and Great Falls. Great Falls has the faster

strip and Billings an atmosphere like that of Hollywood's Old West. To spend a Saturday night on the side of the tracks where the neon sign says "Fire Water" is to feel like a bit player in a John Wayne flick. The track is more of the same. Watch the TOTE BOARD and, if in doubt, take speed on the inside.

MORNING LINE. At this writing, the probable odds printed in the programs at Southern CALIFORNIA tracks represent good handicapping along with an effort to predict what the odds may turn out to be after the throng has had its whack at the mutuel machines. In most other places, handicapping has less to do with the morning lines, which simply predict what the final odds may be, and do not often come close. Lest traffic at the ticket windows be discouraged, programs tend to overstate the probable odds on hot favorites—which generally go off at lower prices than officially predicted. Similarly, the probable odds on hopeless outsiders are understated. The natural 200–1 shot that finally goes off at 99–1 may have been listed in the program at 20–1, inviting tourists to take a flyer. Probable odds given on most sports pages are provided by track publicity departments, which get them from the same party who does the program line. Many newspaper selectors write graded handicaps with their own morning lines, all of which are prepared under the disadvantage of not knowing what the weather will be and which horses will actually run. All this being true, the morning line is of no value in handicapping except, as mentioned, at the very few tracks where a horse at odds materially higher than those expertly predicted in the program can be regarded as an authentic overlay.

MULTIPLE BETTING. Known also as combination betting or exotic betting, this popular development involves wagers on multiple happenings. In conventional betting, the player bets that a horse will win, or finish at least second or at least third. But in the DAILY DOUBLE, the bet loses unless the player selects the winners of two races. EXACTA (perfecta) bets require selection of winner and runner-up in exact order of finish. The quinella (or quiniela) is the same thing, without the requirement of exact order of finish. The TRIFECTA (or triple) wins if the bettor picks the first three finishers in exact order. The Five-Ten or Pic Six asks for the winners of six races in succession. The Big Q is a double quinella that pays off only if the bettor has been right on two designated races. And so forth. The more elaborate the proposition, the greater its resemblance to a raffle. Because the payoffs on $2 or $3 bets often run into the thousands, the incidence of FIXES is higher than in other races and the percentage of winning FAVORITES lower than normal (as documented in this book's article on TRIFECTAS).

Inasmuch as most racegoers approach the game as if it were a roulette wheel and can win only by accident even when playing a single horse at a time, the multiple payoffs are powerfully attractive to them and are employed by track managements and state legislatures to relieve them of their money at an unconscionable rate. Exotic betting pools are invariably subjected to higher taxation than conventional pools. In 1977, the takeout from triple pools at New York tracks was 47 percent higher than the deductions from win, place, and show pools. As suggested elsewhere in these pages, a handicapper may find exactas, quinellas, and doubles rewarding. But more exotic propositions are a ridiculous waste of time and money. The fact that multiple betting now accounts for more than half the daily pari-mutuel handle at many tracks reflects the industry's insane failure to promote handicapping or discourage suicidal gambling.

N

NEBRASKA. Ak-Sar-Ben, near Omaha, is a pleasant track where free parking and courteous employees make the customer feel most unusually welcome. Purses for claiming and allowance races are generally more liberal than those of the top Illinois and Florida tracks, ensuring programs of major-league quality. When dry and fast, the one-mile strip usually favors EARLY SPEED from POST POSITIONS close to the rail. Bad weather sometimes overturns this pattern.

The state also has three minor tracks, each five furlongs long. Atokad Park, near South Sioux City, and Columbus, near the city of that name, are comparable in quality to Waterford Park and Finger Lakes. Columbus is the more hospitable to early speed. Fonner Park, at Grand Island, has a somewhat superior purse schedule, like that of Charles Town. Early speed prospers when the track is wet but has no great advantage at other times.

NEW HAMPSHIRE. Rockingham Park, near the Massachusetts border and about 40 minutes from Boston, is a good place to go racing from early July to late September. With New England virtually defunct as a center of the Thoroughbred sport, Rockingham becomes more attractive than ever. The horses are not top quality but the non-STAKES purses, superior to those of Suffolk Downs, are scaled at the level of Detroit and Albuquerque, slightly below Timonium. During dry spells, EARLY SPEED is generally an asset in sprints. Front-runners win less frequently at longer distances, but are a threat. In wet weather, they do even better. Extreme outside posts are disadvantages on the one-mile strip, but

155

the inside positions are not superior to the middle.

NEW JERSEY. A short ride across the Hudson River from New York City, the Meadowlands offers good racing, mutuel clerks who say, "Thank you," and glass-enclosed stands that shelter horseplayers from the climate. Before the new track's inaugural Thoroughbred race meeting in the autumn of 1977, its ownership (state government), its night racing, canny management, convenient location, modern facilities, and showmanly solicitude for the customer were viewed as dire threats to the already beleaguered Thoroughbred tracks of New York. Within weeks after launching its first harness-race meeting in 1976, the Meadowlands had become established as America's premier Standardbred raceway, its pari-mutuel handle and purses second to none. In combination with the effects of Connecticut's new gambling attraction, jai alai, and OFF-TRACK BETTING in New York, the Meadowlands had left oncemighty Yonkers Raceway drooping on the ropes. The same might happen to Aqueduct and Belmont Park. Would not New York Thoroughbred followers abandon the frigid discomforts of Aqueduct for the warm amenities of the Meadowlands? If this rendered New York unable to maintain its traditionally high purse schedule, would not top stables move to New Jersey, further hastening New York's decline?

The impact of the first Meadowlands meeting was not so devastating as expected. Many faces missing from the Belmont and Aqueduct audiences were visible at the New Jersey plant, yet betting patterns showed that the track's clients were principally newcomers to the game who risked smaller amounts than were customary among hard-bitten New Yorkers. The Meadowlands crowds were bigger than those of Belmont and Aqueduct, but the pari-mutuel handles were lower. In any case, the population of the metropolitan area was large enough to support both New York and New Jersey racing in high style and had been for decades. If Aqueduct and Belmont now languished, the fault would lie not with the Meadowlands but with the New York State Legislature's shortsighted pari-mutuel taxing policies and the New York Racing Association's continued inability to ingratiate itself with horseplayers toward whom it had never demonstrated much warmth in the first place.

Meadowlands purses were high enough to attract SHIPPERS from New York and all other major Eastern tracks during that first meeting, but did not yet compare so favorably as to induce the migration of entire New York stables. This would not happen unless New York's continuingly decreasing attendance forced reduction in its own tracks' purses. So the Meadowlands entered 1978 established as a racing center of major quality, potentially on a par with Hollywood, Santa Anita, and New York.

The one-mile oval was conventionally favorable to EARLY SPEED when dry or sloppy, much less so when drying out after rain. On some evenings, rail positions were all-powerful, on others the middle and outside prospered. Some of these sudden changes were due to a particularly stormy spell of weather during the track's first season, complicated by the settling process that is routine for a new racing surface. It was just as well. Handicappers should never fall into the trap of accepting generalizations about the racing characteristics of any track. Study of recent RESULTS CHARTS and observation of the evening's first races were rewarding to handicappers who took that much trouble at Meadowlands. Less diligent handicappers suffered at the mutuel windows.

Monmouth Park, long the summer showcase of New Jersey racing, is at Oceanport, an hour from New York City. Although the quality of its programs suffered during the horse shortage of the 1970's, the track lost none of the sparkling cleanliness and other visible charms that had long made it a supremely enjoyable place to go. As less viable operations collapse in the dreadful competition of Eastern racing and/or as the horse shortage is relieved, Monmouth surely will recover its proper position as second only to the very best. At this writing, its non-stakes purses placed it on a footing comparable to that of Pimlico, Bay Meadows, and Pomona. The one-mile strip is generally kind to EARLY SPEED but behaves strangely after prolonged rain or drought. The path along the rail may go dead, whereupon smart riders steer their horses to the cen-

ter of the track and lesser riders lose. The best plan here, as everywhere, is to check recent results charts to see whether anything unusual is going on with early speed and posts. The turf course is surprisingly favorable to horses with early speed. Moreover, although inside post positions are all right on the grass, posts seven and eight win more than their fair share of the time.

Atlantic City, a one-and-one-eighth-miler near that seaside resort, encountered hard times during the competitive wars of the 1970's. At this writing, its claiming and allowance purses were distinctly inferior to Monmouth Park's—lower, in fact, than those of any other major Eastern track. The advent of legal casino gambling was expected to help, although no racetrack has ever endured in Las Vegas. The track surface usually rewards sprinters with early foot. Longer races tend to go to the kind that moves slightly in arrears of the front-runner. The turf course favors animals that come from behind in the stretch.

NEW MEXICO. The State Fair runs a brief race meeting each September at Albuquerque, a one-mile track. An unusually long run from the home turn to the finish line (1,114 feet) may explain why fewer than half the races go to horses with EARLY SPEED. The runner that stalks the early pacesetters has somewhat less advantage when the track is wet. Purses for claiming and allowance races compare closely with those at Fair Grounds or Suffolk Downs, making the quality a slice above minor. Quarter-horse racing helps to flesh out the programs here and at the state's three lesser plants: La Mesa Park, a seven-furlong layout near Raton; Santa Fe Downs, a one-miler near that city; and Ruidoso Downs, 70 miles from Roswell. The first two favor early speed. Ruidoso normally does not.

NEW YORK. For more than a century, racing in New York City and the Adirondack watering place, Saratoga Springs, set quality standards for the North American sport. Here were the best horses and riders, the most rigorous rules, the most knowing audiences, the courtliest traditions, and the continent's most august confederation of influential stable OWNERS and BREEDERS—THE JOCKY CLUB. With the economic recession, monetary inflation, and Thoroughbred shortage of the 1970's, New York racing entered heavy weather. To generate revenue for the state treasury, an eight- or nine-month season was stretched into a year-long endurance trial. The DAILY DOUBLE was supplemented with three EXACTAS and a triple (TRIFECTA). What once had been a 10 percent takeout from each wagered dollar now became a punitive 17 percent and, on the triple, a felonious 25 percent. Legal OFF-TRACK BETTING, an inevitability that should have been a tremendous asset to the sport, was enacted by a misbegotten law written without constructive assistance from the racing industry. Administered in almost total ignorance of racing and betting, it encouraged profligate gambling under squalid conditions. While contributing pittances to the tracks, it subtracted from their daily attendance, the decline in which was intensified by the exorbitant takeout, five- and six-horse races, and higher prices for poorer food, drink, and parking services.

The New York Racing Association, under whose leadership all these disasters occurred, came into being as the Greater New York Association in 1953. The old New York tracks were in disrepair, their owners anxious to avoid the costs of expansion and modernization. Purportedly at state behest, The Jockey Club organized the nonprofit association through which some of its foremost members now operate the totally rebuilt Aqueduct and Belmont Park and a somewhat renovated Saratoga. Their arrangement with the state assured NYRA trustees (directors) of appropriate settings and large purses for the championship STAKES races in which they race their own horses and fortify their positions as breeders. In exchange, the state gets three facilities for the large-scale plunder of horseplayers. The NYRA is permitted to keep none of the pari-mutuel take beyond what the state deems necessary for minimum operations including, of course, the aforementioned stakes purses and, for non-stakes races, purses high enough to keep the tracks top drawer. NYRA trustees sometimes refer to the state as their "partner," an apt description. With each party getting exactly what it had bargained for, the joint venture has been happy. That the partners were dealing inconsiderately with their financial backer—the ticket-buying horseplayer—was a matter of outspoken concern only among horseplayers, a strangely alien breed about whose well-being neither partner had ever evinced much curiosity.

By late 1977, with business declining and New Jersey offering superior customer accommodations at the Meadowlands, directly across the Hudson River from New York City, it dawned on the NYRA that the partnership might not endure without concessions to its dwindling clientele. The NYRA suggested a reduced pari-mutuel take. While waiting for the tidy logic of that proposal to penetrate governmental minds, the NYRA sought to boost attendance and betting with free concerts, free admissions, and a brightly redecorated Aqueduct. None of these embellishments attracted many bettors. It was plain that if large numbers of disgruntled New Yorkers deserted to the Meadowlands, New York State would lose enough pari-mutuel income to arouse legislative attention. Would the state reduce the takeout? Would it review the nature of its partnership with the NYRA? Would it wonder if stable owners and breeders were the persons best qualified to administer a tax-collection facility that also was a multi-million-dollar branch of the entertainment industry? Answers can be expected during the 1980's.

For the NYRA trustees and their peers, the high point of the racing year is the Saratoga meeting each August. There they race their best Thoroughbreds in stakes that help settle national championships. They also occupy themselves at auctions of expensively bred yearlings. The old track has a modern racing strip and a marvelously tranquil saddling area among the trees behind the stands. The stands themselves are cramped and congested, with generally poor seating. Saratoga Springs, a pleasant village during the quiet months of September through July, suddenly becomes one of the foremost rip-off centers of Western civilization. Hotels and motels inflate their room rates remorselessly. To get a decent meal at a square price, one must drive for miles. Yet, whoever has not attended the Saratoga meeting has missed some of the best racing in the world. Handicapping and betting demand great caution, because the society stables are forever unveiling upset winners whose entire lives have been directed toward victory at the Spa. Other ready horses ship from all over the continent. Things settle down slightly during the second week, when a horse with a previous race at the meeting has an edge. The mile-and-one-furlong main track used to be heavier and less cordial to EARLY SPEED than the similar strip at Aqueduct, but is now equally glib. Horses that run first, second, or third at the half-mile pole win a respectable share of the races when conditions are dry, and become dominant when the cushion is wet. At some meetings, inside post positions are a great advantage at all distances, and a horse with an outside berth has a built-in excuse for losing. The visitor should study RESULTS

CHARTS of the current meeting to see what has been happening. The turf course favors the three inside post positions and ability to come on in the stretch.

Belmont Park offers non-stakes purses surpassed only at Saratoga and Hollywood Park. It therefore presents programs of topmost quality. Situated on the boundary of New York City and Nassau County, and accessible by car or train, the vast plant is a suitable setting for the important stakes that highlight its seasons—especially when the weather is good. On windy or chilly days, bring a coat and do not be surprised if most of the audience ventures into the outdoor seating areas only during the actual running of races, if then. A trackside dining room is glass-enclosed, blocking the view of the home turn and part of the stretch from many unreserved clubhouse seats but giving diners excellent vantage plus protection from the weather.

The mile-and-a-half main track has long, gradual turns and a backstretch chute for races of as long as nine furlongs around only one turn. Stretch runners come into their own. Early speed wins only when fortified with extra class and assisted by bouncy footing. Post position means little, except during the first September days of the annual fall meeting, when the inside may be deep and deathly slow. Horses that do not go to Saratoga but exercise at Belmont during August pound the inside to concrete hardness. To counteract this,

the track maintenance crew deepens that path just before Belmont reopens. After five or six days of racing, the cushion becomes more uniform. Belmont has two turf courses. On the inner of these, the horses break from a chute that sends them away almost perpendicularly from the stands and discharges them onto the clubhouse turn. An inside post helps, but the paramount consideration is speed enough to capture good position on the turn. Early speed also does nicely on the Widener turf course, which lies between the inner one and the main track.

Aqueduct is the least glamorous, most functionally constructed, and most easily reached of the NYRA facilities. It also is the chilliest and windiest and the one chosen for use during the most severe months of the winter season. On a crowded Saturday, the spaces beneath the stands are as congested as the New York subway and scarcely more elegant. The main track is nine furlongs long and, after three days of dry weather, can usually be expected to favor horses with early speed at six furlongs. At seven furlongs or a mile (which involves only one turn), the advantage is less. In fact, it is not unusual for come-from-behind types to win each of two mile races on a day when all other races go to animals with early foot. When sloppy, Aqueduct is even better for the speedsters. But when drying out after rain, it is tricky. Nobody can be sure what type will prosper until the first couple of races have revealed a trend. At a mile and one-eighth, around two turns, the rail position and early speed are a winning combination.

An inner dirt track, one mile long, is heavily salted against winter freezes and is used exclusively during that season. The horsemen praise it because its cushion seems kindly to legs and hooves. Handicappers like it because it offers a square shake. If the best horse is ridden by a jockey intelligent enough to save ground, it is an excellent bet. Early speed does well for days on end but does not dominate. Inside this track lies a turf course, seven furlongs long, on which a stretch run is usually decisive unless the speed horse with an inside post can get the lead uncontested and coast home.

Upstate, about 16 miles from Rochester and close to Canandaigua is Finger Lakes, which runs about 180 days from March through November. The races are minor-league. The one-mile track tends to help early speedsters when wet but otherwise lacks strong bias.

ODDS. The ability to pick a high percentage of winners signifies an ability to make money at the track only if the winners pay adequate odds. It is no great feat to select as many winners as losers—a winning average of 50 percent—at odds of 3–5, yielding a loss of 20 cents on each wagered dollar. Someone who made selections by stabbing the program with a hatpin would have a fair chance of doing no worse than that. The winning average would be low, but the random character of the selections would produce longshots. A thousand chimpanzees trained to impale programs in that manner would produce selections on which the seasonal returns would cluster around a loss of 18.5 cents per dollar at any track where the government and track management deduct that much from the betting pools.

When the pari-mutuel take, or house percentage, was only 10 percent, it was possible for a first-class handicapper to make a 20 percent profit by picking around 40 winners in every 100 selections, at average odds of 2–1. With the take now about 80 percent higher than that, the same horses no longer pay 2–1 (a $6.00 payoff). They now pay 3–2 (a $5.00 payoff) and to cash 40 percent of the bets leaves the player with neither a profit nor a loss—until the cost of getting to the track, purchasing admission, and buying nourishment are accounted for. Handicappers therefore hunt for overlays—horses that race at liberal odds because their chances have been underestimated by the crowd. Technically and actually, an overlay is a horse whose odds are higher than its winning probability. A natural 2–1 shot is a horse with a 33 percent chance of winning. If, as usual, the bettors collectively recognize this, the animal's odds will not be 2–1 but 3–2, as already noted. But if, as happens, the audience has been misled into support of another horse, and the natural 2–1 shot goes off at 5–2, it is an overlay. To bet on no horses except overlays is to guarantee long-term profits. The situation is directly comparable to the play of a poker hand in which the decision about drawing to an inside straight depends on whether a lucky draw will pay more than 12 times the cost of the card. A series of one-card draws to inside straights at odds of 12–1 or better assures profits. A series of such draws at odds of less than 11–1 assures losses.

The difference between poker and racing bets is, of course, that poker probabilities are well-established statistics. But handicapping has not yet reached the stage at which the actual winning chances of an individual horse can be stated accurately. Progress has been made toward that goal, but a long distance remains. Thus, racegoers tend to speak of overlays after the fact, while tearing up their losing tickets and noticing that the 8–1 winner might just as well have gone at 4–1 and was, in truth, a big overlay. Theoretically, however, a talented and experienced handicapper who has graded a field of horses competently can often tell when one or more of them is overlaid. Profits are possible when bets are placed on all such horses. That is, if the handicapper finds that the field includes three legitimate contenders of which one is going to the post at overlaid odds, a bet on that horse and

all like it all season should yield profits, provided the handicapper can actually identify contenders that well. From this theory comes the betting practice that sustains most successful players: When in doubt about two closely matched horses, they play the one at higher odds. If both are at low odds, they pass the race. But if one is 7–2 or 4–1 or 5–1, they play it. The boundary varies with the individual. Whether the 4–1 shot is an actual overlay or not cannot be determined. But after years of functioning in that way and profiting from it, the player's own records are statistical evidence that a given approach to handicapping and betting has turned up enough overlays and/or a high enough winning average for success at the races. The name of the game.

Although statistical studies invariably have proved that horses at 2–1 win a higher percentage of races than horses at 5–2, which win more often than horses at 3–1, and that flat bets on horses in any odds range must produce long-term losses, it is clear enough that good handicapping overcomes this phenomenon and, with it, the pari-mutuel take that accounts for it. No matter which handicapping doctrine claims the loyalty of the successful player, the resultant selections apparently are so patterned that the horses bet at comparatively high odds win almost as often as those bet at comparatively low odds. Or, if the winning percentage at good odds is substantially lower than at poor odds, it remains high enough to supply the player with profits. This and only this accounts for the success of good handicappers who play the relatively high-odds horse when unable to separate two or three contenders. And it accounts for the corollary phenomenon discussed here under the heading of MONEY MANAGEMENT: Handicapping profits usually trace to winning bets at good odds, with bets on short-priced horses yielding little or nothing. This being so, the seasoned handicapper able to pick a winner in every four attempts may well be entitled to define any selection at 7–2 or better as a nice overlay.

Among efforts to determine the actual winning chances of horses, the best I have found is *Probability Computation,* in which Frederick S. Davis shows how to apply the conclusions reached in his research study, *Thoroughbred Racing: Percentages and Probabilities.* Having ascertained the winning percentages associated with individual handicapping factors, as expressed in characteristics found in the PAST-PERFORMANCE TABLES of individual horses, Davis presented handicapping formulas which combined key factors and their percentages. The mathematics was debatable not because the author's arithmetic was wrong but because statistical objections were possible in terms of the actual independence of the factors and the means used to combine their percentages. But the formulas worked, furnishing the player with a MORNING LINE so accurate that whenever the top-rated horse went at odds higher than stated in the Davis line, it was an excellent bet. Readers interested in experimenting with overlay

identification might like the following formula, a simplification of the original Davis approach. For use in connection with races on dirt tracks only, it adds or subtracts points for CLASS, FORM, consistency, EARLY SPEED, and WEIGHTS. Each starter in a race begins with 10 points.

Class. When handicapping a CLAIMING RACE, add 4 points if the horse has ever finished first or second when entered at today's top claiming price or higher. Subtract 3 points if the horse has not done that. If today's is an ALLOWANCE race, add 7 points if the horse has started in a STAKES race and has not raced in a claimer since then. If the horse has raced only in allowances and non-claiming maiden races, neither add nor subtract. If the horse has raced in a claimer and has not raced in a stakes since then, subtract 4. When handicapping a stakes race, add 6 if the horse has already won a stakes and subtract 4 if it has never raced in a stakes. Otherwise add or subtract nothing.

Finish in Last Race. If the horse has not raced in more than 30 days, skip this altogether. Otherwise use its latest race:

Won	+ 5
Second	+ 7
Third	+ 2
Fourth	0
Fifth	− 1
Sixth	− 2
Worse	− 4

Consistency. Check each horse's six most recent races—fewer if it has raced less than six times. Credit it with 2 points for each win in a non-maiden race at a track of today's quality or higher, and 1 point for a win in a non-maiden race at a minor track (or a track of considerably less quality than your own minor track). Credit it with 1 point for a second-place finish in a non-maiden race at a track of today's quality or higher. Now add these consistency points and modify the horse's previous rating as follows:

Six consistency points or more	+ 8
Five points	+ 6
Four	+ 4
Three	+ 3
Two	+ 1
One	− 2
None	− 4

Early Speed. Find each horse's two best running positions at the first call in past races at today's distance or shorter. Total the numbers. Example: If the horse was first at the first call once and second at the first call on another occasion, 2 + 1 = 3. Find the three horses with the lowest totals. In case of ties, four or more horses may be involved here. Whether three or more are found, give each 3 points. Deduct 2 points from all others.

Weights. After adding to the horses' posted weights whatever APPRENTICE weight allowances have been subtracted, give 4 points to the three horses with the highest weights (four or more horses if ties necessitate). Subtract 3 points from all the other starters.

Computing the Odds. Add all the final ratings. Divide each final rating by the total of all of them. Convert each resultant percentage into its equivalent morning-line odds by using the odds-percentage table that accompanies this book's discussion of DUTCHING.

For races on a turf course, weights and early speed do not apply. Each horse begins with 15 points. Class is handled as in dirt-track races. Proceed:

Finish in Last Race.

Won on grass	+ 11
Second on grass	+ 12
Third on grass	+ 2
Fourth on grass	0
Worse on grass	− 3
Won on dirt	− 2
Second on dirt	0
Third on dirt	− 2
Fourth on dirt	−3
Worse on dirt	−5

Consistency. Referring only to the horse's six most recent races on grass (fewer if it has run less often on that footing), award 2 points for each victory, 1 for each second-place finish. Maiden-race finishes are acceptable.

Six consistency points or more	+ 12
Five points	+ 9
Four	+ 7
Three	+ 5
Two	+ 2
One	0
No turf races or no points	−5

Add all the final ratings and calculate the odds as in main-track racing.

OFF-TRACK BETTING is a pleasant, pervasive, and entirely lawful feature of daily life in most countries with Thoroughbred racetracks. Because of it, British, Australian, and Japanese racing are considerably more popular than our own, and French tracks pay the highest purses in the world. Wherever off-track betting is thoughtfully designed and administered, the sport develops a larger and more sophisticated audience which contributes more revenue to tracks. The chief prerequisite is intelligent collaboration between racing and legislatures.

At this writing, off-track betting is legal in Nevada, New York, and Connecticut. It inevitably will become a taxing device in states throughout the land. Thus far, the U.S. racing industry has been slow to accept this trend. In the manner of King Canute scolding the ocean, an unbudging industry has contributed little but opposition to the laws, submitting few positive proposals of its own. Racing, which should have been a beneficiary of the legislation, therefore became its victim. And why, aside from nostalgia for the past, have the leaders of racing persisted in this negative attitude? They detest all sports betting except the kind legalized at their own tracks. They fear the competition, the possible loss of what they call "the entertainment dollar." They form united fronts with anti-gambling elements— their own enemies—to oppose off-track betting, casinos, football and baseball pools, and all the other kinds of popular wagering that eventually will be sanctioned by tax-seeking legislatures. Predicting doom, they get it in the form of outrageous off-track betting programs that help nobody for long. They then redouble their complaints, apparently without realizing that their bleak prophesies were fulfilled mainly because they did nothing to influence events toward a different course.

The off-track betting procedures legalized in New York (the first racing state to pass such an act) could have been fashioned after the French plan, with the off-track shops serving, in effect, as branches of the tracks themselves. Instead, the New York facilities are remote arms of government, administered by politicians unburdened with knowledge of PARI-MUTUEL BETTING and racing and, in some cases, not even curious to learn. The shops are as cheerless as welfare clinics. Messy, badly ventilated, and staffed by disdainfully irritable bureaucratic types, they offer the handicapper nothing except a deplorably inaccurate MORNING LINE and an opportunity to bet in the blind. But the legislation that spawned them is pioneering legislation, if you please, and is inescapably the model for other states that hope to relieve their own financial problems by exploiting gamblers.

Off-track betting in New York hurts racing by awarding government an exorbitantly large share of the money wagered in the shops and by guaranteeing that any reasonably bright person introduced to racing through OTB will be repelled. The shops also inflict harm on racing by reducing attendance at the tracks—although not as severely as a self-forgiving racing industry would like to believe. New York racing attendance had been in dubious condition before OTB was established. Furthermore, it is patently evident that most OTB patrons are recreational gamblers who lack time, money, or inclination to visit tracks and would not even visit OTB shops if they could find a bookie. The surpassing ignorance of OTB's clientele is evident in the hopeless horses they favor in race after race and the millions of dollars in negotiable place and show tickets that they tear up and throw away after the horses win. Lacking a bookie or OTB, no doubt some of them would find their way to tracks, boosting track revenues to that extent. But this possibility would not matter at all if the OTB law gave tracks an equitable share of the money harvested at the shops.

The New York OTB administration does virtually nothing to educate its legion of suckers. Realizing that a winning handicapper bets more often and in larger amounts, increasing the pari-mutuel profits of whatever agency takes the bets, a race-wise OTB official once proposed that handicapping instruction be made available through literature and lectures. OTB marketing experts rejected the notion, arguing that the handicapping authority who had been nominated for the chore would get too much free publicity. Efforts to explain the relationships among improved handicapping, increased betting, and OTB finances fell on deaf ears.

No handicapper of sound mind can be the steady patron of a betting facility that fails to display the changing odds during the pre-race wagering period. This, plus the failure of the starkly dismal stores to show the actual running of the races on television, makes them indistinguishable from clandestine bookie joints. In one respect they are worse: Levying a 5 percent surcharge on all payoffs, they pay lower mutuel prices than bookies do.

Bad as the situation is in New York, and bad as it threatens to be when organized in that style elsewhere, it is not beyond salvage. A legislature genuinely interested in maximizing tax revenues from racing might learn that the key element must be an effort to increase the game's popularity. The off-track betting establishments could play a central role. The first step would be an upgrading program to make the shops fit haunts for civilized human beings. Necessary information would be furnished to such handicappers as happened to stray into the places when unable to get to the track. Non-handicappers would be educated to win once in a while or, if resistant, would be treated to special wagering (gambling) propositions suitable to that kind of clientele: Perhaps 25-cent bets, as in Australia, and a large selection of MULTIPLE BETTING devices, as in France and England. With the shops refurbished, and their services improved, they would become recruiting centers for racing fans.

And what would induce a new racing fan to go to the track if televised odds changes and televised races and 25-cent bets were offered at OTB? Try this: Track attendance would multiply and revenues soar if pari-mutuel laws and track computers were modified to permit restoration of on-track betting at fixed odds, as in the days before pari-mutuel machines arrived. Whatever odds prevailed when the bet was made were the odds collected by the bettor at the track. A simple computer program could handle that nowadays, especially when assisted by the electronic ticket-selling and ticket-cashing machines used in other countries. But it could not be done so readily without OTB, whose patrons would have to settle for whatever final odds were calculated after all track betting windows closed and the books were balanced. This would be a bonanza for racing. It would rekindle interest among the uncountable tens of thousands of former patrons who have been driven to other pastimes by the increased pari-mutuel takeout. What racing enthusiast would not be pleased to collect a $12.00 mutuel on a horse that only paid $6.40 at OTB?

OHIO. Thistledown, near Cleveland, presents racing all year. River Downs, close to Cincinnati, runs from early May to early September. Beulah Park, outside Columbus, offers one spring and one fall meeting for a total of about 70 racing days. As befits its metropolitan status, Thistledown pays somewhat higher purses and fields slightly better horses than run at the other two tracks. Its quality approximates that of Long-

acres, a thin slice below the tracks of Detroit. With two concentric dirt tracks—one of them a miler, the other seven furlongs long—handicappers face two different kinds of racing. On the main oval, early speed is at a premium in wet weather but is no bargain otherwise, especially in longer races. Having tighter turns, the inner track is more favorable to quick starters. Beulah Park and River Downs form a circuit with Latonia, in Kentucky. Beulah's purse structure resembles those of Cahokia Downs, Caliente, and Florida Downs. River Downs, with a recently improved plant, is at the level of Penn National. The Cincinnati and Columbus tracks are both one-milers that reward early speed. At Beulah, post positions 3 through 6 used to be favorable and may still be.

OREGON. Portland Meadows, a one-miler in the township after which it is named, is a one-mile track on which quarter horses share the programs with Thoroughbreds. Racing runs from January into May and is of minor quality, comparable to that of Finger Lakes. Early speed wins more often in off footing than on dry, when it is best accompanied by a touch of class. At Salem Fairgrounds in Oregon, they scrape the bottom of the Thoroughbred barrel for races on a five-furlong strip. Speed does better here, especially in the wet.

OWNERS. Each year THE THOR-OUGHBRED RECORD publishes a detailed analysis of the previous year's purses and how they were distributed. In 1976, for example, 61,084 Thoroughbreds competed on North American tracks for purse money of $318,680,094. The average runner therefore earned $5,217, which might almost have paid for its keep if it raced on a very minor circuit. But averages are unreliable. Actually, half of all North American horses earned less than $2,100, and 37 percent won $1,000 or less. And only 15.49 percent won $10,000 or more. At that time, it cost at least $10,000 to maintain a horse under the care of a good TRAINER at a major track, and the expenses frequently exceeded $15,000. Ownership of a horse is not certain to be a profitable venture. Neither is owning a lot of horses. In 1975, one of the largest and most firmly established racing and breeding operations, Harbor View Farm, reported a loss of $600,000 on income of about $2,000,000.

The fourth-generation inheritor of a racing dynasty founded with steel, streetcar, subway, railroad, chemical, or banking millions is not in quite the same leaky boat as the newly hatched business tycoon who buys a couple of Thoroughbreds by way of proclaiming to himself and the world that he has indeed Arrived. Each may preside over a losing proposition. But the member of the dynasty is not limited to operation of a racing stable. His or her interests in Thoroughbreds are farther flung. For example, BREEDING. This includes income from the sale of foals dropped by broodmares that established their racing worth in the stable's colors. It also includes membership in syndicates that make millions on the stud services of prize stallions. And, of course, no racing dynasty is complete without positions of authority or privilege in the operation of a few racetracks. Lacking the possibility of such diversification and the revenues and tax benefits that derive therefrom, the small owner may well fold his hand and disappear, as so many do, after the Internal Revenue Service announces that the stable is not a tax-deductible business but a hobby, having earned no profit in years.

It stands to reason that if everyone who owned race horses lost money on that account, the number of actively raced Thoroughbreds would not have doubled between 1960 and 1976. Keen though the sporting instinct may be among persons of affluence, the urge to self-destruct is not normally a part of their makeup. For every new stable that falls by the wayside, another continues year after year, doing the owner more good than harm, regardless of what statistics may show about the average or median earnings of Thoroughbred runners. A good tax lawyer helps. So does a trainer shrewd about the purchase and sale of livestock. And, lest we forget, innumerable horses are owned not by fresh recruits from the outside world but by persons who have lived with Thoroughbreds all their lives and train their own, materially reducing the cost of operations. In addition, trainers frequently accept partial ownership of horses in lieu of fees for service. Other partnerships, often complicated enough to baffle the lawyers who organize them, involve trainers, veterinarians, racing officials, and/or other insiders who own important percentages of stables supposedly the property of others. At the very least, this kind of arrangement minimizes individual loss during an off year.

The handicapper should be aware of all this only because it is part of the setting in which handicapping and betting take place. Otherwise, the name of the owner is seldom germane to the handicapping process. During the heyday of Calumet Farms (Citation, Armed, Whirlaway, Pensive, Coaltown, et al.), the fan convinced of that barn's invincibility would have lost a fortune betting blindly on every Calumet starter. And during the great days when Burt Mulholland trained a division of the horses owned by Mr. and Mrs. George D. Widener, it was not enough to note that a horse was from the Widener barn. To cash in on Mulholland's extraordinary winning average (which seldom fell below 25 percent), it was necessary to make sure that he was the trainer and that the horse was not part of a different Widener division. In the 1970's, when the horses of Dan Lasater set stable-earnings records at tracks throughout the country, the player respected any Lasater starter—not because of the barn's facility for earning purses but because its winning average was phenomenally high. The name and record of the trainer are more important than the name of the owner. And the record of the horse is more important than anything.

P

PACE. After the best horse wins a truly run race, the accomplishment can be described in one of two ways:

1. The winner set an early pace beyond the powers of its opponents, reserving enough energy to maintain its lead to the finish, or

2. The winner overcame the early pace of another horse or horses and reached the front in time.

Where racing luck or riding errors play no part, one of those two descriptions always summarizes the race. But neither description explains anything. Why was the winner able to win? For the answer, the handicapper reviews FUNDAMENTALS. On the particular afternoon, the horse was suited to the DISTANCE of the race, was in adequate FORM, had enough CLASS to handle the field under the WEIGHTS and, as the outcome demonstrated, was at no serious disadvantage in terms of EARLY SPEED, FOOTING, JOCKEY, or POST POSITION.

Because all the fundamentals of handicapping, including close comparison of CONTENDERS, support an effective analysis of pace, that factor forms the basis of an immensely popular approach to the mechanization of handicapping. Some pace handicappers are winners, and deservedly.

Conventional Methods. As noted, the winner of a typical race is the horse able to set or overcome the early pace and be there at the finish. From this comes the traditional pace-rating formula which begins with an assumption as to what the fastest early pace might be and then arithmetically isolates the horse considered likeliest to win after setting or overcoming that pace. For example, assume that three contenders in a typical six-furlong sprint are being compared on grounds of their best recent efforts at the distance:

Horse A	:22.2	:45.2	1:10.2	4^5	3^3	3^2	1^1
Horse B	:22.2	:45.3	1:10.3	1^3	1^2	1^2	1^1
Horse C	:22.0	:45.2	1:10.1	1^1	2^1	3^3	5^5

Presuming that each horse is capable of reproducing the same fractional and final times in the upcoming race, the pace-rating formula compares the official fractional times of each race and the individual final times of each horse. That is, it compares the official quarter-mile and half-mile times published in *Daily Racing Form*'s PAST-PERFORMANCE TABLES and then, after adding one-fifth of a second for each beaten length at the finish, compares the final times of the horses. Official times at each call, like official final times, are the times recorded for whatever horses were in the lead at the given point of call.

For this kind of pace rating, simple arithmetic suffices. Ten points are assigned to the horse or horses whose races involved the fastest quarter-mile and half-mile times, with 1 point deducted for each fifth of a second of slower official time at each of those calls. And the horse or horses with the fastest individual final time gets 10 points, with 1 point per fifth deducted from the scores of horses that logged slower final times. In this example, the official quarter-mile time of C's race was fastest, earning the animal 10 points and each of the others 8. A and C each get 10 points for running behind the fastest of-ficial half-mile time (:45.2), and B gets 9. A gets 10 for winning in 1:10.2, B earns 9 for winning in 1:10.3, and C gets 6 points for finishing in 1:11.1 (five lengths behind a horse that won in 1:10.1 and, therefore, four lengths or four-fifths of a second slower than A).

Adding the points awarded to each horse, we find that A gets 28, B 26, and C 26. This outcome fits one of the stereotyped conceptions of mechanical pace handicapping. The two horses with early speed (B and C) will defeat each other and A, the horse that runs behind the early pace, will come on to win in the stretch, being two points the best. In some circumstances, but by no means in most, the race might actually turn out that way. A careful handicapper would not accept A without digging more deeply. RESULTS CHARTS and a closer look at the past-performance tables might show whether A's rated race was representative of what might be expected of him today. Did he actually overcome the pace of the rated race or did he benefit from racing luck? Might B be too much for A if able once again to get a clear lead at the beginning and continue well in front after a half-mile? Note that B went the half in :45.3, but it took A :46.0 to get there (three lengths

178

behind an official half-mile time of :45.2). And what of C, who is by far the most interesting horse of the three, despite the pace rating? Is C a short-winded animal that always leaves the gate like a rocket and seldom survives in the stretch? Or was he somewhat short of form in the rated race? Might he carry his speed farther today? Was he in good form but victimized by the presence of another quick-starting type that ran him into the ground? Perhaps no such quick starter is on the scene here. If C is any kind of runner, and the track is conducive to early speed, he should romp away from B and leave A far behind. As all this implies, pace analysis is preferable to mechanical pace rating.

Other Pitfalls. The gravest drawback of conventional pace-rating methods is the face-value acceptance of official fractional and final times. On some days, any racing strip is so resilient and the wind so favorable that cheap horses run in stakes-horse time. On other days, at any track, stakes horses log times that, under normal conditions, are within the capabilities of cheap horses. Between these extremes lie innumerable possibilities, complicated by the additional fact that track speed seldom remains constant throughout a racing program. Speed variants are essential to accurate evaluation of running times. Among secondary difficulties which afflict many pace handicappers, these should be mentioned:

1. The typical North American six-furlong sprint takes place on a hard surface with one tight turn. The horses do their fastest running in the first quarter of a mile, decelerating in each subsequent quarter. Both theoretically and actually, most sprints are settled in the first quarter, when a horse either gets a commanding lead and coasts home or front-runners begin to beat each other, setting the stage for a winning stretch performance by a come-from-behinder who happens to be slowing down less rapidly than the others. A familiar variation finds two or three horses fighting for the early lead during the first half-mile, with one of them putting the others away and going on to win. Arithmetical pace-rating methods are based on the supposition that the final time of a race somehow relates arithmetically to the fractional times, but the relationships are more apparent than real. To return to the example above, horse B got loose in :22.2 and won in 1:10.3, which may well have been the best time of his career. If challenged in that race, he might have run the same :22.2 and might have spit out the bit, finishing in 1:12. Indeed, if challenged, he might not have even run the :22.2. Adversaries of pace ratings make much of this phenomenon, tossing out the baby with the bath water. Someone who abandons arithmetic in favor of analytic thought is better off than the pace raters and their critics. A horse who has produced good fractional figures and decent final time can be evaluated quite accurately. His fractions might improve or they might not, depending on the analyst's appraisal of the circumstances in which the race will be run—particularly the horse's present

form, the possibility that he might or might not get better, and the kinds of fractions that might be tossed at him by other horses.

2. A failure to identify contenders before assigning pace ratings leads in many cases to the substitution of pace ratings for even the most rudimentary handicapping. In extreme cases, the pace enthusiast takes the best race for which a running line appears in each horse's past performances. Then, without regard to the recency or whereabouts of each race, and also without accurate speed variants, and often by using inaccurate parallel time charts (see SPEED HANDICAPPING) to compare races at diverse distances, ratings are assigned. The less attention paid to the present relevance of each rated race, the lower the percentage of winners and, of course, the greater the number of longshots. But nobody can stay ahead of the game that way.

3. Contender or not, the horse with the top pace rating is a likely winner only if track conditions favor its running style. If early-speed horses are winning more than their share, the prospects of come-from-behind types diminish, regardless of pace ratings. On tracks of that kind, late-running animals win only by accident. By the same token, when a track is stickier than usual and frontrunners are losing, the highest pace rating is most dependable when it belongs to a fast-closing animal. This argument does not apply, of course, to the rare situation in which a Secretariat faces a field of non-Secretariats and simply outclasses them, irrespective of their running styles.

4. Just as pace ratings should be read in light of track conditions, they should also be influenced by post positions, weights, jockeys, and other factors that may have contributed to the quality of past performances, raising or lowering the pace ratings. Likewise, such factors influence the horse's present prospects and must be taken into account. A high pace rating earned with Willie Shoemaker, Angel Cordero, or Steve Cauthen in the saddle will not necessarily be duplicated under a green APPRENTICE.

5. Reliance on numbers of any kind is warranted only when the handicapper remains alert to their real significance, including their limitations. If two horses get good pace ratings on the basis of (among other numbers) quarter-mile times that turn out to be :22.1 after being modified by speed variants, it is too bad to spoil all that work by assuming that each of the horses will now go to the first quarter in :22.1, perhaps setting things up for some other horse in the homestretch. One of the speedsters may be improving, and quite capable of producing a flat :22.0 and winning in a common canter. That possibility increases if the other horse has been hardraced and fails to duplicate its recent early speed. In any event, it is best to accept pace figures as guides, not blueprints.

Lacking accurate speed variants and the time or willingness to compute them, many pace handicappers improve their results by using three races as the basis on which to rate each contender. Where three sets of local and recent fractional and final times are available, normal variations in track speed may balance each other or, at least, reduce distortions. Some persons who work this way base their calculations not on the customary one-fifth-per-second-per-length formula but a more realistic one in which horses are assumed to travel six lengths per second. One way to do this is to regard each second of time as worth 60 points, with each fifth of a second worth 12. Then, each beaten length is 10 points—the same 60 points per second.

To apply the formula to three contenders, for each of which three races are to be rated, the most convenient method is to assign a figure of 500 to the fastest of the nine listed quarter-mile times. The slower ones get 12 points less per fifth of a second. The same is done for the half-mile times and, in races at a mile or more, three-quarter-mile times. When rating individual final times, begin with the official times, awarding 500 to the fastest—and reduce each slower one by 12 points per fifth. Then deduct 10 points for each beaten length. If none of the rated horses won a race, none will get 500 points for its own final time, but this does not matter. The process ends with the addition of each horse's totals and, one hopes, proper analysis of the highest-rated animal's real prospects.

Still another pace-rating method also uses three races per contender but rates each horse's actual running time at each fraction as well as at the finish. Using PAR TIMES with a value of 100, the handicapper deducts 1 point for each fifth slower at each fraction and at each finish. Or, to calculate on the basis of six lengths per second, each par time is worth 500—with 12 points off per fifth for each slower official fractional and final time, and an additional 10 points for each length behind at each point on the running line. Jayce Killaen, a successful Canadian handicapper, carried this a long step further, eliminating times altogether but using a computer to study the winning probabilities associated with various running positions at each point of call. The computer issued numerical values which Killaen's followers combine to good effect.

In *The Compleat Horseplayer,* I documented excellent results achieved with a stripped-down pace-rating approach that ignored the quarter-mile fraction, using only the half-mile (plus three-quarter-mile in longer races) and individual final times. What saved the method from its oversimplified approach to pace rating was avoidance of difficult races and extreme care about elimination of non-contenders. The procedure seldom unearthed more than two or three playable selections a day. Some of its readers continue to profit from the formula, having supplied missing ingredients like decent variants and quarter-mile times.

In *Ainslie's Private Method,* an attempt to streamline handicapping for the public, no mention was made of pace. I had realized by then that analysis of fundamentals, most especially distance preferences, early speed, and track conditions, took ample care of the pace factor and rendered pace ratings superfluous. Years later, I continue to believe that a handicapper able to differentiate a contender from a non-contender does so only by recognizing that some non-contenders will not be able to keep up during the early running and will not catch up later, while others may run well in the beginning but will fail at the end. That is the foundation of pace analysis, which concludes with a detailed effort to predict not only which horse will win, but how.

PADDOCK AND POST PARADE. The final stages of handicapping are a visit to the saddling enclosure and walking ring, followed by a close look (binoculars will do) at one's choice as it goes to the track, parades in front of the stands, and warms up en route to the STARTING GATE. Properly anxious to avoid needless loss, an inexperienced racegoer will occasionally withhold a bet on a skittish or bedraggled Thoroughbred that belies its unhappy demeanor and wins. But the same racegoer will more often avoid betting on horses that not only look like losers but lose. In this respect, the new handicapper holds a large advantage over the supposed sophisticate who never bothers to inspect horses before a race.

Having handicapped the race on paper, one goes to the paddock hoping that the top selection looks the part. If it arrives calmly, its ears pricked forward, its clearly focused eyes gazing with confident interest at the crowd, its coat agleam with health, its head nodding in comfortable rhythm with its long, easy, uncomplicated stride, it seems very much a ready runner. If it dances on its toes, full of itself, perhaps wheeling playfully without causing its handler major problems, and even if it sweats a bit between its hind legs, it is keyed up. This is a good sign in any athlete, provided that the athlete does not become increasingly tense and leave its race in the paddock. Another welcome sign is a peaceable relationship between horse and GROOM. So is the prompt presence in the saddling enclosure of the TRAINER. If the OWNER and entourage also appear, all decked out for photography in the winner's circle, so much the better. Later, in the post parade and pre-race warmup, it is good to see that the horse earlier so full of its powers is still rarin' to go, leaning on the bit, trying to get to the gate as soon as possible, looking positively aggressive, especially by contrast with troubled opponents whose torment shows in lathered sweat, choppy strides, heads too high, fighting the bit, and often showing such distaste for the matter at hand that they almost must be dragged to the gate.

Naturally, an experienced observer in daily attendance at the paddock has a huge edge, looking for changes in appearance and behavior and evaluating these in light of an animal's physical and mental attitudes on previous occasions. Dozens of professional bettors take careful notes before each race, chronicling the rise and fall of every horse that races at the track and profiting from the effort. In doing this work, they resemble successful TRAINERS whose own paddock observations enable them to tell when a previously lackluster Thoroughbred, finally adjusting to life on the track or recovering from its ailments, is approaching prime condition and, therefore, is worth claiming. At the same time, an ankle puffier than it was last week, or a toe constantly pointed at the ground to avoid pain when the animal stands in its stall, or a noticeably duller coat, or any of numerous other manifestations of distress to be discussed below are enough to warn off shrewd trainer and handicapper alike. Having done my time at many a paddock enclosure with more than a few horsemen and handicappers, I can assure the reader that here, as in every other sector of life, absolute certainty and total competence are rare. And empty pretension abounds. Trainers who constantly enter horses at the wrong distance or in the wrong class or with inadequate form directly attributable to inferior feed, inferior care, and inferior human I.Q., become sages of ostensibly great wisdom at the paddock, scribbling secret memorandums in notebooks as they peer penetratingly at one or another horse. A nice show. Even good trainers make mistakes at the claim box. And an infallible veterinarian has yet to materialize at any track. So the handicapper who decides to fortify personal selections with paddock observation must do so with foreknowledge that the advantages will only be relative. An extra winner

and two or three unbet losers a week are worth the trip.

Before embarking on a review of the signs that warn of possible problems serious enough to make a supposed contender no such thing, we should discuss the sources of the problems. The first of these is fear associated with inexperience. Young Thoroughbreds are easily disturbed by the slightest change in daily routine. On race day, the changes are not slight. Food is withdrawn. Handlers grow tense and communicate their anxieties in myriad ways. The animal is led to the saddling stall past and often through unfamiliar crowds of noisy people. It gets nervous. Before it enters the starting gate 15 or 20 minutes later, it has expended needed energies, if it has not taken leave of its senses altogether. Being herd creatures far more closely attuned to each other than to humans, horses seem to contract pre-race jitters from a jittery horse. It is not unusual to see an entire field of two- or three-year-olds in a nervous snit, even though many of them may have been calm enough before arriving in the paddock.

Another cause of difficulty is fear attributable to too much experience. Horses have long memories. Racing is no lark. A Thoroughbred that associates the withdrawal of food with the agonizing discomfort of past racing experiences can be a basket case even before it heads for the paddock. If apprehensiveness is accompanied by actual pain from a sore joint, aching muscle, or inflamed shin, problems multiply. And then there

183

is the horse gone sour from too much racing and confinement in a tiny stall for at least 22 hours of every day. Finally, one must take account of a large number of highly intelligent Thoroughbreds that have learned the ropes. Knowing that equine rebelliousness does not overthrow the human race but only provokes its wrath, such horses may be the calmest specimens in the walking-ring. But their rotten past-performance records label them as non-contenders and nobody should be misled into supposing that they are ready to run. They run, all right, but no harder than they have to. The jockey who whips them learns to regret it when they duck toward the rail or break stride under his misguided urging. They outfox everybody. More than one Hall of Fame trainer has declared that the last kind of horse he wants in his barn is a smart one.

Here are bad signs conspicuously displayed at the paddock and walking ring:

Fractiousness. Like human beings under stress, some hurting or apprehensive horses try to fight. Others try to flee. Neither type wants to race. A horse is fractious when it fights its handler on the way to the saddling stall. Its ears may lay back or point sideways; its tail may swish angrily from side to side; it may buck, kick, wheel, and scream. The longer this lasts, the more energy is squandered. If the animal continues to resist the whole undertaking in the stall and after the jockey climbs aboard and, worst of all, in the post parade and pre-race warmup, it is not worth a bet unless the handicapper knows for certain that such deportment is its normal way of expressing itself before a winning race. On the other hand, if the horse discharges all its grievances and behaves in more businesslike fashion by the time it leaves the stall under saddle, chances improve that it will run to its handicapping figures. Here again, it helps to know whether an early commotion is part of the horse's normal pattern. Since beginning handicappers invariably are well advised to risk no money except when all systems are go, it pays them to avoid wagers on any horse that throws a fit before its race. To sit out the race and watch the horse lose is to save money. To sit out and watch the horse win is to gain experience.

Nervousness. A fractious horse is nervous, to be sure. So is a frightened horse. The difference is that the fractious one wastes energy in rebellion. The frightened one wastes energy in panic. Its eyes are opaque. It resists the trip to the stall, often digging in its feet and propping its legs like a child being dragged into the doctor's office for a whooping cough injection. When the rider is boosted aboard, frenzy may increase. The animal's head reaches for the sky, ears twitching at odd angles, feet and legs flailing, its entire behavior communicating reluctance while its strength ebbs. When joined by the LEAD PONY for the procession to the racing strip, it lays its head across the pony's neck and withers, as if seeking security. Another sign of nervous irritability is a horizontally swishing tail. In better spirits, a horse flicks its tail vertically. And some horsemen maintain that troubled Thoroughbreds often display a tail that does not fall directly behind the rear quarters, but stands out horizontally for five or six inches at its base. This is most noticeable at the walk and, even when associated with no other unpromising sign, may be taken to mean that all is not perfectly well.

Washiness. Aside from physical resistance to the groom and other handlers, the principal sign of nerves is lathery sweat on neck and flanks and/or between the hind legs (kidney sweat). On hot days, every horse in the field should sweat, but the ones that are seriously upset will produce more copious foam and, in most cases, will manifest distress in other ways. If the top choice seems to be breaking out in a sweat when it comes to the paddock, the handicapper should take pains to see whether the symptom disappears as the saddling routines proceed. Ideally, the horse should settle down before it goes to the track and, once there, should go about its chores with something like willing spirit. Continued production of sweat before the warmup is normal in some highly strung animals, but bad news in most others.

Equipment. If the horse has been unraced for more than a month and now appears for the first time in front BANDAGES or with a new kind of bit or new shoes or a tongue strap, and acts as if it wants to be elsewhere, something is amiss. Unfortunately, only the constant paddock visitor and notebook keeper can recognize innovations in equipment.

Except when BLINKERS are involved, the information is withheld from the public—a policy that should be amended.

Soreness and Lameness. With Butazolidin and innumerable other forms of MEDICATION in general if not always legal use, Thoroughbreds that might be unable to walk straight without chemical assistance can actually race for a while and are less likely to betray their soreness in the walking ring. Nevertheless, hurting horses continue to race with the blessings of veterinarians who reason that they often warm out of the soreness on their way to the gate. If your top choice came to the paddock in cold-water bandages, it may or may not walk sore but it later may warm up sore, and should be watched all the way to the gate. In the paddock stall, see if the handler fusses over some part of a leg or shoulder, and whether the horse responds uncomfortably. In the walking ring, see if the animal seems to stride easily. If its head rises abruptly when a forefoot hits the ground, that member hurts. When the opposite forefoot takes the weight, the horse's head will bob downward on the good side. If hurting badly in a rear leg, the horse will lower its head when the ouchy leg bears weight. Some horses with sore knees walk with forelegs widely spread, as if about to go into a split. Later, in the post parade, a sore horse will often move with its head bowed toward the side that hurts and will warm up in a short, choppy gait as it tries to withdraw its weight from the painful ankle or leg.

Human Failings. Unfamiliar with

equine behavior or not, most adult handicappers have learned enough of the world to recognize a human loser when they see one. Nothing that takes place in the paddock is more revealing about the chances of a horse than the behavior of its GROOM. If that worthy thinks little of the animal's immediate future and resents labor in a losing cause, the attitude will often be evident. Brusque, impatient, disgusted, cruel treatment of the horse give the game away, whether the horse is behaving badly or not. On the other hand, solicitous treatment of a misbehaving Thoroughbred signifies effort to soothe a valued animal and save what might turn into a winning day. With more and more women working as stable hands, the general level of human behavior has improved in that region of the industry. Overwhelmingly, women work in barns because they love horses, both winners and losers. It follows, therefore, that a woman who treats a horse with untypical disdain is browned off at the animal, just like the hundreds of roustabout males who work in mediocre barns and have no use for a horse unless they think they can cash a bet on it.

PARI-MUTUEL BETTING was invented during the 1860's by a Parisian shopkeeper who resented the large profits that local BOOKMAKERS skimmed from betting pools. The higher the percentage withheld by the bookie, the less remained for winning bettors. So Pierre Oller set himself up in business, deducting only 5 percent of each wagered franc for himself and paying the rest to his winning clients. Under the system of what he called "mutual wagers" (or, in French, *pari-mutuels),* everyone was paid off at final odds, which were determined by the ratio between the amount bet on the winning horse and the amounts bet on all the losers. Bettors had never experienced such security. They knew that 95 percent of all the money would go to holders of winning tickets and that they no longer had to contend with hanky-panky by horse-owning, race-fixing bookies, who customarily offered seductively high odds on likely losers and miserly odds on legitimate contenders. In effect, the customers of M. Oller set their own odds.

During the years immediately prior to the beginning of World War I, anti-gambling statutes shut racetracks throughout North America. This was accomplished simply by state prohibition of trackside bookmaking. After severe losses, the industry expedited its return to grace by expelling bookies from tracks and installing the pari-mutuel system. To be sure, pari-mutuel betting was a form of gambling, but it had about it an institutional air. It was antiseptic, mirthless, and entirely mathematical. It could not be tampered with. It guaranteed remittance to the state treasury of every dime prescribed by law. It may well have been the first and only foolproof tax-raising instrument in American history.

If the original formula of M. Oller had remained intact, the only reasonable objection to pari-mutuels would have come from expert handicappers who sensibly preferred to shop for odds among competing bookmakers, buying tickets at the most favorable quotations and, if winners, collecting those exact odds rather than the final-odds payoffs awarded by the pari-mutuel machines. But the formula did not last long. The Frenchman's original 5 percent takeout soon perished. Tracks and governments boosted the take to 10 percent on every mutuel pool and then to 12 and 14 and 15 and 17 and 19 and, on more exotic forms of MULTIPLE BETTING, as high as 25 percent. And, to sweeten the kitty for tracks and states and to spare mutuel clerks the bother of dealing in odd pennies, a feature called breakage was introduced. Breakage confiscates as much as 19 cents from the proceeds of each winning $2 ticket, and is the reason that horses pay off in round numbers at 20-cent intervals—$3.40, $3.60, $3.80, etc.

Think of take and breakage as similar in all fundamentals to the house percentage in casino craps. And consider the random member of the racetrack audience on a day when that audience removes a total of $600,000 from its pockets for use as fresh wagering money. Studies show that a crowd churns (bets and rebets) that amount of money frequently enough and in such amounts that it accounts for a day's mutuel handle of at least $2 million. At a track where the legal take is 17 percent and breakage gobbles another 1.5 percentage points (which actually increases the take by 8.8 percent), total take and breakage on a $2 million mutuel handle

is $370,000. But if the crowd has wagered only $600,000 of the money it brought to the track, building the $2 million by churning, it can be seen that take and breakage have commandeered more than 60 percent of the folks' out-of-pocket betting money. Concede our random member of the crowd only 32 betting opportunities during the afternoon—$2 to win, place, and show on each of nine races, plus $2 each on a DAILY DOUBLE, three EXACTAS, and a TRIFECTA. These bets total $64. If the customer does about as well as the crowd at large, he removes only $20 or so from pocket, churning it into his $64 contribution to the total handle. The track and state get 18.5 percent of the customer's $64—$11.84, which is a cool 59 percent of the poor soul's original $20. To call this a crushingly heavy house percentage is to understate. On 32 rolls of casino dice at $2 per throw, the same customer also churns money, winning some and losing some, but the casino collects less than 90 cents on that action, assuming that the gambler is sensible enough to confine bets to the Pass or Don't Pass lines. Although the customer may be wiped out after 32 rolls, all but 90 cents of his losses will have been conveyed to winning players.

And there's the heart of the matter. A high house percentage penalizes not the losers but the winners. An improvident craps shooter loses his shirt not because the house percentage is high, but because the dice come up snake eyes. At the track, a non-handicapping craps shooter loses not because the take is high but because his horses do not run. Nevertheless, to the degree that pari-mutuel take and breakage subtract from a winning handicapper's profits on successful bets, they make long-term success more difficult to achieve. At casino craps tables, where chance reigns and skill is outlawed, long-term success is impossible in any event. The house percentage finally grinds you down. But at tracks, where skill or the hope of skill are the only basis for frequent attendance and large wagering, the pari-mutuel system (as presently governed) obstructs all but the most skillful players (perhaps less than one in a thousand) from seasonal profits. Thousands of other handicappers, able to maintain their losses at tolerable levels of, say, 5 or 10 cents per wagered dollar, continue to patronize tracks because they enjoy the challenge, hope for better results, and can argue with considerable truth that their skill makes racing an inexpensive entertainment. Good. But every time the state legislature raises the take-out, the entertainment becomes more costly, the number of steady patrons diminishes, and the sport's future darkens.

If there were no such thing as a house percentage, which would be impractical, the pari-mutuel system would make a 5–1 shot of a horse on which 16.66 percent of the money had been wagered. With the 17 percent take which prevails in most places at this writing, the same horse pays not the $12.00 of a 5–1 shot, but $9.80—less than 4–1. This reduces the winning bettor's natural profit by 22 percent. And a natural 4–5 shot, on which 55.5 percent of the money would be bet in a pool unaffected by takeout, pays not $3.60 but $2.80—a 50 percent reduction in profit.

Breakage. Among American refinements of the pari-mutuel system is the refusal to pay winning bettors every penny won. Arguing speciously that handling small change imposes grave inconvenience on mutuel clerks and clientele alike, the tracks and their senior partners in state government require that mutuel payoffs be dispensed in round numbers. Toward that end, the payoffs are rounded downward. The millions of dollars thus confiscated are shared between track and state in some places, and in others are taken by the state alone. At present, a mutuel payoff of $5.40 may be what remains after the pari-mutuel department's computer calculated that the proper payoff was $5.50 or $5.59. Years ago, when breakage began, mutuel prices were calculated by dividing the total betting pool (less the amount of takeout) by the total number of $2 bets (having determined the number of bets that would have been made had there been no bets in amounts larger than $2). If the proper payoff was from $5.51 through $5.59, it was rounded down to the dime: $5.50.

The next stage of elegance was called nickel breakage. The mutuel department now calculated odds at the dollar level. Before breakage, a ticket on the winning horse that had been worth $5.58 for $2 under the old system was now worth $1.79 to $1. The $1.79 was lowered to the next nickel, becoming

$1.75 to $1, meaning $3.50 to $2 and a mutuel payoff of $5.50. This approach gave way in most places to an outright larceny known as dime breakage on dollar odds. The payoff worth $1.79 to $1 in the mutuel pool is now reduced to the next-lower dime—$1.70—and the final payoff is twice that plus the original $2 bet, $5.40. Breakage that had once been eight cents has become 18 cents. In places with 17 percent takeouts, breakage adds about 1.5 percentage points of extra bite, thereby enlarging the takeout by almost 9 percent. The pretense that it is more convenient to pay a winning bettor $5.40 than $5.50 is too absurd to discuss. It becomes more preposterous with the advent of automatic ticket-selling and ticket-cashing equipment.

Odds and Mutuel Prices. The winning bettor retrieves the original cost of the mutuel ticket plus whatever profits the ticket earns at the final odds. Mutuel prices are calculated in terms of the smallest wager accepted, usually $2 but headed higher, no doubt. Here are the mutuel payoffs represented by the figures posted on track odds boards. Horses never pay less than these minimums but, if posted at 4–5 or higher, may pay more.

ODDS	PRICE	ODDS	PRICE	ODDS	PRICE
1–9	$2.20	2–1	$6.00	18–1	$38.00
1–8	2.20	5–2	7.00	19–1	40.00
1–7	2.20	3–1	8.00	20–1	42.00
1–6	2.20	7–2	9.00	21–1	44.00
1–5	2.40	4–1	10.00	22–1	46.00
1–4	2.40	9–2	11.00	23–1	48.00
1–3	2.60	5–1	12.00	24–1	50.00
2–5	2.80	6–1	14.00	25–1	52.00
1–2	3.00	7–1	16.00	30–1	62.00
3–5	3.20	8–1	18.00	35–1	72.00
3–4	3.40	9–1	20.00	40–1	82.00
4–5	3.60	10–1	22.00	45–1	92.00
1–1	4.00	11–1	24.00	50–1	102.00
6–5	4.40	12–1	26.00	60–1	122.00
7–5	4.80	13–1	28.00	75–1	152.00
3–2	5.00	14–1	30.00	99–1	200.00
8–5	5.20	15–1	32.00		
9–5	5.60	16–1	34.00		
		17–1	36.00		

Place and Show Prices. Payoffs for place and show are arrived at by the principles that determine win prices, but the procedures involve extra steps. A place ticket on the winning horse is cashable. So is a place ticket on the horse that finishes second. After the usual takeout from the total place-betting pool, the amounts bet on both the winner and second-place horse are set aside. The remainder is divided in half. One of the halves is distributed to holders of place tickets on the winning horse. The mutuel payoff is calculated by dividing the number of dollars bet to place on that horse into the number of dollars to be distributed as profits, deducting breakage, multiplying by 2 and adding $2. The other half is dispensed in exactly the same way to holders of place tickets on the second horse. In show betting, what remains in the pool after the lawful takeout is divided into thirds for distribution (after breakage) to players with show tickets on the winner and the second- and third-place horses. In case the place or show odds to $1 turn out to be less than 1–20, which would mean a mutuel payoff of less than $2.10, the tracks are required to make up the difference from their own coffers. This is known as a minus pool. To avoid the expense, tracks may refuse to accept show bets on heavy favorites in races with short fields. Minus pools seldom occur in win betting, although Secretariat paid only $2.10 when he won the Arlington Invitational Stakes in June 1973, defeating three other horses in a race without place or show betting.

Mutuel Fields. Pari-mutuel machines accept bets on only 12 horses or entries. In races with more than 12 horses representing more than 12 separate betting interests, the racing secretary combines the extra runners in a mutuel field as if they were a stable entry. A bet on the field pays off if one of the field horses runs that well. Naturally, the racing secretary forms the mutuel field with the horses considered least likely to finish in the money.

The Future. In 1965, the depressing effects on attendance and betting of a 15 percent takeout were noticeable at New York tracks. The state legislature presently intensified the problem by raising the take to 17 percent. By the late 1970's, spokesmen for the New York Racing Association were calling for a reduction to 14 percent. Combined as these pronouncements were with a reduction of admission prices, extra reductions for the elderly, and free rock music for the young, they signified recognition that unless warm bodies could be attracted to the races, STAKES purses would decrease, the BREEDING industry would land on the rocks, and Thoroughbred racing would disappear into the back pastures of the aristocracy, where it originated. The NYRA position accurately represented that of all other elements in racing, including, for a change, horseplayers. There is little doubt that state legislatures can be induced to lower the takes to reasonable levels. They will do so if ever track operators use the same clout in behalf of racing that they exercise in political matters more fundamental to their lives.

See also, PLACE AND SHOW BETTING.

PAR TIMES. To separate CONTEND-

ERS, it often is necessary to compare past performances at different distances, different tracks, or both. If the performances have been at tracks on the local circuit, for example Hollywood Park and Del Mar or Arlington Park and Hawthorne, the handicapper's familiarity with the tracks eases the problem of comparison. But if a SHIPPER from Oaklawn runs a respectable fourth in its debut at Aqueduct and seems ready to improve in its next race, perplexity arises. The horse may now run as well as it did at Oaklawn. How well did it run there? How does one evaluate Oaklawn performances without knowledge of that track and its Thoroughbred colony? Is it possible that the fourth-place Aqueduct finish represented the horse's best effort and that no improvement should be expected?

The safest strategy is to analyze the new horse's local performance in light of what already is known about the horses it opposed and the horses it now will meet. If it displayed enough CLASS and FORM to finish well without undue exertion (the *Daily Racing Form*'s RESULTS CHART supplements the evidence found in the top running line of the PAST-PERFORMANCE TABLE), the handicapper has reason to suppose that the horse may now contend seriously in a race of similar class. But many handicappers want to know more about the horse. In quest of fact, some use tables of par times that permit grossly approximate evaluations of races at distant tracks.

Par-time tables provide a basis for comparison of the track records on which *Daily Racing Form* speed ratings are based. A *Form* speed rating of 100

indicates that the horse tied the track record for the distance. A rating of 96 means that the horse ran four-fifths of a second slower than the record. At a place with a track record comparatively slow by comparison with par, speed ratings are comparatively high at that distance, because horses of ordinary ability are able to run in times closer to the record time. At a track with a comparatively fast track record, the speed ratings at the distance tend to be lower, because the record is that much farther beyond the capabilities of ordinary runners.

Here is a par-time table:

DISTANCE	PAR	DISTANCE	PAR
4½f	:51.2	1mi	1:34.0
5f	:56.3	1mi–40y	1:36.0
5½f	1:02.2	1mi–70y	1:38.0
6f	1:08.2	1-1/16mi	1:40.1
6½f	1:14.2	1-1/8mi	1:46.3
7f	1:20.3	1-3/16mi	1:53.0
7½f	1:26.3	1-1/4mi	1:59.4

If the horse in our example won its final Oaklawn start in 1:11, earning a *Daily Racing Form* speed rating of 90, two seconds slower than the track record, the handicapper knows that the Oaklawn record for six furlongs must be 1:09—10 speed-rating points or two full seconds faster than this horse's 1:11. And 1:09, as the table shows, is three-fifths of a second slower than par. At Aqueduct, on the other hand, the track record for the same distance is 1:08.3, only one tick slower than par. From this, the user of a par table concludes that Oaklawn's comparatively slow track record is more easily approached by any given horse. To bring Oaklawn six-furlong speed ratings into approximate phase with Aqueduct six-furlong speed ratings, the par table orders that the Oaklawn ratings be reduced by 2 points.

Unfortunately, such comparison of track records is fruitless unless the distance in question is one at which both tracks program frequent races for horses capable of breaking records at tracks of highest quality. Otherwise, a slow track record may simply indicate that no fast horses have tried that distance. Or a slow track record may mean a slow racing strip over which champions cannot run as fast as at other tracks. A more sensible basis for comparison of times logged at different tracks or different distances is more difficult to come by. It rests not on track records but on the running times of older, male, middle-grade claiming horses. In 1977, $10,000 claiming four-year-old colts and geldings normally went in 1:11.2 at Oaklawn and 1:11.1 at Aqueduct. It therefore was reasonable to assume that, on an average day, Aqueduct was one tick faster at the distance. Par times for $10,000 males (or whatever grade runs most frequently at major tracks in years to come), can be compiled from results charts or *Daily Racing Form Chart Books,* the newspaper's monthly collection of all North American race results. Having determined, as in the Oaklawn-Aqueduct example, that one track is normally one-fifth-second faster than another, the handicapper may then reduce the horse's official running time at the faster track by one point, or increase a running time at the slower track by one point. If the handicapper prefers to use speed ratings, the same adjustment should be made and the speed rating's built-in distortion by an abnormally fast or slow track record can also be neutralized by use of a conventional par-time table, as above.

Regardless of how par times may be calculated or applied, they remain crude approximations unless supplemented with knowledge of the actual track conditions under which a particular running time was recorded. A horse that earns a 78 speed rating on one day may have run on a much faster surface than delayed a better horse that got only 76 over the same oval on the very next day. Speed variants (more often called track variants) compensate for fluctuations in track speed. The ingenious researcher, William L. Quirin, Ph.D., completed during 1977 a vast computer study which yielded par times for every age-sex-class-distance category at every North American track. The findings included par speed variants compatible with those published in *Daily Racing Form* Eastern editions. Quirin's book, *Winning at the Races: Computer Discoveries in Thoroughbred Handicapping* (William Morrow & Company, 1979), permits unusually accurate time comparisons of past performances, regardless of track or distance. In the absence of that help, handicappers are advised to concentrate on each horse's local form, using conventional par times only to modify speed ratings earned on the local circuit.

A familiar extension of the par-time principle is the parallel time chart, with which generations of hopeful handicappers have been deluded into assuming that, for example, a horse that runs six furlongs in 1:12 at any track can be expected to run nine furlongs in 1:52.3. The charts and those who handicap with them suffer from failure to appreciate (a) the DISTANCE factor and (b) the differences among tracks. The only dependable parallel time chart is one compiled for each distance at an individual track by determining the median times run there by each class of Thoroughbred. Even then, nothing in the chart reveals a single thing about the ability of an individual sprinter to compete at distances of a mile or more.

PAST-PERFORMANCE TABLES.

Each edition of DAILY RACING FORM publishes a past-performance record for each horse entered in each race at each track covered in the particular edition. Depending on available space, the record includes summaries of a horse's eight or ten most recent performances, plus other pertinent material. The larger format of the Eastern editions permits inclusion of data absent from the tabloids of the Middle and Far West and Canada. However, the newspaper is forever tinkering with new typefaces and, during the 1970's, began including in the tabloid editions much information that had formerly appeared only in the East. In previous books I have offered detailed instructions for deciphering the past-performance tables, an ability that

must be cultivated before the newcomer to handicapping can begin to interpret the significance of the information contained in all the abbreviations, symbols, and numbers. But the *Form* is so zealous about amplifying and upgrading the tables that no set of instructions remains current for long. I therefore recommend that anyone not fully conversant with every aspect of the tables obtain the *Form*'s own up-to-date instructional pamphlets, which are available without charge at track newspaper stands or directly from the *Form* itself. As is at least implied on almost every page of this book, the past-performance records are indispensable to handicapping. Occasional advertising claims for miracle systems notwithstanding, nobody can pick winners without the pp's.

PENNSYLVANIA.

Over in Cornwells Heights, just beyond Philadelphia's eastern boundary and not much more than an hour's drive from New York, Keystone runs about 200 days a year, offering glass-enclosed comfort to wind-chilled refugees from Aqueduct and, depending on the time of year, affecting business at tracks in New Jersey, Maryland, and Delaware. Purses are competitive with those at all major tracks outside New York, except Meadowlands, Monmouth Park, and Pimlico. Accordingly, the quality of the racing is respectable, as quality is measured in the 1970's. Shippers from Keystone to any other track, including those of New York, cannot be eliminated. They win their share. The one-mile strip is typical of its kind, favoring EARLY SPEED on most days. Inner post positions generally help.

The state also has three minor tracks. Penn National, a one-miler not far from Harrisburg, offers purses about equal to those of River Downs, a slight cut above Latonia and Fairmount Park. It is a sporting oval on which early speed has less than the usual edge and the best horse can win. Pocono Downs, a five-furlong strip between Wilkes-Barre and Scranton, favors speed on the inside. It compares in quality to Atokad Park, Centennial Park, and Evangeline Downs. Not quite up to Finger Lakes or Portland Meadows. Commodore Downs, in Erie County, is a six-furlong track where early speed helps. Purses are lower than at Pocono.

PLACE AND SHOW BETTING. Payoffs for place and show are justly lower than those for win. The place bettor wins if the horse runs first or second. The show bettor collects if the horse finishes third or better. Involving comparatively small amounts of profit on the wagered dollar, these payoffs suffer most severely from the breakage feature of PARI-MUTUEL BETTING. Designed to pay either flat dollar amounts or intermediate sums at intervals of 20 cents ($4.00, $4.20, $4.40, etc.), breakage may subtract as much as 19 cents from the profit on the bet. Horrible example: The computer finds that the winner of the race should pay $2.39 to place or show. Breakage reduces the price to $2.20, a loss to the bettor of almost 49 percent of the earned profits.

Nevertheless, many racegoers bet only to show, reasoning that the chances of cashing a show ticket are materially larger than the chances of cashing a win ticket. But only a supremely expert handicapper can collect a high enough percentage of show bets to repay losses on the horses that inevitably finish fourth or worse. Professionals who limit themselves to show betting sometimes wait for weeks to find the "sure thing" that will produce the legal minimum of $2.10 and might even soar to $2.20 or $2.40. Less patient show players cash lots of tickets but seldom count themselves seasonal winners.

As the late Robert S. Dowst emphasized: Any handicapper capable of winning money with place or show bets would make more money betting the same horses to win. That observation remains valid half a century later.

In recent years, more than one authority has suggested that it is foolish to bet short-priced FAVORITES to win when a place bet is so much safer. With constant increases in the pari-mutuel take, it will become clearer to everyone that it is foolish to bet short-priced horses to win, place, or show. Unless, of course, one's personality can tolerate sitting around for weeks at a time waiting for a sure-shot show bet. As matters stood in the late 1970's, with six- and seven-horse fields increasingly common at most tracks, and five-horse fields no great rarity, the top-rated horse at a good price was harder and harder to find. Which, in my view, made win and place betting on such horses all the more attractive. To collect $5.00 or $6.00 or even more than that on a place ticket was welcome, whether the horse won or not.

Good handicappers who noticed how often their selections ran second not only were drawn to place betting on horses that ran at decent odds (5–2 or better in a short field, 7–2 or better in a field of seven or more), but began experimenting with betting formulas that called for place bets twice or three times the size of the win bets. When this reduced the size of the win bets, it was not an especially good idea, because it ate into long-term profits. But if money was ample, the procedure increased the volume earned on place bets.

PLAYABLE RACES. A race is playable if it can be handicapped with reasonable confidence and if the handicapping produces a selection at acceptable ODDS. If all starters have raced recently on the present track or in another setting familiar to the handicapper, reasonable suppositions can be made about the FORM, CLASS, and DISTANCE factors. Unless weather or the track maintenance crew has made a mystery of EARLY SPEED or POST POSITION, the race deserves close attention. A race becomes less playable to the degree that basically uninformed guesses must be made about one or more of the horses. Examples are previously unraced animals, or horses returning from absences of several months, or SHIPPERS from distant circuits. The handicapper may simply eliminate such starters on statistical grounds: They seldom win, especially at distances of more than six furlongs. On the other hand, they sometimes win. The handicapper's selection should be especially strong and its odds favorable to justify a bet against first-time starters, absentees, or shippers whose JOCKEYS and TRAINERS are among the local or national leaders. As all this implies, the number of playable races per program increases as the race meeting proceeds and out-of-town shippers and other strangers become less numerous.

POST POSITION. At the typical one-mile track, outside post positions are generally preferable in SPRINTS, but usually are a pronounced disadvantage to quick-starting horses at distances of one mile to a mile and one-eighth. At those longer distances, the horse with EARLY SPEED benefits from an inside post which allows it to reach (or stay on) the inside rail without undue exertion, saving ground and maintaining its lead around the first turn. At BULL RINGS and other tracks of small circumference, inside posts are advantageous at all distances. These generalities become part of audience wisdom at most tracks, thereby accounting for the high mutuel prices paid by winners on days when generalities come unglued. Among the standard routines of winning handicappers is a study of recent RESULTS CHARTS to see whether anything unusual has been happening with early speed or post position. Perceiving a trend away from the norm, or sensing the possibility of one, the handicapper carefully watches the first couple of races of the afternoon (or evening) to see if the trend may be substantial. This kind of vigilance keeps a good handicapper lengths ahead of the other bettors during periods when, for example, the inside posts become abnormally favorable at sprint distances. By the time the crowd at large catches up, the situation is usually approaching its demise, but the alert have made hay.

PROGRAMS. These convenient and pocket-sized pamphlets, printed after SCRATCHES, list the scheduled starters in each race with the identifying numbers that will appear on their saddle cloths, the names of their jockeys, the colors of the riders' silks, the track's MORNING LINE and, in states that permit it, a track handicapper's selections. Other information, such as each horse's age, sex, breeding, owner, trainer, and the conditions of the race itself, duplicate—and occasionally correct—information published in *Daily Racing Form.* Because they enable the racegoer to identify the horses and riders, and provide handy space wherein to note late scratches, jockey changes, or WEIGHTS that turn out to be higher than scheduled, the programs are essential equipment. Their tabulations of jockey and trainer standings tend to be larger and more detailed than those published in newspapers.

The programs also could include handicapping INFORMATION supplementary to that of *Daily Racing Form,* but the industry is not yet sufficiently customer-oriented to render service of that kind. The quality of program handicapping selections varies from place to place and season to season.

PURSES. As this book emphasizes in its articles about racing in the various states, the day-in-day-out quality of competition at an individual track is proportional to the purse money available for CLAIMING RACES, ALLOWANCE RACES, and other so-called overnight events. Because STAKES involve much larger purses, which sometimes attract runners of championship caliber, they increase attendance on the average track's big Saturday or two. Where this is accomplished without lowering overnight purses, so much the better for local racing. But to include $100,000 stakes purses in calculations of the "average" purse at any track is to present a misleading picture.

During the 1960's and 1970's, the custom of dividing a purse among the first four finishers in the race was modified in some places. Traditionally, the winner got 60 percent of the purse, the second horse 22, the third 12, and the fourth 6. Some states modified this, giving the winner 55 percent, the second horse 20, the third 15, the fourth 7.5, and the fifth 2.5. With the costs of Thoroughbred upkeep rising, hard-pressed stable OWNERS and TRAINERS sought additional liberalization of purse-distribution formulas. This was widely deplored as a threat to the sporting character of racing. Inasmuch as all other major industrialized sports customarily paid both winning and losing competitors, the horsemen's arguments were scarcely illogical. It seemed possible that the inevitable transition of racing to full competence as a branch of the entertainment industry would include adequate remuneration for losers as well as winners. A hint of what can be expected was provided in 1977 by the owners of Seattle Slew, the first undefeated Triple Crown winner in American history. Newcomers to racing but hard-nosed wheelers and dealers in their own right, the owners allowed as how Slew was the people's horse and might be kept in action at age four, appearing at tracks all over the land—if guaranteed around $100,000 per race.

Because the level of overnight purses is a good index to the CLASS of a track and of the horses that run there, and because the best horses win the most money, handicappers regard high gross or average earnings as a sign of comparatively high class in any field of horses. As observed in this book's article on class, the approach is statistically valid but has pitfalls, including the variability of purse schedules at a single track or on a single circuit, plus the fact that previously high earnings are an infirm indicator of present FORM and class.

R

RACING LUCK. A handicapper with superhuman patience can achieve profits of at least 20 cents on the wagered dollar by refusing to bet unless the horse is conspicuously best in its field and goes at odds not less than 6–5 under a winning JOCKEY directed by a winning TRAINER. Making perhaps 100 bets a year, this abnormal personality will cash about half of them, having left little to chance. Yet half of these careful selections will lose. Sometimes the horse so conspicuously best is spooked by pre-race sights or sounds and loses its winning FORM during an uncontrollable fit of nerves. Sometimes the best horse has passed the peak of form during its training routines. Sometimes it runs as well as expected but some other animal belies the record and frustrates the analyst with unexpectedly superior form of its own. And sometimes the best horse is knocked off stride or intimidated in a traffic tangle during the race itself. Or finds itself without room behind or among horses. Or steps in a hole and hurts itself. The best horse's unexpected loss of form and the lesser horse's unforeseen access of form may be written off as bad luck, inasmuch as they take place beyond possibility of a handicapper's (or trainer's or rider's) control. And defeat attributable to mischance during the race itself is clearly bad racing luck, equally beyond the handicapper's control, but sure to produce a substantial number of losing bets every season.

Those who believe that all horseplayers die broke generally rest their case on the twin suppositions that (a) recreational gamblers are unstable types likely to make wrong choices and (b) racing luck is a factor so dominant that correct choices depend more on chance than on skill. It would be useful to present statistics on the percentage of races

201

in which loss or victory traces directly to racing luck, but no such statistics exist. On the other hand, other statistics indicate with great clarity that in racing, as in other sports, luck is secondary to skill. For example, the most successful trainers handle horses skillfully enough to win considerably more than their fair share of races. If luck were an overriding influence, the winning averages of top trainers would not differ so dramatically from those of mediocre trainers. The same is true of top jockeys, whose skills enable their agents to obtain the best mounts, producing a situation in which the five or six most respected riders at the average track (about 20 percent of the riding population) account for more than half of all the victories. Finally, skillful handicappers exploit all these realities successfully enough to achieve seasonal profits, despite exorbitant pari-mutuel takeouts and, of course, inevitable losses attributable to handicapping error and bad luck.

RESULTS CHARTS contain information excluded from *Daily Racing Form*'s condensed PAST-PERFORMANCE TABLES. Published in that newspaper a day or two after each racing program for which the particular local edition carries past performance tables, the charts are indispensable for handicappers willing to undertake fully detailed analysis before making selections. At a minimum, the handicapper needs charts of all races run during the regional circuit's current season. A collection of the previous season's charts is additional help.

Among the advantages provided by charts is inclusion of the eligibility CONDITIONS of each race, and the size of its purse. Whereas past-performance records omit the purse and describe each past race only as an ALLOWANCE or $10,000 CLAIMING RACE, the chart tells exactly what kind of allowance runners or $10,000 claimers were eligible. The ability to differentiate the CLASS of one past race from the class of another is, of course, central to profitable handicapping and betting. Players who do not collect results charts should record detailed eligibility conditions in notebooks. An additional value of the charts is the paragraph of comments printed with each. Although those who prepare the charts are humanly frail, they manage to report the names of most horses that run in bad luck and have EXCUSES for losing. The comments also furnish information about the ease, or lack of it, with which horses may have performed in the individual race. This often helps the handicapper to evaluate current FORM.

RHODE ISLAND racing was an early casualty of the Thoroughbred shortage and rising pari-mutuel takeouts that plagued the sport during the 1960's and 1970's. In 1977, the state temporarily disappeared from the racing scene, Narragansett Park having capsized. The old track's overnight purses had dwindled to the point where the quality of the programs resembled that of Assin boia Downs, Commonwealth, Caliente, and Jefferson Downs. Later that year, the place reopened with an incredible 20 percent takeout from the betting pools. It is convenient to Providence and only

37 miles from Boston. It favors EARLY SPEED. In fact, when the horses are the least bit formful, it can be a grand place for a good handicapper. Its prospects of survival would seem to depend on whether the takeout can be reduced sufficiently to attract customers, and the state's share of the proceeds reduced enough to provide the reasonable purses necessary to attract good stables.

ROUTES are races at a mile or more. Except at the few tracks with racing strips of a mile and one-eighth or longer, route distances require the horses and their riders to negotiate two or more turns. It is generally agreed that the mark of an accomplished JOCKEY is ability to rate a horse—husband its resources—sufficiently to have it in energetic contention for first position at the finish wire. This rating may require considerable delicacy on a front-running animal of the type that reacts badly to stern restraint but cannot cover the distance without restraint of some kind. Less impulsive Thoroughbreds also require rating in routes. While allowing the animal to find its stride, the jockey usually tries to steer it close to the rail, saving ground on the turns but hopefully not falling too far behind or, what may be worse, running into an impenetrable wall of horses in the effort to remain close to the leaders. While doing all this navigation, the good rider is careful to change speeds as smoothly and infrequently as possible so that, with room to run in the homestretch, an unflustered mount will enter high gear and challenge for the lead.

Many handicappers regard routes as more difficult analytical problems than SPRINTS. This may well be true, in the sense that many sprints go to horses whose superior EARLY SPEED and final times are identifiable in the PAST-PERFORMANCE TABLES. It should be pointed out, however, that careful attention to DISTANCE, FORM, POST POSITION, JOCKEY assignments, and, when appropriate, WEIGHTS, helps good handicappers to hold their own when trying to pick winners at a mile or beyond. In that regard, I believe it impossible to overestimate the importance of the distance factor. A horse able to win at a mile and one-sixteenth cannot be taken for granted at a mile and an eighth until its record and running styles (and those of its opponents) have been scrutinized.

RULES OF RACING vary from place to place but seldom stray far from this model issued by THE JOCKEY CLUB:

PART I.
Definitions and Interpretations

1. A recognized meeting is:

(a) A meeting held with the sanction of the Commission upon a race course operated by a duly licensed Association, for the time and at the place where such meeting is licensed to be held.

(b) A meeting held in other portions of the United States, or in any foreign country, with the sanction of any turf authority whose jurisdiction over racing of any nature is recognized by The Jockey Club and which gives effect to sentences imposed by The Jockey Club upon those guilty of improper turf practices.

2. An "Association" is a person, or persons, or a corporate body, conducting a recognized meeting.

3. A "Horse" includes mare, gelding, colt and filly.

4. A horse is "bred" at the place of his birth.

5. The age of a horse is reckoned as beginning on the first of January in the year in which he is foaled.

6. A "Maiden" is a horse which, at the time of starting, has never won a race on the flat in any country.

7. A "Race" includes a stake, a purse, a sweepstakes, a private sweepstakes, a match or an overnight event, but does not include a steeplechase or hurdle race.

8. A "Purse" is a race for money or other prize to which the owners of the horses engaged do not contribute.

9. A "Sweepstakes" is a race in which stakes are to be made by the owners of the horses engaged, and it is still a sweepstakes when money or other prize is added, but, within the meaning of this rule, no overnight race, whatever its conditions, shall be considered to be a sweepstakes.

10. A "Private Sweepstakes" is one to which no money or other prize is added and which, previous to closing, has not been advertised, either by publication, or by circular, or entry blank, or in any other way.

11. A "Match" is a race between two horses the property of two different owners on terms agreed upon by them and to which no money, or other prize, is added; it is void if either party dies.

12. An "Overnight Race" is one for which the entries close seventy-two hours (exclusive of Sundays), or less, before the time set for the first race of the day on which such race is to be run.

13. A "Handicap" is a race in which the weights to be carried by the horses are adjusted by the handicapper for the purpose of equalizing their chances of winning.

14. A "Free Handicap" is one in which no liability is incurred for entrance money, stake or forfeit, until acceptance of the weight, either directly or through omission to declare out.

15. A "Highweight Handicap" is one in which the top weight shall not be less than 140 pounds.

16. A "Post Race" is one in which the subscribers declare, at the usual time before a race for declaring to start, the horse or horses they are to run, without limitations of choice other than that prescribed by the rules of racing or the conditions of race.

17. A "Produce" Race is one to be run for by the produce of horses named or described at the time of entry.

18. An untried horse is one whose produce are maidens.

19. (a) A "Claiming Race" is one in which every horse running therein may be claimed in conformity to the rules.

(b) An "Optional Claiming Race" is a race restricted to horses entered to be claimed for a stated claiming price and to those which have started previously for that claiming price or less. In the case of horses entered to be claimed in such a race, the race will be considered, for the purposes of these rules, a claiming race.

20. The "Nominator" is the person in whose name a horse is entered for a race.

21. "Owner" includes part owner or lessee, and singular words include the plural, except where the context otherwise requires.

22. The "Breeder" of a horse is the owner of his dam at the time of foaling.

23. (a) An "Authorized Agent" is a person appointed by a document, accompanied by a fee of $1, signed by the owner and lodged annually at the office of The Jockey Club and approved by it, or if for a single meeting only, with the Clerk of the Course for transmission to The Jockey Club.

(b) An authorized agent may appoint a Sub-Agent only when authorized so to do by the document lodged as above and when the appointment, approved by The Jockey Club, of the Sub-Agent is lodged as above, accompanied by a fee of $1.

Rule 24 (a) and (b). (Stricken out.)

25. "Weight for Age" means standard weight according to these Rules. A "weight for age" race is one in which all horses carry weight according to the scale without penalties or allowances.

26. A "Walkover" is when two horses in entirely different interests do not run for a race.

27. The publications of The Jockey Club are the Racing Calendar and the Stud Book, and such other publications as hereafter may be designated by The Jockey Club.

PART II.

Calculation of Time

28. (a) When the last day for doing anything under these Rules falls on a Sunday, it may be done on the following Monday, unless a race to which such act relates is appointed for that day, in which case it must be done on the previous Saturday.

(b) "A month" means a calendar month; "a day" means twenty-four hours.

PART III.

Regulations for Race Meetings

29. After May 31st in each year, only four overnight events for a distance less than a mile for horses three years old and upwards shall be given on any race day, except upon approval by the Stewards.

30. After June 30th in each year, there shall be no race less than five furlongs.

31. The number of starters in overnight races shall be limited by the width of the track at the starting post, the maximum number to be determined by the Stewards. The number of starters in such overnight races, except handicaps, shall be reduced to the proper number by lot, or by division, also by lot, of the race, at the option of the Association. The division of overnight handicaps shall be made by the Racing Secretary in his entire discretion.

32. By permission of the Stewards of The Jockey Club, races may be run over a race course other than the one over which they have been announced to be run.

33. (a) If a horse runs at any unrecognized meeting, he is disqualified for all races to which these rules apply.

(b) Any person owning, training or riding horses which run at any unrecognized meeting is disqualified, as are also all horses owned by or in charge of any such person.

(c) Any person acting in any official capacity at any unrecognized meeting may be disqualified.

PART IV.
Powers of the Stewards
of The Jockey Club

34. (a) The Stewards of The Jockey Club have power, at their discretion, to grant and to withdraw the approval of The Jockey Club to Associations in the conduct of meetings.

(b) The appointment of a general Racing Secretary, the handicapper, clerk of the scales, starter and judge or judges and all minor racing officials shall be made by the Stewards of The Jockey Club subject, when required by the rules of the Racing Commission, or by the laws, of any State, to the approval of said Racing Commission.

35. The Stewards of The Jockey Club have charge of the forfeit list, the registry office, and the registration of partnerships and other documents required by Rule 86 or other Rules to be registered or filed with The Jockey Club.

36. The Stewards of The Jockey Club have power to make inquiry into and to deal with any matter relating to racing, and to rule off, or otherwise less severely punish, any person concerned in any improper turf practice.

37. The Stewards of The Jockey Club shall hear cases on appeal as provided for in these Rules.

PART V.
Stewards

38. Whenever the word "Steward" or "Stewards" is used, it means Steward or Stewards of the Meeting, or their duly appointed deputy or deputies.

39. (a) There shall be three Stewards to supervise each race meeting. One of such Stewards shall be appointed by the State Racing Commission, one shall be

appointed by The Jockey Club, and one shall be appointed by the Association conducting such race meeting.

(b) The Jockey Club may designate one of its members to visit each race meeting in an honorary capacity in association with the Stewards.

40. Each Steward may appoint a deputy to act for him at any time. If there be but one Steward present, he shall, in case of necessity, appoint one or more persons to act with him. If none of the Stewards are present, the officers of the Association shall request two or more persons to act during the absence of such Stewards.

41. In case of emergency, the Stewards may, during a meeting, appoint a substitute to fill any of the offices for that meeting only.

42. Every complaint against an official shall be made to the Stewards in writing signed by the complainant.

43. The Stewards have power, as they think proper, to make and, if necessary, to vary all arrangements for the conduct of the meeting, as well as power to put off any race from day to day until a Sunday intervenes.

44. The Stewards have control over, and they and the Stewards of The Jockey Club and members of the State Racing Commission of the State wherein the racing is being conducted, or their duly appointed representatives, have free access to all stands, weighing rooms, enclosures and all other places within the grounds of the Associations.

45. (a) The Stewards shall exclude from all places under their control every person who is warned or ruled off.

(b) They may so exclude any person who, by the turf authorities of any country, or by the Stewards of any recognized meeting, has been declared guilty of any improper turf practice.

46. The Stewards have supervision over all entries and declarations.

47. The Stewards have power to regulate and control the conduct of all officials, and of all owners, trainers, jockeys, grooms and other persons attendant on horses.

48. If the Stewards shall find any person has violated these Rules of Racing or has been involved in any improper turf practice, they may impose a punishment no greater than the exclusion of such person from the grounds, or any portion of such grounds, of the association conducting the meeting, for a period not exceeding the remainder of the meeting, or the suspension of such person from acting or riding for a period not exceeding twenty racing days after the meeting, or by fine not exceeding two hundred dollars, or by more than one of such punishments; and if they consider necessary any further punishment, they shall immediately refer the matter to the Stewards of The Jockey Club. Whenever under these Rules of Racing a matter has been referred to the Stewards of The Jockey Club, they shall take such action as they shall deem proper and appropriate.

49. The Stewards have power to determine all questions arising in reference to racing at the meeting, subject to appeal under Part XIX. Should no decision have been arrived at by the Stewards within seven days of an objection being

lodged, the Clerk of the Course shall then report the case to the Stewards of The Jockey Club, who may at their discretion decide the matter, and who, if they consider there has been negligence, may order any additional expense arising therefrom, to be defrayed out of the funds of the meeting at which the case occurred.

50. The Stewards have power to call for proof that a horse is neither itself disqualified in any respect, nor nominated by, nor the property, wholly or in part, of a disqualified person, and in default of such proof being given to their satisfaction, they may declare the horse disqualified.

51. The Stewards have power at any time to order an examination, by such person or persons as they think fit, of any horse entered for a race, or which has run in a race.

PART VI.
Officials of Meetings

52. (a) The Secretary of the Association, or his deputy, shall be Clerk of the Course. He shall discharge all duties, expressed or implied, required by the Rules of Racing, and he shall report to the Stewards all violations of the Rules of Racing or of the regulations of the meeting.

(b) He shall keep a complete record of all races.

(c) He shall receive all stakes, forfeits, entrance moneys, fines, fees, including jockeys' fees.

(d) Within fourteen days, exclusive of Sundays, from the close of the meeting, he shall pay, to the persons entitled to it, all the money collected by him; and at the expiration of the same period he shall notify The Jockey Club of all arrears then remaining unpaid, and all arrears not then reported shall be regarded as having been assumed by the Association.

(e) Before acceptance, he shall submit to The Jockey Club, all entries and transfers of engagements for all races except those opened and decided during the meeting.

53. The handicapper shall append to the weights for every handicap the day and hour from which winners will be liable to a penalty and no alteration shall be made after publication except in case of omission, through error, of the name or weight of a horse duly entered, in which cases by permission of the Stewards the omission may be rectified by the handicapper.

54. (a) The Clerk of the Scales shall exhibit the number (as allotted on the official card) of each horse for which a jockey has been weighed out, and shall forthwith furnish the starter with a list of such numbers.

(b) Any extra or special weight declared for any horse, or any declaration to win, or any alteration of colors shall be exhibited by the Clerk of the Scales upon the Notice Board.

(c) He shall in all cases weigh in the

riders of the horses, and report to the Stewards any jockey not presenting himself to be weighed in.

(d) He shall, at the close of each day's racing, send a return to the office of the Secretary of The Jockey Club, of the weights carried in every race, and the names of the jockeys, specifying overweight, if any.

55. (a) The Judge or Judges must occupy the Judge's box at the time the horses pass the winning post, and their sole duty shall be to place the horses. They must announce their decisions promptly, and such decisions shall be final, unless objection to the winner or any placed horse is made and sustained. Provided, that this rule shall not prevent the Judges from correcting any mistake, such correction being subject to confirmation by the Stewards.

(b) A camera approved by the Stewards of The Jockey Club may be used to make a photograph or photographs of the horses at the finish to assist in determining their positions as exclusively indicated by their noses.

56. The official time of each race shall be determined by the official timer. The time recorded when the first horse crosses the finish line shall be the official time of the race.

57. The Judge or Judges shall, at the close of each day's racing, sign and send a report of the result of each race to the office of The Jockey Club.

58. The Judge or Judges shall determine the order of finishing of as many horses as they may think proper.

PART VII.
Registry Office and Registration of Horses

59. (a) Except as provided in section (b) of this Rule, no horse may start in any race unless duly registered in the Registry Office and duly named.

(b) If for any reason ineligible for registration, or pending inquiry as to eligibility, a horse foaled outside of the United States or its possessions, Canada, Cuba or Mexico, and imported into the United States, may be submitted by the owner for approval solely for racing purposes if the application is accompanied by such information as the Stewards of The Jockey Club shall require;

whereupon if said Stewards shall consider that the horse has an outstanding racing record and that the application and accompanying information meet the requirements prescribed by said Stewards, they may direct the Executive Secretary or other person authorized by them to issue a permit granting racing privileges only for such horse. Application for such a permit for such a horse must be made to The Jockey Club within thirty days of the original arrival of the horse in the United States—the application to be accompanied by a fee of $50, which will include the permit if granted. In case of failure to apply for a permit within the thirty-day period, and upon proof that failure to do so was unintentional or accidental, application for such a permit may be made within three months after original arrival. Such application shall be accompanied by a fee of $200, which will include the permit if granted.

60. The Registry Office, which is the office of The Jockey Club, is established for the identification of all race horses, whether foaled in the United States or its possessions or in other countries, and for the certification of their pedigrees.

61. Except as provided in Rule 65, horses foaled in the United States or its possessions, Canada, Cuba or Mexico must be registered with the Registry Office before October 1st of the year in which they are foaled.

62. (a) The registration shall comprise the name, if any; the color and marks, if any; whether a horse, mare or gelding; and the names of its sire and dam. If the mare was covered by more than one stallion, the names or descriptions in full must be stated.

(b) In any case of doubt regarding the true parentage or identification of an animal, blood tests may be required, and, taking into consideration the results of such tests and/or such other information as may be available, the Stewards may authorize such corrections in the records as may be determined to be necessary or appropriate.

63. The registration fee shall be $30 for each animal, which will include certificate.

64. Only those horses are eligible for registry which authentically trace, in all of their lines, to animals recorded in the American Stud Book or in a Stud Book of another country recognized by The Jockey Club, and which are eligible under the rules and regulations from time to time adopted by the Stewards of The Jockey Club. A horse born in the United States or its possessions, Canada, Cuba or Mexico may not be registered unless both its sire and dam have been previously registered in The American Stud Book. The only exception to this rule is a foal imported in utero whose dam is properly registered in The American Stud Book after importation, and whose sire was not imported but is properly recorded in the Stud Book of a country recognized by The Jockey Club.

65. Upon failure to register a horse before October 1st of the year of his birth, he may be registered prior to January 1st of his three-year-old year by special permission of the Stewards of The Jockey Club, but not thereafter. If the application to register be made prior to the January 1st next following his birth, the payment of a fee of $60 will be required; if made after that date and prior to January 1st of his two-year-old year the required fee will be $150; and if made after that date and prior to January 1st of his three-year-old year, $300.

66. A name for each horse may be claimed gratis through the Registry Office before January 1st of his two-year-

old year. On or after that date, a horse may be named upon payment of a fee of $50 and then only if the name is claimed and allowed at least two days before the date of his first start.

67. (a) All names are subject to approval or disapproval by the Stewards of The Jockey Club.

(b) No name that has been used during the previous fifteen years, either in the stud or on the turf, shall be duplicated, and no name may be claimed for any unregistered horse.

68. By special permission of the Stewards of The Jockey Club a name may be changed but only upon the payment of a fee of $100, except that when a horse's name is changed before January 1st of his two-year-old year, permission is not necessary and the fee is only $10. However, no change of name will be permitted after a horse has started.

69. (a) No horse foaled out of the United States or its possessions, Canada, Cuba or Mexico, shall be registered until the owner has filed in the Registry Office a certificate stating age, color, sex, distinguishing marks, if any, and pedigree as recorded in the recognized Stud Book of its native country or of that country or of that country from which it is exported; or unless, in respect of the age and identity of the horse, the owner has otherwise satisfied the Stewards of The Jockey Club. In both cases there must be filed after importation a veterinarian's certificate of identification.

(b) All such applications must be accompanied by a certified copy of the horse's complete racing record in all countries; such record to state date, the type race, distance and the amount of money won in each race.

(c) This registration must be made at the Registry Office within sixty days after the horse's original landing in the United States or its possessions, Canada, Cuba or Mexico and the registration fee shall be $30 for each horse, which will include certificate of registration.

(d) If it be proved to the satisfaction of the Stewards of The Jockey Club that the failure to apply for the registration of a horse within the 60-day period provided in paragraph (c) of this rule was the result of an excusable inadvertence, such registration may be permitted thereafter, provided, however, that such application to register is made within two years after original arrival in the United States or its possessions, Canada, Cuba or Mexico and provided further that the Stewards are furnished with such authenticated information, in respect of the age and identity of the horse and other relevant matters, as they may require.

If the application to register be made within six months after the original arrival, the fee will be $100 for each horse; if made within one year after original arrival, the fee will be $400.

PART VIII.
Entries, Subscriptions, Declarations
and Acceptances for Races

70. Every person subscribing to a sweepstake or entering a horse in a race to be run under these Rules accepts the decision of the Stewards or the decision of the Stewards of The Jockey Club or the decision of the State Racing Commission, as the case may be, on any question relating to a race or to racing.

71. At the discretion of the Stewards of The Jockey Club or of the Stewards or of the Association, and without notice, the nominations or entries of any person or the transfer of any nomination or entry may be cancelled or refused.

72. A horse is not qualified to run in any race unless he is duly entered for that race.

73. No horse shall be permitted to start unless his certificate of registration or his racing permit is on file at the Identification Office of The Jockey Club, except that the Stewards, in their discretion, for good cause, waive this requirement if the horse is otherwise properly identified.

74. No horse is qualified to be entered or run which is wholly or partly the property of or leased to or from, or in any way under the care or superintendence of, a disqualified person. Disqualification of a husband or wife from racing horses applies equally to both.

75. Any horse which has been the subject of improper practice may be disqualified for such time and for such races as the Stewards shall determine.

76. (a) Entries and declarations shall be made in writing signed by the owner of the horse or of the engagement or by his authorized agent or some person deputed by him; and in order to secure privacy all entries to overnight races must be made at a specially designated booth.

(b) Entries and declarations by telegraph are binding if promptly confirmed in writing.

(c) Entrance money is not returned on the death of a horse nor on his failure to start, whatever be the cause of the failure.

(d) Entries to all races, excepting those which are opened and decided during the meeting, must be posted on the bulletin boards at the track where the meeting is being held.

77. (a) A horse of a partnership cannot be entered or run in the name, whether real or stable name, of an individual partner in accordance with Rule 87, unless that individual's interest or property in the racing qualities of that horse is equal to at least 25 per cent.

(b) All horses owned wholly or in part by the same person or the spouse of any such person or trained by the same trainer, must be coupled and run as an entry.

(c) Not more than one horse owned by the same person or two horses trained by the same person shall be drawn into any overnight race, or on the also eligible list, to the exclusion of another horse.

212

(d) For purposes of paragraphs (b) and (c) of this Rule 77, a horse shall be deemed "owned wholly or in part" by a particular person or "owned" by a particular person if that person holds the entire property interest in the horse or if, by lease or ownership, he controls the racing qualities of the horse or if he holds a proportionate interest of 25 per cent or more in a partnership which either holds the property interest in the horse or, by lease or ownership, controls the racing qualities of the horse.

(e) No licensed or authorized trainer shall have any interest, either by ownership of the horse or by lease of its racing qualities in a horse of which he is not the trainer and which may be racing at the same track where the trainer is licensed or authorized and currently racing.

78. (a) The list of entries for overnight races shall be closed at the advertised time and no entry shall be admitted after that time, except that, in case of an emergency, the Racing Secretary may, with the consent of a Steward, grant an extension of time.

(b) The list of entries for all other races shall be closed at the advertised time and no entry shall be admitted after that time unless the nominator can prove to the Stewards that the entry was mailed before the advertised time of closing; and starters must be named through the entry box by the usual time of closing on the day preceding the race.

79. (a) Except as provided in paragraph (b) of this Rule, entries shall be in the name of one person or a stable name, and shall state the name, or the stable name, of the owner, the name or description of the horse, if unnamed, and if the race be for horses of different ages, the age of the horse entered.

(b) Entries may be made in the name of a corporation or a partnership, but, in order to remain eligible, such entries must be transferred to one name on or before January 1st of the two-year-old year of the horse or horses entered.

80. (a) In entering a horse for the first time, it shall be identified by stating its name (if it has any), its color and sex and the name or description of its sire and dam as recorded in the Stud Book. If the dam was covered by more than one stallion, the names or description of all must be stated.

(b) Except as provided in Rule 81, this description must be repeated in every entry until a description of the horse with his name has been published in the Racing Calendar or in the program or the list of entries of an Association.

(c) In every entry after such publication, his name and age will be sufficient.

81. If a horse be entered with a name for the first time, in several races for the same meeting, closing at the same place on the same day, the description need not be added in more than one of the entries.

82. Upon any change of name of a horse which has run in any country, his old name as well as his new name must be given in every entry until he has run three times under his new name over the course of an Association.

213

Produce Races

83. In making an entry for a produce race, the produce is entered by specifying the dam and the sire or sires.

84. If the produce of a mare is dropped before the 1st of January, or if there is no produce, or if the produce is dead when dropped, or if twins are dropped, the entry of such mare is void.

85. In produce races, allowance for the produce of untried horses must be claimed before the time of closing, and are not lost by subsequent winnings.

Partnerships and Stable Names

86. (a) A horse may be owned by an individual or by a partnership of any number of persons, but no horse shall be entered and run by an owning partnership if it contains more than four members or if the proportionate interest of any member is less than 25 per cent.

(b) A horse owned by a partnership in which the number of members or proportionate interest of any member does not meet the requirements of paragraph (a) of this Rule 86 may be entered and run only by a lessee of its racing qualities, which lessee shall be an individual or a partnership in which the number of members and the proportionate interest of every member meets the requirements of paragraph (a) of this Rule 86. In such a case, the lessee may be a member of or may include one or more members of the owning partnership.

(c) All partnerships having any property, ownership or racing interest in a horse, and the name and address of every individual having any such interest in a horse, the relative proportions of such interest, and the terms of any sale with contingencies, of any lease or of any arrangement, must be signed by all the parties or by their authorized agents and be lodged annually at the office of The Jockey Club or with the Clerk of the Course for transmission to that office, and must be approved by The Jockey Club and a fee of $1.00 per horse be paid, before any horse which is a joint property or which is sold with contingencies or is leased can start in any race.

(d) In the case of a partnership which, by ownership or lease, controls the racing qualities of a horse, all of the partners and each of them shall be jointly and severally liable for all stakes and obligations.

(e) No statement of partnership of a partnership which proposes, by ownership or lease, to control the racing qualities of any horse will be accepted unless proportionate interest of each such partner is at least 25 per cent.

(f) The Jockey Club shall not be required to lodge under paragraph (c) of this Rule 86 any lease of the racing qualities of a horse or horses which is contrary to the law or officially declared public policy of any State in which racing is authorized to be conducted. As a condition of the acceptance of a lease,

The Jockey Club may require lessors and lessees to supply such information concerning the identity of their members or participants as is reasonably necessary to insure compliance with this paragraph.

(g) The Jockey Club reserves the right to disapprove any partnership, sale with contingencies, lease, or other arrangements required to be lodged with and approved by The Jockey Club pursuant to paragraph (c) of this Rule 86 when, in the opinion of The Jockey Club, the effect of the partnership, sale, lease, or other arrangement would be to deceive or improperly mislead the public as to the identity of the persons holding an interest in a horse.

87. All statements of partnerships, of sales with contingencies, of leases, or of arrangements, shall declare in whose name the horse will run, to whom winnings are payable (which must be the name of the nominator), and with whom rests the power of entry.

88. In cases of emergency, authority to sign declarations of partnership may be given to The Jockey Club by a telegram promptly confirmed in writing.

89. No member of a partnership which owns a horse or leases the racing qualities of a horse shall assign his share or any part of it without the written consent of the other partners lodged and approved by paragraph (c) of Rule 86. No assignment of an interest in a partnership, which, by ownership or lease, control the racing qualities of a horse will be accepted, if the effect of the assignment would be to create a partnership, which would not be accepted under the terms of paragraph (c) of Rule 86.

90. (a) An individual may adopt a stable name under which to race horses by registering it annually with The Jockey Club and by paying annually a fee of $100. Such a registration shall be effective only during the calendar year for which it is made, and all such names shall be subject to the approval or disapproval of The Jockey Club.

(b) An individual cannot have registered more than one stable name at the same time, and, so long as an individual has a stable name registered, he shall not use or permit the use of his real name to identify the ownership interest in the racing qualities of any horse.

(c) A partnership which, by ownership or lease, controls the racing qualities of a horse or horses shall race such horses under the name, either real or stable name, of a member of the partnership whose proportionate interest in the horse meets the requirements of paragraph (a) of Rule 77. All horses the racing qualities of which are controlled by a given partnership shall be raced under the same name.

(d) A stable name may be changed at any time by registering a new stable name and by paying the fee of $100.

(e) An individual cannot register as a stable name one which has been already registered, or one which is the name of a race horse, or one which is the real name of an owner.

91. Any individual who has registered a stable name may at any time abandon

it by giving written notice at the office of The Jockey Club; notice of such abandonment shall be published in the next Racing Calendar, after which all entries which have been made in the stable name shall be altered as may be approved by The Jockey Club.

92. No trainer of race horses shall register a stable name, but the partnership of which a trainer is a member may use the stable name of another member, provided the use of such other member's stable name is otherwise authorized by these Rules.

93. (Stricken out.)

94. Provided the identity of the horse is satisfactorily established, incorrect or imperfect description in the entry of a horse or failure to register a partnership, may be corrected at any time before the horse is announced as a starter and his number exhibited for the race concerned; or in a handicap before the weights are announced; but this rule shall not be construed so as to allow any horse to start in any race for which he is not otherwise completely qualified under these Rules of Racing.

95. Except in overnight races, if the hour for closing of entries or for declarations be not stated, it is understood to be midnight of the day specified.

96. In the absence of notice to the contrary, entries and declarations of forfeit, due on the eve of and during a meeting, are due at the office of the Clerk of the Course where the race is to be run.

97. A person who subscribes to a sweepstakes may, after approval by the Stewards, transfer his subscription.

98. An entry of a horse in a sweepstakes is a subscription to the sweepstakes. Such an entry or subscription may, before the time of closing, be altered or withdrawn.

99. Subscriptions and all entries or rights of entry under them shall not become void on the death of the person in whose name they were made or taken. All rights, privileges and obligations shall attach to the continuing owners including the legal representatives of the decedent.

100. No horse shall be considered as struck out of any of his engagements until the owner or his authorized agent shall have given notice, in writing or by telegram, promptly confirmed in writing, to the Clerk of the Course where the horse is engaged.

101. (a) The striking of a horse out of an engagement is irrevocable.

(b) Omission by the vendor to strike a horse out of an engagement, not sold or transferred with him, does not entitle his owner to start him, or to the stakes if he wins.

102. (Stricken out.)

103. (a) If a horse is sold by private treaty, or at public auction, or claimed out of a claiming race (unless the conditions of the claiming race stated otherwise) the written acknowledgment of both parties is necessary to prove the fact that it was transferred with its engagements.

(b) When a horse is sold with his engagements, or any part of them, the seller cannot strike the horse out of any such engagements.

(c) If only certain engagements be

specified, those only are transferred with the horse.

104. A sale to a person ruled off, or to an unqualified or disqualified person, will not entitle such person to be recognized as an owner under these Rules of Racing.

PART IX.

Stakes, Subscriptions, Etc.

105. In the absence of conditions or notice to the contrary, entries for overnight races are to be made at the office of the Clerk of the Course by 2 P.M. on the day before the race.

106. Every horse shall be considered as having started and be liable for whatever is due for so doing, when its jockey has been weighed and its number displayed, unless the Stewards shall otherwise determine.

107. (Stricken out.)

108. No horse shall be allowed to start for any race and no jockey shall be weighed out for any horse until there have been paid or guaranteed to the Clerk of the Course

(a) Any stake or entrance money due by the owner in respect to that race.

(b) The jockey's fee.

PART X.

Rules 109 through 116 were repealed by The Jockey Club years ago.

PART XI.

Qualifications of Starters

117. (a) A horse shall not be qualified to start in any race unless, not less than 30 minutes before the time set for the race, his presence on the grounds of the Association be reported to the paddock judge, he be announced to the Clerk of the Scales as a starter, and the name of his jockey given to the latter official.

(b) Any subsequent change of jockeys must be sanctioned by the Stewards, who, if no satisfactory reason is given for the change, may fine or suspend any person they may think culpable in the matter.

(c) All horses must be saddled in the paddock.

(d) The paddock judge shall be in charge of the paddock and inspect all race horses and their equipment prior to each race, and shall report forthwith to a Steward any violation observed by him.

(e) No one not actually connected with its stable shall touch a horse while in the paddock preparatory to starting a race, except as provided in Rule 117(f).

(f) A representative of the Association conducting a meeting shall inspect the plating and bandaging of each horse as it enters the paddock before the race, and record the plating on a board provided for the purpose in the paddock.

118. The Stewards may permit or direct the withdrawing of a horse after weighing out.

119. The time fixed for the first race shall be printed on the program.

Post time is the time designated by the Stewards at which horses are to arrive at the post for each race, and such time shall be shown on the dial provided for that purpose.

PART XII.

Weights, Penalties and Allowances

120. (a) The following weights are carried when the weights are not stated in the conditions of the race:

SCALE OF WEIGHTS FOR AGE

DISTANCE	AGE	JAN.	FEB.	MAR.	APRIL	MAY	JUNE	JULY	AUG.	SEPT.	OCT.	NOV.	DEC.
Half Mile	Two years	x	x	x	x	x	x	x	105	108	111	114	114
	Three years	117	117	119	119	121	123	125	126	127	128	129	129
	Four years	130	130	130	130	130	130	130	130	130	130	130	130
	Five years & up	130	130	130	130	130	130	130	130	130	130	130	130
Six Furlongs	Two years	x	x	x	x	x	x	x	102	105	108	111	111
	Three years	114	114	117	117	119	121	123	125	126	127	128	128
	Four years	129	129	130	130	130	130	130	130	130	130	130	130
	Five years & up	130	130	130	130	130	130	130	130	130	130	130	130
One Mile	Two years	x	x	x	x	x	x	x	x	96	99	102	102
	Three years	107	107	111	111	113	115	117	119	121	122	123	123
	Four years	127	127	128	128	127	126	126	126	126	126	126	126
	Five years & up	128	128	128	128	127	126	126	126	126	126	126	126
One and a Quarter Miles	Two years	x	x	x	x	x	x	x	x	x	x	x	x
	Three years	101	101	107	107	111	113	116	118	120	121	122	122
	Four years	125	125	127	127	127	126	126	126	126	126	126	126
	Five years & up	127	127	127	127	127	126	126	126	126	126	126	126
One and a Half Miles	Two years	x	x	x	x	x	x	x	x	x	x	x	x
	Three years	98	98	104	104	108	111	114	117	119	121	122	122
	Four years	124	124	126	126	126	126	126	126	126	126	126	126
	Five years & up	126	126	126	126	126	126	126	126	126	126	126	126
Two Miles	Three years	96	96	102	102	106	109	112	114	117	119	120	120
	Four years	124	124	126	126	126	126	126	125	125	124	124	124
	Five years & up	126	126	126	126	126	126	126	125	125	124	124	124

(b) In races of intermediate lengths, the weights for the shorter distance are carried.

(c) In races exclusively for three-year-olds or four-year-olds, the weight is 126 lbs., and in races exclusively for two-year-olds, it is 122 lbs.

(d) In all races except handicaps and

races where the conditions expressly state to the contrary, the scale of weights is less, by the following: for fillies two years old, 3 lbs.; for mares three years old and upward, 5 lbs. before September 1, and 3 lbs. thereafter.

(e) Welter weights are 28 lbs. added to the weight for age.

(f) In all overnight races except handicaps, not more than six pounds may be deducted from the scale of weights for age, except for allowances, but in no case shall the total allowances of any type reduce the lowest weight below 101 lbs., except that this minimum weight need not apply to two-year-olds or three-year-olds when racing with older horses.

(g) In all handicaps which close more than 72 hours prior to the race the top weight shall not be less than 126 lbs., except that in handicaps for fillies and mares, the top weight shall not be less than 126 lbs. less the sex allowance at the time the race is run; and scale weight for fillies and mares or three-year-olds may be used for open handicaps as minimum top weight in place of 126 lbs.

(h) In all overnight handicaps and in all claiming handicaps, the top weight shall not be less than 122 lbs.

(i) In all overnight races for two-year-olds, for three-year-olds, or for four-year-olds and upward the minimum weight shall be 112 pounds, subject to sex and apprentice allowances. This rule shall not apply to handicaps, nor to races for three-year-olds and upward.

Estimated Winnings

121. (a) In estimating the value of a race to the winner, there shall be deducted only the amount of money payable to the owners of the other horses and to other persons out of the stakes and out of the added money.

(b) In estimating foreign winnings, the current rate of exchange at the time of such winnings shall be adopted.

(c) The value of prizes not in money will not be estimated in the value of the race to the winner.

(d) In estimating the value of a series of races in which an extra sum of money is won by winning two or more races, the extra sum shall be estimated in the last race by which it was finally won.

122. In all races, should there be any surplus from entries, or subscriptions over the advertised value, it shall be paid the winner, unless stated by the conditions to go to other horses in the race.

123. (a) Winnings during the year shall include all prizes from the 1st of January preceding to the time appointed for the start, and shall apply to all races in any country; and winning shall include dividing or walking over.

(b) Winning of a fixed sum is understood to be winning it in one race, unless specified to the contrary.

124. (a) In a case of a walkover, one-half of the money offered to the winner is given.

(b) When a walkover is the result of

arrangement by owners of horses engaged, no portion of the added money nor any other prize need be given.

125. Any money or prize which by the conditions is to go to the horse placed second, or in any lower place in the race, shall, if the winner has walked over or no horse has been so placed, be dealt with as follows:

(a) If part of the stake, it shall go to the winner; or

(b) If a separate donation from the Association or any other source, it shall not be given at all; or

(c) If entrance money for the race, it shall go to the Association.

126. If a race never be run or be void, all moneys paid by an owner in respect to that race shall be returned.

127. A race may be declared void if no qualified horse covers the course according to rule.

Penalties

128. No horse shall carry extra weight, nor be barred from any race for having run second or in any lower place in a race.

129. When the winners of claiming races are exempted from penalties, the exemption does not apply to races in which any of the horses running are not subject to being claimed.

130. Penalties and allowances are not cumulative, unless so declared by the conditions of the race.

Allowances

131. (a) Any male between the ages of sixteen and twenty-five years who has never previously been licensed as a jockey in any country, and has of his own free will and, if under age, with the written consent of his parents or guardian, bound himself to an owner or trainer for a term of not less than three nor more than five years (subject to written extension if made for less than five years) by written contract approved by and filed with The Jockey Club, and after at least one year service with a racing stable, may claim in all overnight races, except handicaps, the following allowances:

(1) Ten pounds until he has ridden five winners and seven pounds until he has ridden an additional 30 winners; if he has ridden 35 winners prior to the end of one year from the date of riding his fifth winner, he shall have an allowance of five pounds until the end of that year.

(2) After the completion of conditions above, for one year he may claim three pounds when riding horses owned or trained by his original contract employer provided his contract has not been permanently transferred or sold since he rode his first winner.

(3) The holder of the contract at the time the boy rides his first winner shall be considered the original contract employer.

(b) All holders of apprentice contracts shall be subject to investigation as to character, ability, facilities and financial responsibility; and shall, at the time of making the contract, own in good faith a minimum of three horses in training, or, if a trainer, shall operate in good faith a stable of at least three horses.

(c) Contracts for apprentice jockeys shall provide for fair remuneration, adequate medical attention and suitable board and lodging for the apprentice; and approved provision shall be made for savings out of his earnings.

(d) Under exceptional circumstances which would prevent an apprentice jockey from riding during the full periods specified above, such as (a) service in the armed forces of the United States; (b) personal injuries suffered in the course of his occupation or otherwise; (c) a disabling illness; (d) restrictions on racing; (e) or other valid reason, the Stewards may extend said period and the term of his contract to compensate therefore.

(e) No apprentice shall be permitted to acquire his own contract.

(f) All apprentice contracts described in this rule shall be filed with The Jockey Club within thirty days after execution thereof or upon filing application for license with the New York State Racing Commission.

(g) The failure of an owner or trainer to file such contract or to obtain the approval of The Jockey Club thereto, may subject such owner or trainer to the revocation or suspension of his license or to such other disciplinary action by the Commission as in its judgment may seem proper.

132. No horse shall receive allowance of weight, or be relieved from extra weight, for having been beaten in one or more races; provided that this rule shall not prohibit maiden allowances, or allowances to horses that have not won within a specified time, or that have not won races of a specified value.

PART XIII.
Weighing Out

133. (a) Every jockey must be weighed for a specified horse not less than 30 minutes before the time fixed for the race, and the number of the horse shall be exhibited officially as soon as possible.

(b) Only equipment specifically approved by the Stewards shall be worn or carried by a jockey or a horse in a race.

(c) Every jockey, apprentice jockey and other rider, whether in a race or when exercising or ponying a Thoroughbred horse, shall wear a safety helmet of a type approved in writing by the Stewards; and no change shall be made in any such helmet without the approval of the Stewards.

134. If a horse run in muzzle, martingale, breastplate or clothing, it must be put on the scale and included in the jockey's weight.

135. No whip, or substitute for a whip, blinkers or number cloth shall be allowed on the scales, nor shall any bridle

221

or safety helmet approved by the Stewards be weighed.

136. If a jockey intends to carry overweight, he must declare the amount thereof at the time of weighing out, or if in doubt as to his proper weight, he may declare the weight he intends to carry.

137. If a jockey intends to carry overweight exceeding by more than two pounds the weight which his horse is to carry, the owner or trainer consenting, he must declare the amount of overweight to the Clerk of the Scales at least 45 minutes before the time appointed for the race, and the Clerk shall cause the overweight to be stated on the Notice Board immediately. For failure on the part of a jockey to comply with this Rule he may be punished as provided by Rule 48.

138. No horse shall carry more than five pounds overweight except in races confined exclusively to amateurs or to riders who are Officers of the United States Army or Navy or of the National Guard.

139. The owner is responsible for the weight carried by his horse.

PART XIV.
Starting

140. (a) The Starter shall give all orders necessary for securing a fair start.

(b) He shall report to the Stewards by whom or by what cause any delay was occasioned, and any cases of misconduct by jockeys when under his orders.

141. If a horse whose number has been exhibited or whose starting is obligatory does not start and run in the race, the Stewards may fine or suspend any person or persons responsible therefor.

142. After the horses are ordered to the starting post, and until the Stewards direct the gates to be reopened, all persons except the racing officials shall be excluded from the course to be run over.

143. A bell shall be rung to indicate the time to saddle and a bugle sounded to indicate the time to go to the post.

144. (a) All horses shall parade and, under penalty of disqualification, shall carry their weight from the paddock to the starting post, such parade to pass the finish line.

(b) When by permission of the paddock judge and upon payment of $10 a horse is led to the post, he is excused from parading with the other horses, but nevertheless he must, on his way to the post, pass the Steward's stand.

145. (a) The position of horses when starting shall be determined by a lot, i.e., a numbered ball shall be drawn from a bottle by the Clerk of the Scales.

(b) The Starter may place vicious and unruly horses on the outside and behind the line.

(c) A horse in the hands of the Starter shall receive no further care from anyone at the starting post except the assistant starters, provided that if any accident happens to a jockey, his horse or his equipment, the Starter may permit any jockey or jockeys to dismount and the horses to be cared for during the

222

delay; otherwise no jockey shall dismount.

146. (a) Except in cases provided for in paragraph (b) of this Rule, all races shall be started by a starting gate selected by the Association conducting the meeting if approved by the Stewards of The Jockey Club.

(b) By permission of the Stewards, a race may be started without a gate.

(c) When a race is started without a starting gate, the start shall not be official until, and there shall be no recall after, the recall flag has been dropped in answer to that of the starter.

147. A start in front of the post is void, and the horses must be started again.

148. All horses shall be schooled properly before starting and, upon the report of the Starter, the Stewards may fine or suspend any trainer who, after being notified, shall start any unruly horse.

149. The horses shall be started as far as possible in a line, but may be started at such reasonable distance behind the starting post as the Starter thinks necessary.

150. (a) The Starter may fine or suspend a jockey for disobedience of his orders at the starting gate or for attempting any unfair advantage; and the Starter may impose upon an offender a fine not exceeding $200 and suspension not exceeding ten days, with or without reference to the Stewards for further action, but such suspension shall not take effect until after the last race of the day of his suspension.

(b) All fines and suspensions by the Starter must be reported in writing by him to the Clerk of the Course, and they may be modified or remitted by the Stewards only.

151. The concurrent statements of the Starter and his assistant as to incidents of the start are conclusive.

PART XV.
Rules of the Race

152. An owner running two or more horses in a race may declare to win with one of them, and such declaration must be made at the time of weighing out, and it is to be immediately posted on the Notice Board. A jockey riding a horse with which his owner has not declared to win must on no account stop such horse except in favor of the stable companion on whose behalf declaration to win has been made.

153. (a) When clear, a horse may be taken to any part of the course provided that crossing or weaving in front of contenders may constitute interference or intimidation for which the offender may be disciplined.

(b) A horse crossing another so as actually to impede him is disqualified, unless the impeded horse was partly in fault or the crossing was wholly caused by the fault of some other horse or jockey.

(c) If a horse or jockey jostle another horse, the aggressor may be disqualified, unless the impeded horse or his jockey was partly in fault or the jostle was wholly caused by the fault of some other horse or jockey.

(d) If a jockey wilfully strike another horse or jockey, or ride wilfully or carelessly so as to injure another horse which is in no way in fault or so as to cause other horses to do so, his horse is disqualified.

(e) When a horse is disqualified under this rule, every horse in the same race belonging wholly or partly to the same owner, in the discretion of the Stewards, may be disqualified.

(f) Complaints under this rule can only be received from the owner, trainer or jockey of the horse alleged to be aggrieved, and must be made to the Clerk of the Scales or to the Stewards before or immediately after his jockey has passed the scales. But nothing in this rule shall prevent the Stewards taking cognizance of foul riding.

(g) Any jockey against whom a foul is claimed shall be given the opportunity to appear before the Stewards before any decision is made by them.

(h) A jockey whose horse has been disqualified or who unnecessarily causes his horse to shorten his stride with a view to complaint, or an owner, trainer or jockey who complains frivolously that his horse was crossed or jostled, may be fined or suspended.

(i) The extent of disqualification shall be determined by the Stewards as in these rules provided.

154. If the Stewards at any time are satisfied that the riding of any race was intentionally foul or that any jockey was instructed or induced so to ride, all persons guilty of complicity shall be suspended and the case shall be reported to the Stewards of The Jockey Club for such additional action as they may consider necessary.

155. If a horse leaves the course, he must turn back and run the course from the point at which he left it.

156. If a race has been run by all the horses at wrong weights or over a wrong course or distance, and an objection be made before official confirmation of the number of the horses placed in the race, or if a Judge is not in the stand when the horses pass the winning post, the race shall be run again after the last race of the day, but in no case less than 30 minutes after the finish of the wrongly run race.

Walking Over

157. In a sweepstake, if only one horse remains to start, the Stewards may dispense with a walkover.

PART XVI.
Weighing In

158. Every jockey must, immediately after pulling up, ride his horse to the place of weighing, dismount only after obtaining permission from the official in

charge, and present himself to be weighed by the Clerk of the Scales; provided that if a jockey be prevented from riding to the place of weighing by reason of accident or illness by which he or his horse is disabled, he may walk or be carried to the scales.

159. Except by special permission of the official in charge, every jockey must, upon pulling up, unsaddle his own horse, and no attendant shall touch the horse, except by his bridle. Upon the returning of a jockey to the winner's circle to dismount after a race has been run, no one may touch the equipment of the jockey until he has been weighed in, except upon the approval of the official in charge.

160. If a jockey does not present himself to weigh in, or if he be more than one pound short of his weight, or if he be guilty of any fraudulent practice with respect to weight or weighing, or, except as provided in Rule 158, if he dismount before reaching the scales, or dismount without permission, or if he touch (except accidentally) before weighing in any person or thing other than his own equipment, his horse may be disqualified and he himself may be fined or suspended, as provided by Rule 48.

161. If a horse carry more than two pounds over his proper or declared weight, his jockey shall be fined, suspended or ruled off, unless the Stewards are satisfied that such excess weight has been caused by rain or mud.

PART XVII.
Dead Heats

162. When a race results in a dead heat, the dead heat shall not be run off, owners shall divide, except where division would conflict with the conditions of the race.

When two horses run a dead heat for first place, all prizes to which first and second horses would have been entitled shall be divided equally between them; and this applies in dividing prizes, whatever the number of horses running a dead heat and whatever places for which the dead heat is run. Each horse shall be deemed a winner and liable to penalty for the amount he shall receive.

When a dead heat is run for second place and an objection is made to the winner of the race, and sustained, the horses which ran the dead heat shall be deemed to have run a dead heat for first place.

163. If the dividing owners cannot agree as to which of them is to have a Cup or other prize which cannot be divided, the question shall be determined by lot by the Stewards.

164. On a dead heat for a match, the match is off.

PART XVIII.

Claiming Races

165. (a) In claiming races any horse may be claimed for its entered price by any owner presently registered in good faith for racing at that meeting who has nominated a starter up to or including the race in which the claim is made, or by his authorized agent, but for the account only of the owner making the claim, or for whom the claim was made by the agent; provided, however, that no person shall claim his own horse or cause his horse to be claimed directly or indirectly for his own account.

(b) The minimum price for which a horse may be entered in a claiming race shall be twelve hundred dollars, but in no case shall it be entered for less than the value of the purse to the winner.

(c) If a horse is claimed, it shall not start in a claiming race for a period of 30 days from date of claim for less than 25% more than the amount for which it was claimed.

(d) If a horse is claimed, it shall not be sold or transferred to anyone wholly or in part, except in a claiming race, for a period of 30 days from date of claim, nor shall it, unless reclaimed, remain in the same stable or under control or management of its former owner or trainer for a like period, nor shall it race elsewhere until after the close of the meeting at which it was claimed.

166. All claims shall be in writing, sealed and deposited in a locked box provided for this purpose by the Clerk of the Course, at least fifteen minutes before post time. No money shall ac-company the claim. Each person desiring to make a claim, unless he shall have such amount to his credit with the Association, must first deposit with the Association the whole amount of the claim in cash, for which a receipt will be given. All claims shall be passed upon by the Stewards, and the person determined at the closing time for claiming to have the right of claim shall become the owner of the horse when the start is effected whether it be alive or dead, sound or unsound, or injured before or during the race, or after it. If more than one person should enter a claim for the same horse, the disposition of the horse shall be decided by lot by the Stewards. An owner shall not be informed that a claim has been made until after the race has been run, and any horse so claimed shall then be taken to the paddock for delivery to the claimant.

167. No person shall claim more than one horse in a race.

168. Each horse shall run for the account of the person in whose name it starts.

169. When a claim has been lodged with the Secretary or Clerk of the Course, it is irrevocable, and is at the risk of the claimant.

170. In case of a dead heat, each of the dividing horses is the winner for the purpose of these rules.

171. (a) Should the Stewards be of the opinion that any person is claiming a horse collusively for the benefit of another interest or in order to evade the

provisions of Rule 165, they may require him to make an affidavit that he is not so doing, and if upon proof it is ascertained that he made a false affidavit he shall be referred to the Stewards of The Jockey Club for further action.

(b) Should the Stewards within twenty-four hours after the running of a race be of the opinion that the lease or the entry of a horse was not made in good faith but was made for the purpose of obtaining the privilege of entering a claim, then in each case they may disallow or cancel any such claim and order the return of a horse that may have been delivered and refer the case to the Stewards of The Jockey Club for further action.

172. A horse's liability to be claimed is not affected by his walking over, but he shall receive all the money offered by the conditions of the race to the winner.

173. No horse shall be delivered except on a written order from the Secretary or Clerk of the Course.

174. Any person refusing to deliver a claimed horse shall be suspended and his case may be referred to the Stewards of The Jockey Club. The horse is disqualified until he is delivered to the purchaser.

175. (a) When a stable has been eliminated by claiming, the owner so affected, if he has not replenished his stable before the close of the meeting, may obtain a certificate from the Stewards of the meeting, and on presentation thereof the owner shall be entitled to claim during the next thirty racing days at any recognized meeting operating under the jurisdiction of The Jockey Club, until he has claimed a horse. Stables eliminated by fire or other hazards may also be permitted to claim under this Rule by the discretion of the Stewards.

(b) Any person who shall attempt to prevent another person from claiming any horse in a claiming race, or any owners running in claiming races who may make an agreement for the claiming of each other's horses, may be fined or suspended by the Stewards and referred to the Stewards of The Jockey Club for further action.

PART XIX.

Disputes, Objections, Appeals, Etc.

176. When a race is in dispute, both the horse that finished first and any horse claiming the race shall be liable to all the penalties attaching to the winner of that race until the matter is decided.

177. Every objection shall be decided by the Stewards, but the decisions shall be subject to appeal to the Stewards of The Jockey Club so far as relates to points involving the interpretation of these rules, or to any question other than a question of fact, on which there shall be no appeal unless by leave of the Stewards and with the consent of the Stewards of The Jockey Club. Notice of appeal must be given in writing to the Clerk of the Course within forty-eight hours of the decision being known.

Objections, When and Where Made

178. Every objection must be made by the owner, trainer or jockey of some horse engaged in the race, or by the officials of the course, to the Clerk of the Scales or to one of the Stewards, or an objection may be made by any one of the Stewards.

179. All objections except claims of interference during a race must be in writing signed by the objector.

180. An objection cannot be withdrawn without leave of the Stewards.

181. All costs and expenses in relation to determining an objection or conducting an inquiry shall be paid by such person or persons, and in such proportions as the Stewards shall direct.

182. Before considering an objection, the Stewards may require a deposit of $25, which shall be forfeited if the objection is decided to be frivolous or vexatious.

183. If an objection to a horse engaged in a race be made not less than 15 minutes before the time set for the race, the Stewards may require the qualification to be proved before the race, and in default of such proof being given to their satisfaction, they must declare the horse disqualified.

184. An objection to any decision of the Clerk of the Scales must be made at once.

185. An objection to the distance of a course officially designated must be made not less than 15 minutes before the race.

186. An objection to a horse on the ground of his not having run the proper course, or of the race having been run on a wrong course, or of any other matter occurring in the race, must be made before the numbers of the horses placed in the race are confirmed officially.

187. (a) An objection on the ground

(1) Of misstatement, omission or error in the entry under which a horse has run; or

(2) That the horse which ran was not the horse nor of the age which he was represented to be at the time of entry; or

(3) That he was not qualified under the conditions of the race or by reason of default; or

(4) That he has run in contravention of the rules of partnership or registration, may be received up to 48 hours exclusive of Sunday after the last race of the last day of the meeting.

(b) In any other case an objection must be within 48 hours of the race being run, exclusive of Sunday, save in the case of any fraud or willful misstatement, when there shall be no limit to the time of objecting provided the Stewards are satisfied that there has been no unnecessary delay on the part of the objector.

188. The Stewards are vested with the power to determine the extent of disqualification in case of fouls. They may place the offending horse behind such horses as in their judgment it interfered with, or they may place it last, and they may disqualify it from participation in any part of the purse.

189. If by reason of an objection to a

horse a race or place is awarded to another horse, the money for such race shall be distributed in accordance with the final placing, and the owner of a horse to which the race or place is finally awarded can recover the money from those who wrongfully received it.

190. Pending the determination of an objection any prize which the horse objected to may have won or may win in the race, or any money held by the association holding the meeting, as the price of a horse claimed (if affected by the determination of the objection) shall be withheld until the objection is determined.

PART XX.
*Licenses or Authorization:
for Participants in Racing*

191. Except as provided in Rule 192, no person shall be allowed to start, ride or train horses, and no person may pursue any other occupation or be employed at race meetings, in any State where it is or shall be required that such person be licensed, or obtain an authorization, in order to pursue his occupation or employment upon the grounds of an Association, unless such person shall have been licensed or shall have obtained such authorization.

192. Unless otherwise provided by the rules of the Racing Commission, or by the laws, of the State concerned:

(a) No jockey license or authorization shall be granted to anyone less than sixteen years of age;

(b) Each owner, to be eligible for a license or authorization, shall be required to submit an affidavit, as to his ownership or lease of all horses in his possession;

(c) Boys never having ridden in a race may be allowed to ride twice, if approved by the Stewards, before applying for a license or authorization; but a license or authorization shall not be granted to boys who have never ridden in a race;

(d) In an emergency, the Stewards may permit owners, trainers, assistant trainers and jockeys and others to start, train or ride or pursue their other occupations or employments pending action on their applications; and

(e) Any amateur wishing to ride in races on even terms with jockeys shall obtain leave, good until revoked, from the Stewards of The Jockey Club;

(f) No person shall be eligible for an owner's or trainer's license or authorization, if, during the term of such license or authorization, he would practice as farrier or veterinarian with horses racing under the jurisdiction of The Jockey Club; provided, however, that a duly licensed or authorized owner may personally shoe a horse owned by him upon applying for and receiving a certificate of fitness therefor from the Stewards;

193. Trainer and assistant trainers are responsible for the condition of horses in their care and are presumed to know these Rules.

Jockeys' Betting, Etc.

194. (a) No jockey shall bet on any race except through the owner of and on the horses which he rides, and any jockey who shall be proved to the satisfaction of the Stewards to have any interest in any race horse, or to have been engaged in any betting transaction except as permitted by this Rule, or to have received presents from persons other than the owner, may be punished as provided by Rule 48.

(b) Any person knowingly acting in the capacity of part owner or trainer of any horse in which a jockey possesses any interest, or making any bet with or in behalf of any jockey except as provided in Rule 194 (a), or otherwise aiding or abetting in any breach of these Rules of Racing, may be punished as provided by Rule 48.

195. (a) No jockey shall be the owner of any race horse.

(b) A jockey may not ride in any race against a starter of his contract employer unless his mount and his contract employer's starter are both in the hands of the same trainer.

196. (a) A jockey or trainer under suspension in any state or foreign country, shall not be permitted to train or ride in a race for anyone during the period of his suspension. Any person who shall employ a jockey or trainer in contravention of this Rule may be punished as provided by Rule 48.

(b) All fines imposed upon jockeys must be paid by the jockeys themselves. Any other person found paying the same shall be punished as well as the jockey.

197. In the absence of a specific contract, jockey's fees shall be as follows:

PURSE	WINNER	SECOND	THIRD	LOSER	PURSE	WINNER	SECOND	THIRD	LOSER
$400	$25.00	$15.00	$12.00	$10.00	$1,200–1,300	$42.00	$27.00	$23.00	$18.00
500	26.00	16.00	13.00	11.00	1,400–1,500	44.00	29.00	24.00	19.00
600	27.00	17.00	14.00	12.00	1,600–1,700	47.00	32.00	25.00	20.00
700	34.00	21.00	19.00	15.00	1,800–1,900	50.00	35.00	27.00	22.00
800–900	37.00	22.00	21.00	17.00	2,000 & up	50.00	40.00	30.00	25.00
1,000–1,100	39.00	24.00	22.00	17.00					

198. (a) The terms of all contracts between jockeys and their employers shall be filed with The Jockey Club, accompanied by a fee of $1, and must be approved by it (in the cases of apprentices, before a license or authorization be granted), and such contracts shall contain a provision that in case a jockey's license or authorization be revoked or suspended, the salary of the jockey shall in the former case cease, and in the latter case cease during the time of his suspension. The terms of all contracts between jockeys and jockey agents shall be filed with The Jockey Club accompanied by a fee of $1 and must be approved by it before being effective.

(b) A jockey shall be compensated and insured by either the owner or trainer of the horse according to which one is the employer as defined by the applicable Workmen's Compensation Law.

199. If a jockey engaged for a race, or for a specified time, refuses to fulfill his engagement, he may be punished as provided by Rule 48.

200. Employers retaining the same jockey have precedence according to the priority of the retainers as specified in the contracts.

201. Conflicting claims for the services of a jockey shall be decided by the Stewards.

Stable Employees

202. No owner or trainer shall engage any person who has not a written discharge from his last employer, but any person prevented by this rule from obtaining or retaining employment shall have the right of appeal to the Stewards against the person withholding his written discharge.

203. Any owner or trainer employing a person in violation of any of Rules 191 to 202, inclusive, may be punished as provided by Rule 48.

PART XXI.
Racing Colors and Numbers

204. (a) Racing colors shall be registered annually on payment of $5, or for five years on payment of $15. Colors so registered shall not be taken by any other person. All disputes as to the right to particular colors shall be settled by the Stewards of The Jockey Club.

(b) No person shall run a horse in colors other than those registered in his own or a stable name without special permission of the Stewards.

205. Jockeys must wear a number on the saddle cloths corresponding to the numbers of the horses as exhibited after weighing out.

206. Any deviation from the recorded colors of the owner that may be granted by the Stewards is to be immediately posted on the Notice Board.

207. Under special circumstances, a horse may be permitted by the Stewards to run in colors not those of the owner.

PART XXII.
Corrupt Practices and
Disqualifications of Persons

208. (a) If any person give, offer or promise, directly or indirectly, any bribe in any form to any person having official duties in relation to any race or race horse, or to any trainer, jockey or agent, or to any other person having charge of, or access to, any race horse; or

(b) If any person having official duties in relation to any race track, race or race horse, or if any trainer, jockey, agent or other person having charge of, or access to, any race horse, solicit, accept, or offer to accept any bribe in any form; or

(c) If any licensed person, or person

permitted within the grounds of any Association, shall be approached with an offer or promise of a bribe or with a request or a suggestion for a bribe or for any improper, corrupt or fraudulent act or practice in relation to a race or racing, or that any race shall be conducted otherwise than fairly and in accordance with these Rules of Racing, and if such licensed or other person shall not immediately report the matter to the Stewards; or

(d) If any person wilfully enter, or cause or permit to be entered, or to start, in any race a horse which he knows or has reason to believe to be disqualified; or

(e) If any person shall have in his possession in or about any race track, or shall use, appliances—electrical, mechanical, or otherwise—other than the ordinary equipment, of such nature as could affect the speed or racing conditions of a horse; or

(f) If any person be guilty of any improper, corrupt or fraudulent act or practice in relation to racing in this or in any other country, or shall conspire with any other person to commit, or shall assist in the commission of, any such act or practice;

Any person found by the Stewards to have violated Rule 208(a), (b), (c), (d), (e) or (f) shall have such penalty imposed upon him and the Stewards shall take such other action in the matter as they may deem proper under any Rules of Racing, including reference to the Stewards of The Jockey Club.

(g) If the Stewards shall find that any drug has been administered or attempted to be administered, internally or externally, to a horse before a race, which is of such a character as could affect the racing condition of the horse in such a race, such Stewards shall impose such penalty and take such other action as they may deem proper under any of these Rules of Racing (including reference to the Stewards of The Jockey Club) against every person found by them to have administered, or to have attempted to administer or to have caused to be administered or to have caused an attempt to administer, or to have conspired with another person to administer such drug.

The trainer, groom, and any other person, having charge, custody or care of the horse, are obligated properly to protect the horse and guard it against such administration or attempted administration and, if the Stewards shall find that any such person has failed to show proper protection and guarding of the horse, they shall impose such penalty and take such other action as they may deem proper under any of the Rules of Racing, including reference to the Stewards of The Jockey Club.

The owner or owners of a horse so found to have received such administration shall be denied, or shall promptly return, any portion of the purse or sweepstakes, and any trophy in such race, and the same shall be distributed as in the case of a disqualification. If a horse shall be disqualified in a race because of the infraction of this Rule 208(g), the eligibility of other horses which ran in such race and which have started in a subsequent race before announcement of such disqualification, shall not be in any way affected.

(h) No person within the grounds of a racing Association where race horses are lodged or kept, shall have in or upon the premises which he occupies or has the right to occupy, or in his personal property or effects, any hypodermic syringe, hypodermic needle, or other device which could be used for the injection or other infusion into a horse of a drug without first securing written permission from the Stewards. Every racing Association, upon the grounds of which race horses are lodged or kept, is required to use all reasonable efforts to prevent the violation of this Rule. Every such racing Association, the Commission, and the Stewards, or any of them, shall have the right to permit a person or persons authorized by any of them to enter into or upon the buildings, stables, rooms or other places within the grounds of such an Association and to examine the same and to inspect and examine the personal property and effects of any person, within such places; and every licensed person and person authorized to pursue his occupation or employment within the grounds of any Association, by accepting his license or accepting such authorization, does consent to such search and to the seizure of any such hypodermic syringes, hypodermic needles or other devices, and any drugs apparently intended to be used in connection therewith, so found. If the Stewards shall find that any persons have violated this Rule

208(h), they shall impose such penalty and take such other action as they may deem proper under any of the Rules of Racing, including reference to the Stewards of The Jockey Club.

(i) Every person ruled off the course of a recognized Association is ruled off wherever these rules have force.

(j) Anyone who has been ruled off or who has been suspended, whether temporarily for investigation or otherwise, and anyone penalized as above by the highest official regulatory racing body having jurisdiction where the offense occurred, shall be denied admission to all race tracks until duly reinstated.

(k) A person whose license or authorization has been revoked or has been suspended, whether temporarily for investigation or otherwise, and so long as his exclusion or suspension continues shall not be qualified, whether acting as agent or otherwise, to subscribe for or to run any horse for any race, either in his own name or in that of any other person.

(l) All horses in the charge of a trainer who has been ruled off or has been suspended, whether temporarily for investigation or otherwise shall be automatically suspended from racing during the period of the trainer's exclusion or suspension. Permission may be given by the Stewards for the transfer of such horses to another trainer during such period, and upon such approval such horses shall again be eligible to race.

(m) In the event that a horse establishes a track or other record in a race and it should be determined by competent authority that the chemical analysis of any sample taken from such horse shows the presence of a drug which is of such character as could affect the racing condition of the horse in such race, then such record shall be null and void.

PART XXIII.
Discretionary Powers

209. If any case occurs which is not or which is alleged not to be provided for by these Rules, it shall be determined by the Stewards or by the Stewards of The Jockey Club, as the case may be, in such manner as they think just and conformable to the usages of the turf.

210. These Rules of Racing or any rules, not consistent therewith, made by the State Racing Commission of the State concerned, supersede the conditions of a race or regulations of a meeting when they conflict.

211. The Stewards shall not entertain any disputes relating to bets.

212. The Jockey Club may contract with racing authorities, racing Associations and other bodies for the rendition of such advisory or other services as may be desired.

PART XXIV.
New Rules

213. No new Rules of Racing can be adopted by The Jockey Club nor can any of its Rules be rescinded or altered unless the proposed new rule, rescission or alteration shall have been previously advertised twice in the Racing Calendar nor unless notice shall have been given in such advertisement of the meeting of The Jockey Club at which it is to be acted upon, except that:

(a) In the event of an "Emergency," so declared by the Stewards of The Jockey Club, new rules may be passed and any existing rule rescinded or altered at a meeting of The Jockey Club called upon twenty-four hours' notice, which notice shall contain the reason for the meeting.

(b) The Stewards of The Jockey Club may sanction variations in these Rules to conform with local conditions.

234

SCRATCHES. Early in the morning of every racing day, stable representatives, jockey agents, and track officials gather at the racing secretary's office to find out which of the horses listed on the day's program will actually run, and who will ride. Where Thoroughbreds are plentiful and more entries are received than can be accommodated in the STARTING GATE, stables can withdraw horses from races at will. The scratched (or "declared") animals are then replaced by others from an "also-eligible" list. More typically in modern racing, however, fields are sparse and tracks are reluctant to permit scratches for other than medical reasons. Thus, a TRAINER who has tried to withdraw a horse may hear in the morning that the animal is "stuck," which means that if it can run it is required to do so. Late scratches posted on track bulletin boards and announced over the public-address systems are frequently stuck horses whose unfitness has been confirmed by the track veterinarian. On the other hand, stuck horses sometimes win the races from which their handlers have sought to declare them. This is interpreted as evidence of animal perversity but actually tells more about humans than horses. A trainer may try to scratch a racing-sound horse in hope of cashing a larger or easier check in a race several days later. If the names of stuck horses were publicized, audiences would become indignant when an occasional stuck horse won. But in more cases, handicappers would be warned that a horse with a recently unimpressive record was sufficiently out of sorts to be no threat. Or that a presumed CONTENDER was probably not. In this process, the hallowed custom of permitting scratches for non-medical reasons would become an embarrassment to tracks. In self-protection, they would clamp down on the practice, thereby depriving OWNERS and TRAINERS of a prized tactic in their daily efforts to mislead each other and confuse the betting public. As far as I know, no track identifies stuck horses in the printed programs sold to racegoers.

Because handicapping is more fun and more effective when undertaken at leisure, enthusiasts usually prefer to study DAILY RACING FORM on the evening before the races or in the morning before leaving for the track. Without an informative friend in some barn, a handicapper arrives at the track without knowing which horses will run and which have been scratched. In big cities, scratch sheets may be available at newsstands in mid-morning. These report the scratches and final jockey assignments, facilitating the selection process. Whether informed of scratches early or after entering the track, a careful handicapper is attentive to their possible effect on the running of each race. Perhaps the withdrawal of a horse with EARLY SPEED is all that may be needed to establish one's own choice, another speedster, as a likelier selection than ever. On the other hand, if the personal choice is a come-from-behind type, the absence of one quick starter may provide another with such a PACE advantage that the slow starter's prospects diminish.

SELECTION SYSTEMS. Expert handicapping is the comprehensive, orderly comparison of the records of horses entered in a race. It is systematic. So are the hundreds of selection systems published each year. But selection systems are retailed as substitutes for handicapping. As the direct-mail circular promises, no judgment is required. By following a few simple rules, everyone picks the same horse. Riches ensue. The last time I was in the newspaper section of the Library of Congress, most of the seats were occupied by persons poring over bound volumes of *Daily Racing Form* in quest of the miraculously effective system that would liberate them from whatever they hoped to be liberated from. Presumably, each of these questers had already tried to beat the horses with mail-order systems and had abandoned that particular blind alley.

I have no doubt that computer studies have already equipped some individuals with systems that turn a profit without burdening them with the exertions and anxieties of handicapping. The exertions, as implied above, are those of comprehensive study. The anxieties come from risking money on choices that derive from personal judgment. An effective computer-developed system would be a great relief. A computerized selection process would be even better, spewing out the day's choices after the names of the horses were cranked in. Dream on. The day will come.

In the meantime, I agree with those who insist that nothing accurately described as a selection system actually works. That is, none yet seen survives the test of time. The fundamental problem is that the systems attempt to detour the complexities of a complex game. Most begin and end with prescription of two or three past-performance characteristics which are to be accepted as reasons to bet on a horse. Yet, details are the very essence of handicapping. To isolate a horse as a bet without considering its record in comparison with those of its opponents is to carry simplification across the border of fantasy. Numerous authors, myself included, have therefore tried to help new handicappers with elaborate sets of rules known as "methods"—so called because they fall approximately midway between full-dress handicapping and oversimplified systems and deserve to be differentiated from the latter. Their rules pilot the reader through most foreseeable problems but cannot possibly cover all contingencies. Eventually, rules fall short and handicapping judgments are necessary.

SHIPPERS. Each season, some New York horses win their first starts at Santa Anita and other New York horses fail to run a yard, even after racing at the California track often enough to become acclimated. And some California horses win at first asking in New York, while others finish nowhere. In 1976, the stable trained by Frank Martin won everything in sight during the early weeks of the Aqueduct meeting. The feat was even more remarkable than it seemed, because the same horses had done nothing but lose before shipping east from Santa Anita. Horses that cannot win at Detroit Race Course become tigers at higher-class Sportsman's Park. Horses that run for Sweeney at Fair Grounds display miraculous improvement after shipping north to compete for better purses in Arkansas or Illinois. To explain these conflicting phenomena in terms of the patterned strategies of individual TRAINERS is interesting but does not necessarily illuminate the future. The patterns are impermanent. A trainer who loses race after race at a balmy winter track while legging up his cavalry for all-out springtime effort in the north may win consistently at some future meeting in the south, the composition of his stable or the preferences of his OWNERS having changed. Similarly, the fact that some horses ship well and others do not is demonstrated by the individual horse only after it has shipped and won (or lost). In other hands, it might have shipped less successfully, or more so, as it sometimes proves after changing stables. Another complication arises in trying to handicap the prospects of a horse shipped only a short distance. For example, horses with splendid 1976 and 1977 records at Atlantic City attracted lots of betting when they vanned up the road to Monmouth Park, a trip of not more than 120 minutes. But they usually lost because the opposition at Monmouth was sterner than that to which they were accustomed.

The appearance of an out-of-town horse in its first local race is therefore a special handicapping problem. If the horse has traveled from a distant track of quality equal to or higher than the local track's, the handicapper must decide whether it is likely to be in winning form, a matter about which no evidence will be available unless the horse's visible record includes previous performances under similar conditions. The handicapper also must attempt to divine the intentions of the trainer. If the barn has shipped to the local oval *en masse,* to remain for the entire meeting, the performances of its other horses in their own first outings are helpful clues. The trainer may have decided to shoot for all the money from the very start or, not yet ready, he may allow the livestock to become accustomed to the new surroundings while racing into form. In any event, the safest long-run approach is to avoid playing races in which the prospects of any new shipper cannot be dismissed because of something unpromising in its recent record. After the shipper has raced over the track a time or two, it can be rated on its local form and whatever signs of improvement it may have offered.

SHOES protect the delicate tissues of Thoroughbred hooves and feet from full impact with the racing surface. They also hold hooves together, lessening the possibility of spreading or cracking. And when properly designed and fitted, they provide the balance without which a horse cannot approach its full potentiality as a racer. A change of as little as one-sixteenth of an inch in the contour of a single shoe can transform a clumsy loser into a graceful winner. Or vice versa. Which is why the farrier (blacksmith) is a decisively important figure in the backstage maneuvers of racing. Modern shoes are usually aluminum, less often steel, and sometimes are cushioned with felt or plastic. To help a horse gain purchase on slippery footing, they may be embellished with raised rims, calks (rounded metal projections), stickers (sharper than calks), or inserts (extra-long shoeing nails that protrude below the shoe). Whether any of these are used depends partly on the condition of the racing strip, partly on the TRAINER's appraisal of the individual horse's needs and partly on whatever measures of the kind may be fashionable at the time. Some successful barns use plain shoes in all circumstances. Others change shoe styles with every change in weather or TRACK CONDITIONS. At most tracks, a shoe board advises the audience as to which horses are shod with, for example, mud calks and which are not. If most are equipped with a given style of shoe, and the exception is a chronic loser from a losing barn, the failure to adhere to style may be accepted as another reason why horse and barn keep losing. Far more valuable for handicapping purposes than shoe boards would be published information about modifications in the design of a horse's foot gear, and the reasons for the change. No information of that kind ever escapes the privacy of the barn but there can be no doubt whatever that many a longshot victory is attributable to a sudden improvement in the animal's shoes.

SOUTH DAKOTA racing takes place for about 35 days per summer at Park Jefferson, a half-miler in Jefferson, near Sioux City, Iowa. The purses are about as low as can be found in the United States. The horse with EARLY SPEED and an inside POST POSITION wins far more than its reasonable share of the races.

SPEED HANDICAPPING. Long before development of the electronic devices that time races at modern tracks, bookmakers and other interested parties used personal stopwatches to learn more about horses than others could possibly know. They were the first speed handicappers. The few who understood how to relate variable race times to the actual capabilities of horses were true experts. Their theory and technique were perhaps not full-fledged secrets but were tightly held and discussed as sparingly as possible. Outsiders learned the craft only through independent study of a most prolonged, arduous, and creative kind. Published revelations were few and had little effect. Scarcely any readers could find time to study and practice this most rarefied branch of the handicapping art.

In the 1930's, previously guarded material appeared in the anonymously written *How To Select Winning Horses,* published by TURF & SPORT DIGEST in an undated volume which attracted small attention and has long since gone out of print. In 1963, Robert Hebert, the eminent writer-handicapper of the *Los Angeles Times,* included certain basic facts in *Bob Hebert's Secrets of Hand-icapping* (Prentice-Hall, Englewood Cliffs, N.J.). In 1975, Andrew Beyer of the Washington *Star-News* aroused wide interest with an advanced procedure advocated in his *Picking Winners* (Houghton Mifflin, Boston). This brought speed theory out of hiding. In 1976, *Gordon Jones To Win!* (Karman Communications, Huntington Beach, Cal.) presented a more conventional formula which may have omitted elaborations employed by that handicapper in his own justly celebrated selections for the Los Angeles *Herald-Examiner.* More recently, Dr. William L. Quirin, of the mathematics faculty at Adelphi University, Garden City, New York, wrote *Winning at the Races: Computer Discoveries in Thoroughbred Handicapping* (William Morrow & Company, 1979). This generous work includes new, original, labor-saving contributions to speed-handicapping technique.

To set the scene for review of the present state of speed-handicapping knowledge, a few assertions are in order:

1. The traditional reluctance of expert speed handicappers to share their ideas derives from fear that educated bettors might ruin the mutuel prices on certain winning horses. But significant numbers of racegoers are unlikely to devote themselves to the years of work that precede mastery of speed handicapping. For example, no evidence indicates that Andrew Beyer's book has affected the payoffs at any track. On the other hand, the published selections of speed handicappers like Russ Harris of the New

York *Daily News,* Gordon Jones, and the East Coast's *Clocker Lawton* influence thousands of bettors and deflate mutuel prices. So do various mail-order services that sell accurate speed figures to subscribers. In a real sense, the cat has been out of the bag for years.

2. Real speed handicapping bears only coincidental resemblance to the activities of horseplayers who try to pick winners by comparing official running times and/or the speed ratings published in *Daily Racing Form.* It relates but remotely to oversimplified selection methods that use ratings found on canned, hopelessly inaccurate time-distance charts. It requires thorough acquaintance with the recent and prospective abilities of hundreds of horses. It requires keen, experienced judgment. It requires daily study of results in an effort to factor out the effects on running time of wind, the texture of the racing strip, PACE, jockeying, and RACING LUCK. It is most effective when limited to comparisons of CONTENDERS previously identified by reference to the FUNDAMENTALS of handicapping.

3. Horsemen and handicappers who grumble that running time is no indicator of CLASS or FORM do not understand the variable but indissoluble relationship between time-at-the-distance and Thoroughbred quality. Or, understanding that much, they have not learned how to deal with the variables.

Parallel-Time Charts. Imitation speed-handicapping methods are sold as quick, convenient means of picking winners. The customer clips a time-distance-rat-ing chart (known as a parallel-time chart) from the magazine or book and, indeed, finds it easy to use. To make a selection, one merely notes the latest running time of each horse (regardless of track or DISTANCE), finds the corresponding numerical rating on the chart, and makes whatever adjustments may be prescribed for shifts in WEIGHTS or the supposedly permanent and changeless speed differences among tracks (a myth). In a few seconds, all the horses are rated. The one with the highest number is the choice, without regard to its probable form, its distance preferences, the likely role of EARLY SPEED or, worst, the actual racing ability represented by the running time on which each rating was based. The crucial relationship between running time and ability is discussed below, in connection with speed figures. Such basics aside, handicapping of the sort just described contains little nourishment. Like any other handicapping that neglects fundamentals, it cannot work.

Even accomplished handicappers sometimes become so enchanted by the magical powers of a parallel-time chart that they risk subordinating the form and distance factors to the numbers printed on the piece of paper. Where a reasonably accurate chart (see below) lists the median times in which each class of runners travels each programmed distance at a particular track when the strip is normally fast, and may assign ratings to those times, many handicappers decide that the chart is capable of predicting the time in which a

$9,000 sprinter will run nine furlongs, or in which an allowance router will go six. Nothing could be much less realistic than that. Charts or not, Thoroughbreds have individual distance preferences. To make a sensible forecast about the running time of a horse at a new distance, it is necessary first to wonder whether the animal will go the distance in anything like its standard form. No chart can do that.

And no chart is serviceable at all tracks, even though most purport to be. Tracks differ in circumference, in width, in the geometry of their turns, and in the inherent resilience of their racing surfaces. This produces irregular time-distance relationships. A claiming horse capable of 1:11.1 for six furlongs on the Aqueduct main track might earn, let us say, a rating of 80 from some universal time chart. Under normal conditions at Keeneland, however, the same animal would finish in 1:11, earning an 81. Yet, if able to hold its speed for an extra 110 yards, it would travel six and a half furlongs in 1:17.3 at Aqueduct, earning perhaps a 79, and would require 1:17.4 for the distance at Keeneland, a 78. Keeneland is normally faster than Aqueduct at the one distance and slower at the other, making a 78 horse out of one that deserves an 81. In a game of split seconds and inches and, more particularly, in the only kind of handicapping potentially able to translate these small margins into numbers, a three-point error is lethal. The differing lengths of time it takes one horse to cover two congenial distances under

normal circumstances at two different tracks are enough to invalidate any universal time-distance chart.

For accurate calculation, the parallel time chart must be compiled for use at one track only, from normal running times recorded at that track in each age-sex-class-distance category. To list all those times, find their averages or medians, and plot the local chart is a blindingly tiresome job. But with the numbers finally in hand, the toiler is able to produce speed variants and rate individual performances with a precision beyond reach of less diligent handicappers. Thanks to the computer studies of Dr. William L. Quirin, hours of library research need no longer precede the drafting of good parallel time charts for the local circuit. Having supplied his machine with the facts about tens of thousands of races at all North American tracks, Quirin discovered that running times at all distances improve in a standard pattern from the lowest to the highest classes. Regardless of the idiosyncracies of the particular racing strip, the normal clockings for all classes of claiming horses become known as soon as the handicapper establishes averages for one grade of claiming race at all distances. Times for non-claiming races, such as allowances and stakes, also adhere to standard patterns. If the worker determines the correct fast-track times for non-claiming maiden races involving but not necessarily restricted to older males at all distances, the normal times for higher classes automatically fall into place. The accompanying charts are abstracted from Dr. Quirin's book.

The large chart applies only to claiming races in which the competitors include male Thoroughbreds aged four or more. For convenience, it supposes that races for $10,000 animals of that description are sufficiently common to serve as a numerical base for major-track charts. At minor tracks, races at a lower claiming price might be more numerous and therefore more serviceable as a source of normal times. But the pattern remains the same. In calculating the average running time for whatever grade of race will serve as the foundation of the chart, the researcher notes the official times of a representative sample of races in which older males of the appropriate claiming price participated at each programmed distance at that track on days when the strip was described as fast. It is all right to use races in which three-year-olds also competed. Eight or ten races per distance should suffice. After crossing out the two fastest and slowest times at each distance, the worker averages the others and inscribes each average in its proper place on the chart. The rest of the chart develops with subtraction of the indicated number of fifths of a second for each higher (and faster) class, and addition of fifths for lower and slower classes. The same procedure constructs a separate chart for non-claiming races. The abbreviation "NW 1" indicates allowance races for horses that have not yet won an allowance race. "Clf" refers to the highest grade of allowance race, for horses in the local classified division,

having won too often to be eligible for allowance races restricted to limited winners.

When researching the time bases for the individual chart, and later in using the charts to calculate speed variants and handicap ratings, the handicapper assumes that a race with a top-eligibility claiming price of $10,500 or $9,500 belongs in the $10,000 category. Similar flexibility is required at all claiming levels. A STARTER handicap is presumed to be worth twice the claiming price written in the conditions of the race. Standard adjustments for races restricted to fillies and mares or maiden claiming runners accompany the fundamental charts, as do the seasonal adjustments for races in which three-year-olds run against each other, without competition from older horses.

Example: The local par time is 1:12 for six-furlong races with fields that include older males entered to be claimed for $10,000. What then is the six-furlong par for three-year-old maiden fillies and mares entered to be claimed for $7,500 on a day in June? Simple:

$7,500:	+ 2
Fillies:	+ 2
Maidens:	+ 5
June three-year-olds:	+ 2

The total adjustment is eleven-fifths of a second—two and one-fifth seconds slower than the 1:12 par for older males. The par time therefore is 1:14.1.

CLAIMING RACES
(Older Males)

CLASS	3½f	4f	4½f	5f	5½f	6f	6½f	7f	1m	1-1/16	1-1/8
$50,000	−3	−4	−5	−5	−6	−6	−6	−7	−9	−9	−10
$40,000	−3	−4	−5	−5	−6	−6	−6	−6	−8	−8	−9
$35,000	−3	−4	−5	−5	−5	−5	−5	−5	−7	−7	−8
$30,000	−3	−4	−5	−5	−5	−5	−5	−5	−6	−6	−7
$25,000	−2	−3	−4	−4	−4	−4	−4	−4	−5	−5	−6
$20,000	−2	−2	−3	−3	−3	−3	−3	−3	−4	−4	−4
$18,000	−2	−2	−2	−2	−2	−2	−2	−2	−3	−3	−3
$15,000	−1	−1	−2	−2	−2	−2	−2	−2	−2	−2	−2
$13,000	−1	−1	−1	−1	−1	−1	−1	−1	−1	−1	−1
$10,000	0	0	0	0	0	0	0	0	0	0	0
$8,500	+1	+1	+1	+1	+1	+1	+1	+1	+1	+1	+1
$7,500	+1	+1	+1	+2	+2	+2	+2	+2	+2	+2	+2
$6,500	+1	+1	+1	+2	+3	+3	+3	+3	+3	+3	+3
$5,000	+2	+2	+2	+3	+4	+4	+4	+4	+4	+4	+4
$4,000	+3	+3	+3	+4	+5	+5	+5	+5	+5	+5	+5
$3,500	+3	+3	+3	+4	+5	+5	+5	+5	+5	+6	+6
$3,200	+4	+4	+4	+5	+6	+6	+6	+6	+6	+7	+7
$3,000	+4	+4	+4	+5	+6	+6	+6	+6	+7	+8	+8
$2,500	+5	+5	+5	+6	+7	+7	+7	+7	+8	+9	+9
$2,000	+5	+5	+6	+7	+8	+8	+8	+8	+9	+10	+11
$1,750	+6	+6	+7	+8	+9	+9	+9	+9	+10	+11	+12
$1,500	+6	+6	+7	+8	+9	+9	+9	+10	+11	+12	+13
$1,250	+6	+7	+8	+9	+10	+10	+10	+11	+12	+13	+14
$1,000	+6	+7	+8	+9	+10	+10	+10	+11	+13	+14	+15

THREE-YEAR-OLDS

At the beginning of the year, three-year-olds normally are much slower than older runners of the same sex and class. This table shows the standard time differences, and the dates on which the differences diminish.

	6f	6½f	7f	1m	1-1/16m	1-1/8m	
+9						Jan. 1	+9
+8						Feb. 1	+8
+7					Jan. 1	Mar. 15	+7
+6					Feb. 15	May 1	+6
+5				Jan. 1	Apr. 15	June 1	+5
+4		Jan. 1	Jan. 1	Apr. 15	June 1	July 1	+4
+3	Jan. 1	Feb. 1	Mar. 15	June 1	July 1	Aug. 1	+3
+2	Apr. 15	June 1	June 15	July 15	Aug. 15	Sept. 15	+2
+1	July 1	Aug. 1	Aug. 15	Sept. 15	Oct. 15	Dec. 1	+1
0	Nov. 1	Dec. 1	Dec. 15	———	———	———	0

NON-CLAIMING RACES

	SPRINTS	ROUTES
Maidens	0	0
NW 1	−2	−3
NW 2	−4	−5
NW 3	−5	−7
Clf	−7	−10
Stakes	−9	−12

FILLIES AND MARES

The normal times for sprints restricted to females are two-fifths of a second slower than the times for males of the same class and age group. In races at a mile or longer, the times for females are three-fifths of a second slower.

MAIDEN CLAIMERS

Maiden claiming sprints normally are a full second slower than non-maiden claimers for horses of the same age, sex, and claiming price. Maiden claiming races at a mile or farther are seven-fifths slower.

Speed Ratings. The running lines in *Daily Racing Form* PAST-PERFORMANCE TABLES include numerical speed ratings that measure the number of fifths of a second between the individual horse's running time and the track record for the distance. A rating of 100 means that the horse equalled the record. A 79 shows that it finished 21 fifths—four and one-fifth seconds—behind the record. Among the difficulties of speed ratings based on track records is one that complicates efforts to compare ratings

earned at different distances and/or different tracks. Track records at a comparatively long distance are farther beyond the reach of most horses than are track records at shorter distances. A *Form* speed rating of 75 for a race at a mile is more impressive than a 75 at six furlongs. To compare the values, the handicapper needs accurate speed variants plus a means of compensating for abnormally fast or slow track records. If the local mark happens to have been established by a superhorse like Secretariat, a *Form* speed rating of 80—only four seconds slower than Secretariat—is worth more than the unwary might imagine. Its value soars by comparison with that of a speed rating earned at an infrequently run distance, the local record for which may have been set by a cheap claimer. A table of universal PAR TIMES helps adjust gross discrepancies of this kind. Ratings taken from a parallel-time chart compiled at the local track are much more dependable, especially after application of a speed variant. On Dr. William L. Quirin's time charts, the norm times for older $10,000 males are assigned a rating of 100 at each distance, with one point added for each fifth of a second of faster time, and one point subtracted for each tick slower. These intervals of one point per fifth (and one fifth per beaten length) are traditional in the field, and eminently serviceable.

Nevertheless, few Thoroughbreds travel as slowly as five lengths per second (one length per fifth), even when staggering across the finish line in a woeful state of deceleration. Speed handicappers long have wondered if a more valid time-lengths formula might not produce more accurate ratings. In a field where more precision defeats less, the question is appropriate. One fairly satisfactory but cumbersome way to deal with it is to avoid ratings altogether, dealing entirely with the times on a properly researched local parallel-time chart (as modified by good speed variants), and noting whether one horse's adjusted times stand on higher lines of the chart than do the adjusted times of the other horses. This detours the distortions inherent in the supposition that one rating point equals one length and/or one-fifth of a second of racing time. But it does so only if the handicapper stops charging a horse with one-fifth of a second for each beaten length. Since most Thoroughbreds measure about eight feet in length from nose to rear when standing quietly, and stretch out to about nine feet when running full tilt, it becomes clear that they race at speeds in the vicinity of six lengths per second—or about 1.2 lengths per fifth. The associated decimals may become an annoyance for someone who tries to use them to locate the line of the parallel-time chart on which a horse's adjusted running time belongs.

Years ago, I proposed an arithmetical alternative that translates the concept of six-running-lengths-per-second into numerical ratings. Let 60 points represent one second of race time. Then, each fifth of a second is worth 12 points and each beaten length is worth 10 (one-sixth of a second per length). Arbitrarily assigning 500 points to some centrally located line on the parallel-time chart, the handicapper would add 12 points for each fifth faster, and subtract 12 for each fifth slower. If some winner's time (adjusted by speed variant) were worth 464, a horse beaten by one length in that race would get 10 points less, or 454. The logic is impeccable, but other problems arise. These are the exaggerated values imparted to ratings that use large numerical intervals to describe small differences in racing ability. For example, on a conventional rating scale such as Dr. Quirin's, a horse that earns 100 is rated only 5.3 percent above one that earns a 95. On the 12-point-per-fifth or 10-point-per-length scale, however, with the winner at 500 and the loser at 440, the difference between the ratings would be 12 percent, an unreal value. The unreality multiplies as time differences enlarge. To be sure, scale distortion would be minimized for someone willing to deal in decimals—6 points per second, 1.2 points per fifth of a second, and 1 point per beaten length. On such a scale, the winning horse in our example might get 100 and the other 94, a difference of only 6.3 percent. But if the winner's time were two-fifths of a second faster than the time to which a rating of 100 was awarded, its rating would be 102.4 and the other horse's 96.4. Numbers of that kind have a maddening effect on some handicappers, who often abolish the annoyance by rounding the decimals into whole numbers, thereby defeating themselves. Anyone tolerant of small decimals might find this scale more satisfactory than the one-point-per-fifth-per-length, if only because it is founded in actuality.

The most exaggerated scale distortion yet presented to handicappers was mighty seductive at first glance. It suggested that each fifth of a second be weighted separately at each distance, according to the ratio between one fifth and the total running time. For example, a horse that finished six furlongs in 1:13 had raced for 365 fifths. One fifth was 1/365 or .0027. To facilitate operations, these unmanageably small percentages were multiplied by 1,000 and rounded. In mathematical consequence, superior running times were overvalued and slower ones undervalued. Moreover, the distortions multiplied as distances shortened. At two furlongs, for example, a running time of 22 seconds earned a point value 835 times as large as the rating for 26 seconds. And so the hunt continues for simple but undistorted rating scales based on accurate lengths-time relationships. In the meantime, the old one-point-per-fifth and one-fifth-per-length formulas serve more than adequately, perhaps because their manifold errors tend to cancel each other.

Speed Variants. The horse was clocked in 1:11.3, but how good was the performance? Might its time be credited to an abnormally glib racing strip and a following wind? Conventional speed handicappers, including some mighty successful ones, find their answer in a daily track variant—the number of fifths of seconds of untypically fast or slow running time per average race on a single day's or evening's program. Eastern editions of *Daily Racing Form* supplement the paper's speed ratings with a daily variant figure which states the average number of fifths that separated that day's official winning times from the corresponding track records. Because cheap horses are less likely than better ones to approach record clockings, and because all horses of less than top quality fall farther behind record times as distances increase, the *Form* variant is a partial reflection of the general quality of horseflesh that competed on the given day, and a dim reflection of the speed of the track. Unless the variant is remarkably small—less than 10—or unusually high—25 or above—one cannot be sure that the track was notably fast or slow. Even when the variant is extraordinarily large, its class component frustrates the handicapper's desire to know by how many fifths of a second the track itself deviated from norm. For that reason, most speed handicappers prefer to calculate their own variants by comparing the running time of each race with its norm, as shown on a parallel-time chart. After recording the number of fifths by which each race deviated from par, the handicapper strikes an arithmetical average—the daily variant. This numeral goes into a notebook for reference when handicapping the horses that happened to perform on the specific day. Example: If the handicapper's variant for a day was +2 (for slow-by-two-fifths), a horse with an official time of 1:36 or a speed rating of 85 will be credited with 1:35.3 or 87, on the assumption that normal conditions would have enabled it to finish two ticks earlier.

Handicappers careful about the fundamentals of their game do very nicely if they carry speed ratings and variants no farther than that. Yet their calculations involve much compromise. On a day when six of the races are slower than par, three may be faster. The usual solution is to lump all the pluses and minuses and compute their average without additional analysis. Other handicappers prefer additional sophistications. To bring their daily variants into closer phase with the six-furlong running times that are most numerous on racing programs, they do not calculate the daily average until they have reduced by 33 percent any plus (for slow) deviations from par noted in the times of races at a mile or longer. Later, when confronted with a past performance earned in a route race, they simply increase the variant by adding 50 percent to the notebook figure for that day. This maneuver reduces the distortions introduced into the average daily variant by lumping abnormal running times at diverse distances, and it permits a generally more satisfactory variant figure for the modification of official running times in longer races. Numerous other refinements, though possible, are seldom found at this level of speed analysis. We shall discuss them in connection with the techniques that produce authentic speed figures.

The real defect of a daily speed variant is that it substitutes arithmetic for reality. To suppose that the inherent speed of a track changes but once a day is a large convenience but fallacious. To suppose also that the condition of the strip not only changes on an exclusively daily basis but changes uniformly around its entire circumference is equally unrealistic. Shifting winds, the increasing or disappearing moisture of the racing surface and, by no means least, the between-race ministrations of the maintenance crew often produce several significant changes in track speed during the course of a single program. In the gustily inclement Northeast, several wide swings from abnormally fast to abnormally slow may occur at a single track on any afternoon or evening. To do full justice to an analysis of running times, it is necessary to press beyond the daily variant. As we shall now see, this is achieved with remarkable precision by the extremely few handicappers who produce good speed figures. Whereas daily variants try to determine the condition of a track, speed figures give that up as a bad job and concentrate on the class and condition of horses.

Speed Figures. The best speed handicappers are masters of all fundamental factors, which they use both in identifying contenders and in making their final selections. Accurate speed figures enable them to pick more winners at higher prices than other handicappers can hope to find. The figures are generated without recourse to daily variants and seldom involve the use of parallel-time charts. The charts come into play in certain maiden races and, less often, in other races among horses of unknown ability. Most often, speed figures derive entirely from the handicapper's knowledge of individual horses and, in specific circumstances, what they can be expected to do. The basis is indisputable: The better a horse, the faster it runs. Whoever knows what times to expect of as many as two or three horses in a race can evaluate the time of that race and of all the horses in it. This is done by comparing the running times of the known horses with their predicted times and factoring out all discernible influences on running time except the quality of the horses themselves. Like all other handicappers, these are confronted with the unexpected improvement of a previously belittled animal, or the sudden departure from form of a horse expected to run well. To assign a value to a race, they concentrate on horses that actually fire, running well enough to affect the outcome and the running time, win or lose. Having handicapped each race beforehand, they handicap it again after it is over, paying close attention to such inducers of abnormal running time as wind, track texture, RACING LUCK and, as happens once in a while, an artificially fast or slow early PACE.

To undertake this kind of handicapping, the minimum prerequisites are: (1) thorough knowledge of handicapping as such, as demonstrated by ability to pick winners, and (2) the best possible parallel-time chart for each track on the local circuit. In the beginning, the charts must be used. As the handicapper develops familiarity with the capabilities of individual horses, the charts go to a back burner. Wise beginners facilitate their own development with a file of index cards, one per horse. The card lists the animal's running times, adjusted to compensate for circumstances that may have caused it to run faster or more slowly than normal. Thus, the card is a history of the horse's form cycle and of its improving or declining class. Perhaps the card lists adjusted times alone. Perhaps it also lists ratings taken from whatever scale pleases the worker. It also may include notations that the horse had an excuse in a race, or was carrying too much weight. Whether the handicapper adjusts the animal's postrace ratings to reflect those disadvantages or not is a matter of choice.

A notebook or a file of RESULTS CHARTS contains the ratings for all past races at the meeting, plus whatever supplementary comments and/or ratings may be assigned to individual horses whose performances could not be assessed accurately on the basis of beaten lengths alone. Indeed, the story of the race and its running time is less often told by the performance of the winner than by the times of horses that finish in a cluster for second, third, or fourth. This is conspicuously true in races that end for all practical purposes during the first quarter-mile when some cheap speedster manages to get loose on the front end, galloping home without opposition in faster time than it has ever run before or will ever run again. On the winter tracks of the Northeast, such horses sometimes win by 20 lengths or more. To take their running times seriously is to undermine one's handicapping. Next time out, at a higher claiming price, some other horse runs with the recent 20-length winner during the early going and discourages it into dropping out of contention on the turn for home, if not sooner.

The first stage in the development of speed figures for a field of horses is, of course, the pre-race handicapping. Assuming that the handicapper has been at it for a few weeks, file cards probably exist for several of the entrants in the race, and the parallel-time chart can be ignored. Let us imagine that horse A has been going in about 1:12, is improving, has a top rider, and seems at no disadvantage with respect to early speed, post position, or TRACK CONDITIONS. It might get 1:11.4. Horse B seems to be a 1:11.3 at best, but tossed in a dubious performance last out and may be off its feed. In other words, it might run in 1:12.0 or 1:12.2. None of the other known quantities in the field seems of sufficient class or form to challenge either of these two. The track is labeled fast, which means something other than sloppy or muddy or slow, but can produce abnormal times over a wide range. The flag on the backstretch indicates that a considerable wind is blowing into the horses' faces as they leave the gate and go down that long straightaway to the turn. Horse A and a shipper from some distant circuit come out of the gate like bullets and race noses apart until the head of the homestretch, when the outlander stops.

Horse A holds on to beat the fast-charging horse B by a short neck in an official time of 1:12.2. The winner ran a dead-game race under adverse circumstances that included a stern challenge for a full half-mile, plus the kind of backstretch head wind that often defeats front-runners. It appears that horse A ran at least as well as predicted. Its performance might be worth 1:11.3 or 1:11.4. Because of the wind and other influences, like the depth of the racing cushion, the track was slow. Was it slow in the previous race? Or in the following race? Having answered those questions, and having conceded that horse B ran a fine race, belying its indifferent performance last out, the handicapper might decide to give both animals 1:11.3 or 79 or 524 or whatever rating scale creates the most confidence. Note that the handicapper's chief concern was not a track variant or the numbers on a parallel-time chart. The concentration in this kind of handicapping is on the difference between the horses' running times and the times that a close observer expects of them.

When a horse fails to run as well as expected, has no excuse, and does not finish in the money or in a cluster of horses contending for second, third, or fourth, the handicapper ignores it when evaluating the race. Later, its rating will be determined by the number of lengths that separated it from the winner or, just as likely, from the horses on whose times the race itself was rated. Naturally, if the times of the second and third horses are used for rating purposes, an arbitrary rating is awarded the winner. Unless the winner was the undeserving beneficiary of racing luck, its rating will surpass those of the horses that ran behind it, but not always at the rate of a full point per length or 10 points per length or whatever the rating scale normally demands. Here, as in every other sector of this work, the judgment of the handicapper is crucial. The rating of a horse includes the handicapper's projection of the horse's next performance (if properly placed as to distance and class and not out of action so long as to cast doubts on its form). Thus, when a high-class animal wins by a large margin without apparent exertion, defeating other good runners that appear to have done their predicted best in the struggle for second money, the winner's figure may be enlarged arbitrarily to reflect its immensely superior class. Handicappers who added extra points to winning performances by Count Fleet, Secretariat, Ruffian, and Seattle Slew were correct in doing so.

The best speed handicapper I know, or have even heard of, is Henry Kuck, a New Yorker who produces speed figures (five points per second) for every race at every major Eastern track—as many as six tracks a day. Working from past-performance tables, results charts, and personal observation of four or five days of racing per week, Kuck knows what to expect of thousands of horses. Even when a shipper arrives from distant parts, he has something of a line on the animal, knowing the quality of some of the horses that have been beating it, or running behind it. He completes his daily chores in about 90 minutes. But before anyone sends the boss a farewell note and clears the deck to compile speed figures and lifetime riches, I should point out that Henry Kuck has been turning out speed figures for 20 years and did not reach his present pinnacle until about 10 years ago.

Two-Year-Olds. No parallel-time chart and no formula for calculating daily speed variants includes races for two-year-olds. But speed handicappers who function at that level generally use their daily variants to modify two-year-old running times for handicapping purposes. Persons who deal in real speed figures seldom know what running times to expect of green two-year-olds before their races, but modify the official running times in keeping with their best estimate of the comparative slowness or bounciness of the track. On dead or otherwise slow tracks, by the way, two-year-olds slow down much more dramatically than do older runners, probably because they are not yet strong enough to race uphill. And the running times of improving two-year-olds become dramatically better from race to race.

Turf Racing. Few speed handicappers touch turf races, theorizing that it is impossible to calculate a daily speed variant from the running times recorded on so bumpy and unpredictable a surface as grass. But persons who specialize in speed figures have no difficulty whatever. Being less concerned with the bounciness of the footing than with the performances of horses, they appraise each grass race strictly in terms of the individual runner's apparent improvement or lack thereof, considering how it ran and where it finished and how it had been rated before the race. Time itself does not often complicate these analyses. If a horse is an improving 84 and defeats a solid 83 by two lengths, it probably gets an 85 and the other continues at 83—other things being equal, of course. Very few horses run as well on grass as on dirt, or vice versa. Those that specialize in grass running and hate the main track must be handicapped entirely on the basis of their grass figures.

Mud. The speed figurer learns in time whether some horses move up in muddy going, and makes due allowance in pre-race projections and post-race analyses. It is a poor idea to use wet-track figures in handicapping fast-track races, except for a horse that runs equally well on either footing.

Weights. Many speed handicappers modify their ratings to reflect shifts in weight assignments. Most employ the formula traditional among racing secretaries: At sprint distances, four pounds slows a horse by one length or one-fifth second. Three extra pounds mean one length at a mile. Two pounds have that effect at a mile and an eighth. One pound equals one length at a mile and a quarter. My own preference is to note the weight at which a given horse appears to have difficulty at the upcoming distance. Some seem unable to carry more than 115 pounds. Others handle 120 or more when properly situated in all other respects. Weighted beyond its apparent tolerance and running against

other contenders not so overburdened, a horse can be expected to lose. The steadying impost, as it is called, then becomes an acceptable excuse for the loss. It also becomes an element in the handicapper's appraisal of the horse's chances in its next start. How strenuously did the jockey drive the horse in an attempt to carry the high weight all the way? Did the effort drain the animal and knock it off form? When a rider lets an overweighted mount run on its own courage and do the best it can without undue punishment, chances increase that the horse will have something left for its next race. The high-weight excuse is then worth extra points on the speed rating earned in the losing race. The number of extra points may be found in one of the pound/distance formulas mentioned above. Or, less mechanically, it can be whatever number of points restores the horse's normal rating, modified by added or subtracted points to express the handicapper's evaluation of the animal's impending prospects.

Excuses on Turns. The circumference of a track is measured not at the inside rail but about three feet away. A horse that cruises along the rail throughout a six-furlong race travels exactly three quarters of a mile to the finish wire from the starting point outside the gate. Horses that break from outer post positions lose negligible amounts of ground in their more-or-less diagonal efforts to reach the inside before arriving at the turn. At a typical one-mile track, the horses in a six-furlong race run along a 1,650-foot backstretch before entering the turn. A horse that begins the race 24 feet from the rail and manages to navigate an absolutely diagonal path to the rail position at the beginning of the turn has run less than 1,651 feet. But the geometry of circles penalizes outside running position on turns, which are semicircles. Traveling a full turn in a position directly outside the rail-running horse requires 9.4 feet of additional ground. Running outside two horses means 18.9 extra feet. To go the entire turn outside three horses wastes 28.25 feet. Inasmuch as 11 feet of running distance represents about one-fifth of a second of running time in a six-furlong race, careful race-watching enables speed handicappers to adjust the figures of horses whose official running times may have included extra fifths lost on turns. Whether it wins its race or not, a horse that loses substantial ground on turns should be credited with faster time. Retaining its form and getting an easier trip next time out, it will finish in better time.

SPRINTS By common consent, a race of less than one mile with not more than one turn is regarded as a sprint. Thus, at tracks a mile or more in circumference, a sprint may be as long as seven and a half furlongs. The most usual distance, of course, is six furlongs. At one-mile tracks, sprints of that distance or longer begin in a chute—an extension of the backstretch—from which the horses run directly onto that straightaway and thence to the turn that takes them into the homestretch. Although some accomplished sprinters lag behind their fields in the early running and win by coming from far off the pace to overtake the leaders in the final yards, most have enough EARLY SPEED to contend for the lead at the beginning or, failing that, to race in the forward half of the field within easy striking distance of the front-runners. The usual emphasis on early speed relieves riders of the need to "rate" their mounts with as much precision as is demanded in longer races. Quick-starting sprinters go as fast as they can down the backstretch and, if able to gain a clear lead, may be restrained by the riders in hope of conserving some energy for the final furlongs. Under a skillful jockey, a slower-starting sprinter may not be rated at all, except in the sense that the rider allows it to settle into stride in its own tempo until ready to give chase during the stampede around the turn.

At BULL RINGS of less than a mile, sprints as short as four furlongs may include more than one turn. A runner able to take the lead at the beginning and save ground on the rail holds great advantage over its opponents. Among the unsound horses that usually race at such tracks, turns often are a physical problem which becomes more severe for those struggling against centrifugal force while turning in traffic on the middle of the racing strip. After the ordeal of two turns, a horse that has not been close to the rail and close to the leader can seldom generate enough energy to close the gap during the final run down the short stretch.

STAKES. To run their prize Thoroughbreds in the richest and most important races of the year, OWNERS usually are required to post fees. The first of these is paid when the animal is nominated for the event. In futurity stakes, nominations are made and the first fees posted before the horses have ever competed in a race. Subsequent fees are levied from owners who want to keep their horses eligible during the final months and weeks before the race. A last contribution permits actual participation on the big day. These payments are the modern equivalent of the person-to-person wagers, or stakes, on which the sport was based before the days of enclosed tracks and paying customers. All fees become part of the purse, to which the track itself adds a guaranteed amount (which is what is meant by the familiar "$100,000 added"). Stakes are run under various conditions. Some are allowance races, the WEIGHTS for which are determined by variable earnings formulas that saddle the more successful entrants with heavier burdens than are required for horses of less accomplishment. Other stakes are handicaps, in which the weights depend entirely on the racing secretary's appraisal of the horses. The most interesting and generally most significant stakes of the year are weight-for-age, with each starter carrying the impost prescribed by THE JOCKEY CLUB in the scale of weights set forth in its RULES.

Since victory or an in-the-money finish in a stakes is a powerful testimonial for a potential stallion or brood-mare, the owners and BREEDERS who set policy at many tracks try to arrange all the stakes races they can. Another encouragement of stakes races is the understandable tendency of newspapers and television to give more publicity to a rich race than to the sport at large. During the late 1970's, therefore, almost 2.5 percent of all North American races were stakes. In a typical year, more than 600 Thoroughbreds won such races. This meant that most stakes races were of substandard quality, because there simply were not that many authentic stakes-class horses on the continent. Indeed, some stakes, including a few with large purses, were won by nondescript animals with mediocre records in allowance and claiming company. This might have been a matter of small moment if it did not proclaim a general lowering of the industry's quality standards and, more harmfully, if the money added by tracks to stakes pots did not subtract from the purses paid to hard-pressed claiming stables.

To delineate high-class stakes from the others and restore a measure of probity to the advertisements of the breeding industry, the Thoroughbred Owners and Breeders Association undertook an annual grading of the big races. In 1977, it designated 65 as Grade I, 99 as Grade II, 105 as Grade III, and left the remaining 1,300 races ungraded. Among tracks with Grade I stakes, the leader was Belmont Park, with 17. Aqueduct had three, Saratoga four. Santa Anita was credited with ten and Hollywood Park with eight. Monmouth Park had five,

Atlantic City two, Laurel three; Delaware, Hialeah, Gulfstream, and Keeneland two each; Pimlico, Arlington Park, Churchill Downs, Woodbine, and Garden State one apiece.

As handicapping propositions, higher-class stakes races are perhaps less rewarding than allowances and claimers. In the year of a great champion, or a year of close competition among the top runners of one or another sex or age group, the stakes are exciting to watch and discuss, but may not offer many predictable winners at good prices. Well-regarded SHIPPERS often complicate the handicapping. On the other hand, a publicized stakes attracts tourists, whose contributions to the mutuel pools fatten the prices available in other races on the program. If you can get a decent seat, the day of an important stakes race is a day to be at the track.

STARTER RACES are ALLOWANCE or HANDICAP affairs for animals that have started for specified claiming prices during the previous year or so. The purses and the horses that compete for them are usually far superior to those associated with the specified claiming prices. When the starter races were more popular than they now are in New York and California, TRAINERS traveled large distances to enter good runners in races at low claiming prices without losing them to other barns. This made the animals eligible for easy starter competition at their own tracks. In the East, the actual CLASS of a starter handicap restricted to horses that have run for $10,000 claim-

ing prices is generally equivalent to that of a straight $20,000 claimer. In California, where starter allowances were once preferred, the usual practice was to encourage fair competition by setting a top limit on the claiming price at which an entrant had won. If the race was open to horses that had started for a claiming price of $5,000 or less, it was closed to such of them as had managed to win for $6,500 or more. This provided better races and discouraged the peculiar maneuvers that found Eastern barns winning $3,500 starter handicaps with $12,000 runners. When those handicaps appeared on two or three programs a week, the only way to beat them was to bet proportioned amounts on whatever horses had won their last starter handicaps. Some of them won five or more in succession, under increasingly high weights.

STARTING GATE. Before the development of this contraption, false starts plagued Thoroughbred racing programs with lengthy delays and well-founded rumors of chicanery. Nowadays, each runner awaits the start in a separate stall. When the track's official starter believes that all the horses and riders are facing in the right direction and ready to compete, he pushes the button that trips the latch that opens all the stall gates simultaneously, preventing any horse from gaining unfair advantage by beating the gun. Occasionally, a horse is less ready than expected, and leaves the gate tardily. This may be due to a lapse by the rider or sudden distraction of the animal or, as happens, the failure of an assistant starter to let go of the horse's tail. But complaints about bad starts are no longer a major problem. On the other hand, the mad dash from a standing start may inflict undue strain on Thoroughbred legs. Some horsemen and veterinarians believe that horses would last longer if a way could be found to start their races more gradually.

The worst prospect at any track is a horse chronically slow out of the gate but unable to compete successfully in the ROUTE races which impose less penalty on early sluggishness. A slow-starting sprinter is in deep trouble. The other horses are running faster than they will in the later stages, and the late starter must immediately collect itself and run faster than any of them if it is to be within reach of the lead during the final furlong. This extra exertion is almost invariably more than the horse can supply. Therefore, when a handicapper notices that a sprinter's latest defeat was associated with a slow start, it is important to make sure that starts of that kind are not the horse's standard. If prompt departure from the gate is more characteristic of the animal, a slow start in the last outing is a legitimate EXCUSE which may add a couple of points to today's mutuel price.

STATE-BRED RACES are for horses bred in the track's own state. Numerous legislatures have been persuaded to create funds for the encouragement of Thoroughbred breeding. Among the inducements are higher PURSES for state-bred races than for open races of comparable class, plus bonuses to the breeders of horses that win state-bred STAKES. At this writing, although programs of this kind have not yet transformed places like New Jersey and New York into threats to the breeding supremacy of Kentucky, they have indeed improved the quality of the horses bred in those states. The situations there and in other states being in steady flux, it is impossible to propose a dependable formula for CLASS comparison of an open allowance or claiming race with one for bred-in-state animals. The open race is almost sure to be of higher quality, but the degree of difference can be determined only by close analysis of the horses themselves. Because purses paid to state-breds are inflated, average or gross earnings have become an even less trustworthy class index than in the past.

STEEPLECHASES. To see Thoroughbreds and their riders race long distances over brush fences and water hazards is an experience to raise the hair. Steeplechasing and its less spectacular junior version, the race over low hurdles, are ancient and honorable sports which may deserve more popularity than they now enjoy in North America. Formerly a colorful feature of the most glamorous race meetings in New York, New Jersey, and Delaware, the jumpers now turn up only occasionally. Largely because it mystifies horseplayers, including expert handicappers, jumping attracts less pari-mutuel revenue than does the six-furlong sprint for $5,000 maidens. So the jump stables find most of their competition in more leisurely settings, including brief hunt meetings and, on occasion, competitions at private estates. Some of America's most accomplished horsemen train jumpers, and some of our bravest and most intelligent jockeys ride them (at WEIGHTS higher than are assigned to runners on the flat). To handicap them, the safest procedure is to look up the lists of leading steeplechase TRAINERS and JOCKEYS, and watch the TOTE BOARD.

STEWARDS. At most tracks, three experienced officials function as a panel of presiding judges charged with enforcement of the RULES OF RACING. Customarily, one steward is appointed by the state racing commission and the other two by the track operators. To assure the close but widespread observation needed for effective enforcement, the stewards are assisted by official veterinarians, the starter, patrol judges posted at points of vantage on the race course, paddock judges, placing judges (who help read the photographs of close finishes), and a clerk of scales whose staff supervises the jockey room and the scales where riders weigh in before the race and weigh out afterward. Because the position of steward is often a reward for decades of unquestioning obedience at less authoritative levels of racetrack employment, few stewards are noted for independence or zeal.

T

TEXAS is horse-breeder, horse-raiser, and horseplayer country which has not had legal racing and betting for decades but seems certain to repair the omission during the 1980's. It is difficult to imagine Texans entering this field on a small scale. Formation of a major circuit with Oaklawn (ARKANSAS) and Ak-Sar-Ben (NEBRASKA) might devastate ILLINOIS, LOUISIANA, and MICHIGAN racing and would pose large challenges to Southern CALIFORNIA and NEW YORK. There simply are not enough good Thoroughbreds. Neither is there a foreseeable prospect that BREEDERS will reorganize to relieve the shortage. Someday, each half of the DAILY DOUBLE may be a race for maiden Appaloosas.

THOROUGHBRED RECORD, THE. This weekly covers much the same ground as THE BLOOD-HORSE but the differences are sufficiently numerous to make both magazines required reading for persons who need to know what is afoot in Thoroughbred racing. *The Thoroughbred Record* publishes an enormous annual supplement, its *Statistical Review* of the previous year's racing and breeding. During the remainder of the year, it frequently offers illuminating statistical studies of trends in racing. A regular feature, *The Racing Calendar,* relays notices from THE JOCKEY CLUB. As standard practice, each issue contains competent reports about STAKES at major tracks in America and Europe. In general, the *Record* is less critical of the policies of racing's upper crust than is *The Blood-Horse,* but it stands second to none in indignation about the sorry state of the non-racing world, particularly Washington, D.C.

TIP SHEETS. Hawked at track entrances and available at nearby newsstands, these colorfully printed leaflets spare non-handicappers the task of making selections. Prepared after SCRATCHES on the morning of the races, the best are more helpful than newspaper handicaps compiled many hours earlier. Offering as many as three horses in DAILY DOUBLE, EXACTA, and TRIFECTA races and not less than two in other races, the sheets seldom fail to name a few winners, although they rarely select enough to repay the cost of wagering on, for example, all 27 of the horses named at a track that programs two trifectas, five exactas, and a double. The really good ones, such as *Clocker Lawton* (excellent East Coast selections usually based on SPEED HANDICAPPING), have a profoundly depressing effect on mutuel prices. One of the most interesting, and consistently on the winning side of the ledger, is the *Woodbine Journal,* published under the auspices of the Ontario Jockey Club and known also as the *Fort Erie* or *Greenwood Journal,* depending on which of the circuit's tracks is in operation at the time. The handicapper, James E. Bannon, supplies the bettor with an analysis of each starter's prospects and appends his selections in order of preference. And in Southern California is *Today's Racing Digest,* not really a tip sheet but a compendium of handicapping information more substantial and considerably more helpful than anything published elsewhere.

TOTE BOARD. The large, illuminated display of odds in the racetrack infield is the totalisator board, named for the old-fashioned calculating machinery that did the arithmetic of PARI-MUTUEL BETTING until replaced by computers. Nowadays, the boards at larger tracks show the changing pre-race win odds on each horse; the amounts of money bet on each for win, place, and show; the numbers of the four leading horses at each stage of an ongoing race; the fractional times of the race; and afterward, the winning numbers and mutuel prices. The most elaborate displays also include probable daily double and exacta payoff possibilities.

Having made a choice in a race, or torn between two horses, the handicapper refers to the odds display to see whether one or both of the horses may pay enough to deserve support. That process may also include calculation of the possible place prices. For that purpose, the total amount in the place pool is reduced by 18 percent—or whatever percentage is consumed by the official take. From the remainder, one subtracts the amounts bet on one's choice and the probable favorite in the race. Or, if the horse under consideration is the favorite, the amount bet on it to place is subtracted with the amount bet on the horse with the next largest share of the place pool. After dividing the remainder in half, the handicapper divides one of the halves by the number of dollars that the crowd has bet on the chosen animal. That quotient is the smallest odds that the horse would pay to place if the race were to be run immediately and the horse were to finish first or second. Naturally, if some horse at longer odds shares in the place payoff, the return on one's bet will exceed the minimum.

The board also reveals trends in betting. Some handicappers become uncomfortable when their own choices attract little betting action. A horse held at 5–1 in the MORNING LINE may be posted at 6–1 in the first flash of tote-board information after betting begins, and may stay at that level until betting ends. If any number of insiders or other substantial bettors really liked the animal's chances, its odds would drop at some point. Should the handicapper change horses or simply pass the race? Or should the opinions of other bettors, insiders or not, make no difference? The answer is found in the personal history and individual temperament of the handicapper. Someone who is no great shakes as a selector should be complimented for having no illusions on that score. To demand tote-board confirmation of a handicapping selection is an understandable preference. It also is an uncomfortable and ultimately an unprofitable way to spend one's time. Far better to deemphasize betting while improving the handicapping procedure and developing the confidence that leads to full enjoyment of the game. Genuinely expert handicappers are happiest when the odds on their selections increase, signifying that not many other members of the audience have recognized the possibilities. One kind of selection on which an odds drop may be welcome is the first-time starter. Another is the longshot whose recent lack of competitive sparkle can be attributed to stable manipulations such as races at the wrong distance or on the wrong foot-

ing. When the odds fall from 10–1 to 7–1 to 5–1, the handicapper presumes that the stable and its well-wishers are sending in some money, having recognized with the handicapper that today is the day.

Literally hundreds of board-watching systems help hopeful horseplayers to find heavily bet and therefore supposedly well-meant horses. For example, in a place where the morning line is reasonably dependable, the player may jot down the first odds displayed after the morning line is removed from the board. Then, at five minutes before post time, the player may settle on the horse whose odds at that time represent the largest percentage reduction from the morning line and/or the odds at the first flash. This works at all tracks, but not consistently enough. The player ends by backing too many overbet horses—underlays that win too infrequently and pay too little for long-term profit. At best, the tote-board player handicaps human beings—other bettors. But this is a game that can be won only by astute handicapping of horses and careful consideration of odds.

TOUTS. The financial section of any Sunday newspaper in a large metropolitan area is replete with advertisements from Wall Street investment counselors whose claims resemble those made by racetrack touting services. The difference is one of form rather than substance. Financial counseling is socially accepted but turf counseling is not. Handicappers concerned with reputation in the sport or standing in the community do not sell racing selections by mail or telephone. They leave that remunerative field to less scrupulous types, some of whom can handicap and most of whom are concerned only with vacuuming the pockets of suckers. This is too bad. In England and France, reliable betting advice is sold publicly and respectably. And in North America, discreet, unadvertised touting takes place at all levels of racing. Some stable OWNERS pay large money for expert selections delivered shortly before post time. Many a TRAINER, GROOM, and JOCKEY supplements earnings with payments from betting clients.

Racetrack security personnel expel persons caught touting on the premises. The usual tout enchants his or her pigeons by claiming inside connections with betting stables, naming five horses per race (one per sucker), and demanding a percentage of the proceeds when one of the animals wins. Some touts work in teams. The well-dressed one loudly berates the other for constantly hanging around in search of inside information. After his confederate slinks away, the tout has established credibility with the innocent bystander for whom the squabble was staged. The quality of real or fancied inside INFORMATION being as poor as it is, even when delivered with good intentions, it follows that no handicapper of sound mind will fall prey to a racetrack tout. As to those who peddle their miracles by phone or mail, I have never met one who was not himself a customer of touts. Indeed, they even advertise that they spend large sums of money for inside information. If true, the ad means that somebody in some barn is touting the tout. An occasional tout may be a competent handicapper, which would make his selections no better than those of TIP SHEET handicappers whose own choices also are made in the morning instead of a couple of minutes before post-time and a look at the horse and its odds.

TRACK ACCOMMODATIONS. Anyone who doubts the profound appeal of Thoroughbred racing might ponder the fact that hundreds of thousands of human beings from all walks of life go to the races at every opportunity for decades on end without ever experiencing the pleasure of a decent seat. The best seats are high enough for a view of the entire racing strip, and forward enough for vision unobstructed by persons who stand on their chairs when the horses enter the homestretch. The location should be near the finish line, for a clear idea of which nose arrives first in a close race. At some tracks, such accommodations are available only in enclosed dining rooms to which admission requires purchase of a premium-priced clubhouse ticket, a tip for the functionary in charge of table reservations, another tip for the roustabout who escorts the customer to the table, a cover charge per person, overpriced food of little distinction, and a tip for the waiter. Elsewhere, ideal vantage is reserved for a private sanctum known, perhaps, as a turf and field club and open only to persons who pay a seasonal tariff for the privilege. Or the best seats may be in private boxes, also rented seasonally. Seats of secondary quality often may be had at extra expense in reserved sections of the grandstand or clubhouse. For a handicapper visiting an unfamiliar track, early arrival is prudent. Depending on the current state of the personal budget, the best available seat may be obtained in a reserved section, after which a brief tour will establish the whereabouts of the paddock, the mutuel windows, and the lengths of time needed to reach both places from the seat. On slow days, many tracks allow the ushers in charge of private boxes to rent unoccupied ones for tips. This frequently is the best possible arrangement.

Before eating at a strange track, it is advisable to scout the entire premises and determine the possibilities. These vary from track to track and, for that matter, at individual tracks. Automobile parking seldom offers options, but should be explored on the first visit. With "preferred" parking now available for a price at many tracks, it is possible to discover whether it is worth the extra charge or whether one might as well walk a quarter of a mile to the gate rather than pay extra to walk only a furlong. Finally, it does not take long to locate the civil mutuel clerk whose smilingly prompt and honest service helps one bear in mind that racing is one of the world's pleasures.

TRACK CONDITIONS. The descriptions of track texture posted on infield

TOTE BOARDS are always of interest to the handicapper but should not be accepted as dependable indicators of how EARLY SPEED and POST POSITION should affect selections. After rain has deposited puddles of standing water on a racing strip, and for the hours or days that may elapse before the surface has returned to its normally dry and resilient state, close observation of races is the only productive way to deal with those questions.

Here are the official descriptions of track conditions and what they usually mean:

Fast. The strip is dry and the footing firm. It may be so dry that the watering trucks sprinkle it several times during the program. Or it may be "wet-fast," which indicates the presence of insufficient moisture to invalidate the "fast" sign on the infield board. "Wet-fast" is not used on those boards but sometimes appears on bulletins under the stands. Whether fast or wet-fast, the track's effects on horses with early speed may vary. At tracks that usually favor quick starts, the first "fast" day after a siege of rain and a period of drying out may produce a situation in which speed horses do less than expected during the early races but begin to recover their normal advantage later in the program.

Good. Wetter than wet-fast, but not as wet as muddy or sloppy. Often describes a track no longer fast but on the way to sloppy under prolonged, light rain. The description also appears during the drying out process from muddy to slow to good to fast. After heavy rain in New

York, it is taken for granted that "good" can mean bad. The track-drainage systems on that circuit are so extremely efficient and the racing cushions so full of sand that an amount of moisture warranting the description of "good" may indicate overloaded drains, a softened base, and a drying track that tires front-runners.

Slow. Wetter than good, but not as soft as muddy. In the old days, a slow track was a great help to come-from-behinders, and often produces that effect on modern strips.

Muddy. The water has soaked into the base beneath the cushion, with an effect that often confers advantage on Thoroughbreds with small, cup-like feet and tires those with larger, flatter ones. Contrary to the lore of the past, a muddy track is not always a haven for horses that lag behind in the early stages. A muddy track may be an advantage to a quick-starting animal able to kick wet soil in the faces of its rearward opponents. Here again, the handicapper's main recourse is observation of early-speed performances.

Sloppy. The track usually is covered with puddles but the base is hard. In most places, this helps the early speedsters.

Heavy. Seldom seen nowadays, this describes a track drying out after a lengthy spell of mud and means a stickiness likely to tire horses that run too fast too soon.

Having emphasized the need to watch the races closely before making assumptions about the running style likely to be favored by the texture of the strip, I shall now list tracks which, at least during the 1970's, were generally more favorable to early speed when wet than when dry and fast:

Albuquerque, Aqueduct, Assiniboia Downs, Atokad Park, Bay Meadows, Belmont Park, Bowie, Calder, Detroit, Ellis Park, Fair Grounds, Finger Lakes, Florida Downs, Fonner Park, Fort Erie, Greenwood, Hazel Park, Hialeah, Keeneland, La Mesa, Penn National, Pimlico, Portland Meadows, Salem Park, Saratoga, Sportsman's Park, Suffolk Downs, Thistledown, Woodbine.

Those that often produced the opposite effect, tending to slow front-runners when wet, were Ak-Sar-Ben, Beulah Park, Cahokia Downs, Charles Town, Delaware Park, Great Barrington, Jefferson Downs, Latonia, and Monmouth Park.

As to post position, it is necessary to remember that a racing strip drains from its raised crown near the center of the track to lower territory along the fences. The crown may be dry and firm while the path along the inside rail is still gummy with mud. Comes freezing weather and the wet loam on the inside may become a rock-hard highway, a winning advantage to horses with early speed. Here again, careful reading of results charts and close heed to changes in the weather combine with observation of a few races to equip the handicapper for the day's play.

TRAINERS. If one could name the hundred most expert Thoroughbred horsemen and women in North America, the list would include at least 90 who have not made the grade as trainers. Successful management of a racing stable requires no little luck plus assorted talents more various than those of horsemanship. The primary need is ability to form and maintain mutually respectful relations with stable OWNERS who, as footers of the bills, often express wishes in tones of command without necessarily knowing one end of a horse from the other. Another imperative is intelligent recruitment and supervision of dependable barn personnel, a large order in a field notorious for low pay, long hours, and unenviable working conditions. Still another need, as important as the others, is ability to superintend the preparation of Thoroughbreds for entry in races that they can win. Some trainers fall short in the preparation department. Others enter fit horses in the wrong races. Trainers able to handle both responsibilities cannot rest there. With the CLAIMING horses that compose most stables, they need to be immensely resourceful about avoiding the loss of improving animals to other outfits, while trying to get rid of depleted horses and, of course, swooping into the claim box to capture good additions to their own strings.

Some trainers are consummate professionals who function effectively with Thoroughbreds of all kinds. They can school yearlings, oversee their physical development and, barring unavoidable accident, bring them to the races ready to run. When relations with the owner permit, they can coddle an unsound AL-LOWANCE or STAKES runner, spacing its starts at the lengthy intervals needed to keep it afloat. Having won more money with it than would have been possible with less perceptive management, they know enough to turn it out for the winter before overexertion can terminate its career. Their hallmarks are patience and the aforementioned ability to find and hold the kinds of sponsors and stable help with whom patience can be practiced. A majority of trainers are less experienced or less gifted. They are best described as administrators who do their best work with animals developed by others. Many, including some with impressive records, leave the preparation of horses entirely to assistants. They concentrate on the care and cultivation of owners, shrewd sale and purchase of livestock and, with advice from a stable agent or other trusted colleague, entry of horses in the right races.

From the viewpoint of a handicapper concerned mainly with transactions at the mutuel windows, the best trainers are those who, regardless of personal abilities, manage to win at least 15 percent of their attempts. Given a choice between two CONTENDERS, one from a barn with a good winning percentage and the other from an outfit whose horses usually come up short, successful handicappers favor the one saddled by the successful trainer and are right much more often than wrong. With that in mind, it pays to carry handicapping research beyond the published lists of leading trainers. Smaller operators may not enter many races and therefore may not win often enough to qualify for the list, yet may win consistently. Some handicappers press even farther than that, attempting to ferret out the individual pattern of past performances and/or WORKOUTS that identify a trainer's way of preparing for a win at a price. That kind of study is especially useful when it reveals the reluctance of some stables to try with first-time starters and the propensity of others to win such races; or the tendency of some to win with newly claimed animals while others seem to postpone all-out effort until the horse runs at a lower claiming price than was paid for it; or how some barns win mainly with top JOCKEYS, losing with others; or the frequency with which certain barns win on the first or second attempt with horses that have been freshened for months; or the curious inability of some trainers to win with FAVORITES. To the degree that knowledge of that kind is based on meaningful statistics and current behavior, it strengthens the handicapping arsenal. The dangers, of course, are the human tendency to confuse fleeting impressions with statistical facts and, in this game, to substitute peripheral ANGLES for the FUNDAMENTALS of handicapping. Early in the 1970's, prominent enthusiasts of trainer patterns were advising their followers that Lazaro Barrera was unable to leg up sprinters for competition in ROUTES. This judgment could not possibly have derived from substantial knowledge of New York and California racing, in which Barrera had

long since established himself as a fully competent horseman subject, like all others, to the ups and downs of changing circumstances. In 1976, Barrera flustered his detractors by winning the Kentucky Derby and Belmont Stakes with Bold Forbes, a sprinter dyed in wool. I mention this not to inflict embarrassment but to emphasize that trainers, like horses, are best evaluated in terms of the conditions that prevail at the time. A trainer on a hot streak is a hot trainer. A trainer who led the standings at Saratoga will be a candidate for such leadership again when gifted with the horses to do it. In the meantime, handicappers are best situated when they concentrate on comparative analysis of Thoroughbred past performances, supplemented with careful consideration of prevailing conditions likely to influence EARLY SPEED and POST POSITION. At that point, knowledge of current trainer and jockey statistics comes into play, along with whatever actual knowledge about the present capacities of those human beings may seem relevant.

TRIFECTAS. In this form of exotic betting, the horseplayer tries to pick the first three horses in their exact order of finish. In New York, the proposition is known as the triple. In a few other places, it is a trizacta. It is a highly popular gamble because winning tickets sometimes pay tens of thousands of dollars. From time to time, jockeys have been accused of rigging this kind of race. Certain statistics suggest that the actual FIXES far outnumber the accusations. As everyone should know, FAVOR-ITES normally win about 32 percent of races. The percentage remains quite steady regardless of the CLASS of race. A corollary statistic establishes that favorites finish first or second about 60 percent of the time, and first, second, or third about 70 percent of the time.

During the months of October and November 1976, a study of all results at Aqueduct, Belmont Park, Keystone, Monmouth Park, Bowie, Pimlico, Laurel, and Calder—the major tracks covered in my edition of *Daily Racing Form*—produced melancholy statistics. In 1,783 DAILY DOUBLE and EXACTA races and races that involved no MULTI-PLE BETTING of any kind, favorites won 597 times for a respectable 33 percent. Of the 242 trifecta races on the same programs, only 71 went to favorites—29.3 percent. Mathematicians will note that favorites were almost 14 percent more successful in non-trifecta races, a large difference.

Favorites finished first or second 59.3 percent of the time in races without multiple betting and did not do quite that well in exacta races: 55.3 percent. But in trifectas, they ran second or better only 46.7 percent of the time, a miserably low average. Still worse, they ran as close as third only 59 percent of the time, as compared with a perfectly normal 69.7 percent in races without multiple betting. Keen readers who would prefer comparison of trifecta results with non-multiple-betting races involving fields of eight horses or more (trifectas almost always field a minimum of eight horses),

will find little consolation: The favorites finished first, second, or third in an acceptable 68 percent of more crowded races that lacked multiple betting, as compared with the wretched 59 percent in trifectas.

Without belaboring the point, it should be pointed out that the most effective rigging of a high-payoff trifecta requires that the favorite finish fourth or worse. The poor performances of trifecta favorites resist explanation of any other kind. Assuming that the two-month 1976 statistics hold true over a longer period, could bettors make money by eliminating favorites from their trifecta transactions and cashing in on many of the 41 percent of races in which favorites run out of the money? I doubt it. Purchase of multiple combination tickets involving every possible order of finish among the five or six likeliest non-favorites might result in a good winning average, but the mutuel prices are simply not high enough for profits. The reason for this is that take and breakage on trifectas exceed 25 percent—a prohibitive bite. I know bettors who have cashed numerous trifecta tickets, including some that fetched thousands of dollars. But none of these punters has actually made more on winning trifecta tickets than has been spent on losing ones. I doubt that it can be done.

TURF & SPORT DIGEST. Founded in 1924, this nationally circulated monthly magazine has undergone numerous changes under its several publishers but, as of 1977, was producing lively and informative material for racing fans, including handicappers. In bygone years, it had been America's foremost publisher and analyzer of superior SELECTION SYSTEMS, some of which appeared with confirmatory lists of winners and losers representing tests of as long as a year. Nowadays, after many vicissitudes, the magazine once again features good writing about matters of interest to fans, including occasional backstage views of the sport and, to help handicappers, discussions of the unique properties of individual racing strips. Published at 511 Oakland Ave., Baltimore, Maryland 21212.

TURF RACING. Some horses do well on the dirt tracks over which most North American races are run. Others prefer the grass of the infield turf courses that have become busier and more numerous during the latter half of the twentieth century. Not many horses are equally comfortable on both kinds of FOOTING. Some horsefolk and handicappers find that horses with large, flat, low-heeled feet usually prefer grass. Others maintain that nobody knows how a horse will perform on that surface until it has been given its chance. Still others see grass talent as largely a question of BREEDING. All three schools of thought are right, but none is right in all cases. As Dr. William L. Quirin demonstrates in his *Winning at the Races: Computer Discoveries in Thoroughbred Handicapping*

(William Morrow & Company, New York), certain sire lines have produced many generations of superior turf runners. For example, a horse with Prince Rose blood is a bright prospect in its first start on grass, especially if nothing else in the field has demonstrated a liking for the stuff. In turf races for more experienced runners, the likeliest prospects are those that have established winning consistency on that footing, seem to be in FORM, and are at no disadvantage in CLASS, POST POSITION, JOCKEY, and WEIGHTS.

Handicappers seriously interested in the bloodlines of first- or second-time starters on the turf are liable to frustration when an animal of unfamiliar parentage runs in at a whopping price. To avoid such surprises and cash in on some of them, players on comfortable budgets should consider purchasing *Sires and Dams of Stakes Winners*, published expensively every few years by the Thoroughbred Owners and Breeders Association and available from THE BLOOD-HORSE, Box 4038, Lexington, Kentucky 40504. This large directory lists every stakes winner of the preceding half-century under the names of its sire and dam. A little digging in the book and in more recent supplements published by *The Blood-Horse* often reveals the high-class turf breeding of the sire, dam, or broodmare sire of a newcomer to grass. Needless to say, one must begin the digging with firm knowledge of the bloodlines associated with grass-running ability.

WASHINGTON. One of the most intelligently managed, and therefore one of the more enjoyable tracks in America is Longacres, a one-miler conveniently located near Seattle and the Seattle-Tacoma airport. The horses are no great shakes, running for claiming and allowance purses at the Suffolk Downs or Louisiana Downs level, but customer relations are first-class. Cordial service, reasonable prices, actual handicapping classes, an emphasis on straight rather than MULTIPLE BETTING, and excellent television-monitor and public-address communications demonstrate genuine respect for racing and its clientele. The backbone of the usual 100-day meeting is Washington's energetic STATE-BRED program, which already has turned up some fair Thoroughbreds and promises to upgrade the local sport in due course. Tourists lacking necessary knowledge of the state's top stallions, broodmares, and breeders can obtain that information at the handicapping seminars and cash some nice bets. The racing strip sometimes is world-record fast but varies considerably from day to day. In general, it offers the best horse a decent opportunity to win, even if short of extreme EARLY SPEED. Inner post positions usually are best, although the variations in track texture suggest cautious observation of the first couple of races before taking large risks. Two lesser Washington tracks are Playfair, a five-eighths-miler in Spokane, and Yakima Meadows, a one-miler at Yakima.

WEIGHTS. In the middle of the last century, the most authoritative figure in British Thoroughbred racing was Admiral John Francis Rous, a flinty individual devoted to the integrity of the sport. In 1850, he produced a scale of standard weight assignments intended to equalize competition among horses of different AGE or sex. This was not the first attempt of its kind. Horsemen had known for centuries that runners tired more severely under high weights and that the effect increased in ratio to the distance of the race. They knew also that younger horses could not be expected to compete successfully at equal weights with mature ones of equal CLASS, and that females suffered similar disadvantages against males. The signal contribution of Rous was a scale that changed with the calendar. As the year proceeded and three- and four-year-olds grew in size, strength, and stamina, the Rous scale gradually reduced the weight concessions granted them during earlier months. After much tinkering by the admiral and others, the new scale was officially adopted by the British Jockey Club in 1878. The United States version, which appears in this volume's RULES OF RACING, has been changed frequently, most recently in 1966. It serves the sport well, although some suspect that it may impose unfairly high weights on four-year-olds racing against older animals early in the year, and probably is overindulgent to three-year-olds in weight-for-age STAKES during the fall.

Championships are settled in competition under scale weights at taxing distances. In 1972, Secretariat became the champion two-year-old by destroying the best colts of that age at distances up to a mile and one-sixteenth. He carried 122 pounds on each occasion, and

so did his opponents. In 1973, he won the three-year-old championship by winning the Triple Crown—the Kentucky Derby (one mile and a quarter), Preakness Stakes (one mile and three-sixteenths), and Belmont Stakes (one mile and a half)—under 126 pounds, the same weight that burdened the animals he defeated. Before retiring to stud, he capped his career by defeating older horses in races at scale weights and also won the Marlboro Cup Handicap while giving his elders what is known as "weight on the scale." That is, scale weight for three-year-olds at one mile and an eighth in September was 121 pounds, and for older horses 126. Secretariat carried 124 pounds—three pounds over scale, but the older Riva Ridge ran second under 127, only one over scale. The third horse, Cougar II, ran at scale weight of 126. The ability to give good horses weight on the scale and beat them is accepted as a hallmark of greatness. Thus, horsemen hailed Forego's 1976 Marlboro Cup victory as one of the outstanding performances of all time. On that day, he carried 137 pounds for a mile and a quarter, defeating the respectable three-year-old Honest Pleasure, weighted at 119. Scale weights were 126 pounds for Forego and 121 for the younger horse, a difference of only five pounds. Forego therefore gave Honest Pleasure 13 pounds on the scale.

Many times before and after that historic victory, Forego lost HANDICAP RACES that he could have won at scale weights. On days when the old warrior was in good FORM and liked the FOOT-

ING, the horses that defeated him were able to do so only because of the advantageous weight assignments. Clearly, if the central purpose of racing were to identify and celebrate the best horses of the year, all major races would be contested at scale weights. Hardly anyone would attend, because the best horse would win race after race at miserably low odds. Betting interest would be inadequate to finance the sport. Accordingly, aside from the most prominent events for two- and three-year-olds, scale-weight stakes are few and far between. To generate the popular confusion that produces attractive odds and long lines at mutuel windows, most races—including the CLAIMING RACES that outnumber all other kinds—are run under ALLOWANCE or handicap conditions. The belief that "weight brings them all together" runs deep in the minds of horsemen and racegoers. That high weight sometimes defeats the best horse is evident enough in the history of Forego and other handicap stars. But few horses are called upon to face such challenges, carrying more than 130 pounds at long distances against the best competition available on the continent. In day-in-day-out racing, weight seldom bulks large enough to negate the more essential factors of DISTANCE, FORM, and CLASS.

Those factors are by no means obliterated in rich handicaps. During 1976, of 47 major handicaps in which the highest assigned weight (in terms of the standard age scale) was carried by not more than two horses, animals so burdened won 22 races—or 47 percent. Thus, the effort to "bring them all together" heightens the possibility of closer finishes, but does not always stop the best horse. Every year, high-weighted horses win a large enough percentage of the nation's richest handicaps to put money in the pocket of anybody far-flung enough to be able to bet on them all. The best horse is hard to beat. To enlarge the chance that it will not be beaten, OWNERS and their TRAINERS traditionally avoid handicaps in which their own horses are assigned forbiddingly heavy weights. For every Forego whose management sportingly accepted challenges like 137 pounds, one could name hundreds of champions and near-champions who shipped elsewhere when asked to carry more than 126.

At races below stakes class, weights occasionally become a handicapping concern:

1. Regardless of distance, horses vary in their ability to carry weight. Each has a limit beyond which it does not get there in time unless dropped in class or shortened in distance. The PAST-PERFORMANCE TABLES often reveal that some quick-starting filly never seems to hold her speed to the wire when carrying more than 116 pounds. Or that some other horse has not yet been asked to bear more than 120 but has won authoritatively under that weight and, at today's distance, should be able to handle the 122-pound assignment.

2. Most handicappers regard 120 pounds as the threshold of trouble at all distances. After proper comparison of

275

CONTENDERS on other grounds, they usually are reluctant to select an animal at 120 or more that has not been showing plenty of energy at 117 or 118. Wariness increases as distances stretch beyond six furlongs. At a mile or longer, the prevailing tendency when evaluating two otherwise closely matched contenders is to avoid the one entered at a new high weight of 120 or more if the other is in with four or five pounds less and, furthermore, has already run well under such poundage.

3. Weight in the 120-pound range becomes a greater detriment when the track is gummy and other contenders are not heavily weighted.

4. At a mile or beyond, and to a lesser extent in sprints involving closely matched animals, weight shifts may tip the balance. If one horse beat the other by a nose last week but was carrying four pounds less than the loser, and if the weight advantage no longer exists today, last week's finish should be reversed. Racing secretaries and other professionals generally regard four pounds of weight as equivalent to a length at sprint distances. Three pounds are worth the same at a mile. Two pounds are a length at a mile and a furlong, and one pound is a length at a mile and a quarter. Some depart from that ancient formula and do quite well with one or two pounds per length at a mile or longer.

5. Weights almost never are a factor in two-year-old races at less than six furlongs.

6. To keep horses from breaking down under heavy weights, imposts are scaled as low as possible. But jockeys are larger than ever. At some tracks it is not unusual for the public address announcer to name four or five horses with overweight riders in a single race. In bygone years, the presence of a rider heavier than necessary was a sign that the barn expected little and had not exerted itself to find someone who could make the assigned 104. Nowadays, overweights are routine. Unless the horse figures to be neck-and-neck with another contender in a stretch run so close that a pound or two might matter, overweights can be ignored.

And so, despite all the foregoing detail, can weights be ignored in most other situations. When an animal handicaps as best and is not apparently overburdened, it can be bet without a lot of flyspecking about poundage. In that spirit, I cite the research of Frederick S. Davis, who found that if weight were the only handicapping criterion, the best bet in any race would be the animal with the highest impost. Logically, race conditions are written to place the heaviest burden on the best horses. It may not help them win, but it does not defeat them frequently enough to neutralize their superiority.

The subject of weights should include consideration of the horse's own weight, a statistic of much greater importance than the 115 pounds on the animal's back. As any veterinarian or horseman can attest, loss of weight associated with appetite dulled by AILMENT, INJURY, or overexertion is often the first unavoidable sign of distress. The opposite condition, in which gluttony or inactivity produces fat, is equally undesirable for racing purposes. Hence, when all due allowances are made for the normal growth of a young runner, it can be seen that each horse, like every human athlete, has its optimum competitive weight. Published as part of the standard handicapping information in Japan and Chile, current body weights are a powerful assistance to careful handicappers in those places.

WEST VIRGINIA. Charles Town, Shenandoah Downs, and Waterford Park each offer year-round night racing with glassed-in protection from the elements. Charles Town (a 6-furlong bull ring) and Shenandoah (a 5-furlong) are next-door neighbors which share racing dates about 30 miles from Dulles Airport. When last sampled, their food and service were considerably superior to the begrudged offerings at some of the more celebrated tracks in the East. The short racing strips are havens for horses with EARLY SPEED and inside posts. The bread-and-butter purses rank with those of minor tracks like Florida Downs, Fonner Park, and Turf Paradise. Waterford Park, accessible from Pittsburgh; Youngstown, Ohio; and Wheeling, West Virginia is about a mile in circumference, with a tight clubhouse turn, a more gradual turn for home, and a long enough run to the wire to give come-from-behind horses a fighting chance. Nevertheless, early speed is usually best. The quality of the horseflesh is below

that of Charles Town and Shenandoah, ranking with Atokad Park, Evangeline Downs, Pocono Downs—not quite as good as Finger Lakes.

WORKOUTS. The frequency, length, times, and the degrees of effort expended in workouts are crucially important to the FORM of any horse able to tolerate training. For that reason, wherever dependable workout information may be available, it deserves the handicapper's keenest attention. Unfortunately, the competence of CLOCKERS is as variable as the state regulations governing (a) their work, (b) the responsibility of TRAINERS to exercise accurately identified horses in public view, and (c) the veracity of the workout information transmitted to the racing press. As of 1977, workout rules in CALIFORNIA were probably best of a bad lot, although many stables in that state continued to outsmart clockers and bettors in the traditional effort to put something over. At the minimum, no previously unraced horse should be eligible to race until it either has competed in a training race at the track or has worked out there at least twice. The facts about such training races and workouts should be part of the animal's record in *Daily Racing Form*. Previously raced SHIPPERS or horses that have been away from the wars for a month or longer should be barred from competition unless they have worked out publicly at some track during that time. Lack of workouts might be excused for medical reasons, which would then be published in the *Form*'s entry lists or PAST-PERFORMANCE TABLES. A stable that preferred to train its horses at a private farm would not be exempt from these requirements. All information in the *Form*'s daily reports of such activity would include not only the distance and time of each workout, but the weights carried, the horse's distance from the rail on turns, and, for longer workouts, the quarter-mile and half-mile times. Further to prevent the secrecy in which betting stables specialize, and to discourage commercial arrangements between such stables and clockers, prevailing ground rules should be amended to make the trainer (rather than the clocker) responsible for accurate identification of an exercising horse. Assuming that any of these reforms could be enacted, which is not immediately foreseeable, they would impose great burdens on STEWARDS and other supervisory personnel. That would be a small price to pay for improved communications between the sport and its audience.

As matters stand, a handicapper's attitude toward workout information depends on the incidence of horses whose *Form* records show no workouts and no races in three or more weeks. To suppose that none of these animals has exercised is a mistake. But no outsider can tell which has worked and which has been unable. In circumstances of that kind, workouts cease to be a crucial factor in handicapping, although it is always nice to see that the horse with the best racing record has stretched itself on the track at intervals of from four to eight days since its last start. And a blow-out of three furlongs during the week or ten days since the latest good race is a positive indicator of form.

Where information is more copious and few recently unraced Thoroughbreds go postward without publicly noted works, the *Form*'s daily workout tabs (a separate column of distances, times, and occasional commentary) become seriously useful. Many handicappers clip and file the reports to ascertain, for example, whether a lightly regarded MAIDEN busted the clocker's stopwatches six weeks ago but lately has been dawdling to produce unimpressive times in the few recent works published beneath its name in the past-performance table. A file of the work tabs may also show whether some cheap claiming animal's normally slow work was actually within a tick or two of that morning's fastest effort at the distance. To understand the relevance of these tidbits, it is necessary to understand that competent trainers are able to prepare Thoroughbreds for winning efforts in SPRINTS and, in special cases, even in ROUTES on workouts alone. The names of local trainers who qualify on that score soon become familiar to handicappers careful about remembering those that win with horses that have not raced in more than a month. With horses running four or five times a month in the general attempt to relieve the shortage of ambulatory livestock, a prevalent practice is to race them into winning shape, and out of it as well. But better barns continue to win with absentees. Where workout information is offered about a horse of that kind, it can be quite illuminating. And where such animals win without published workouts after doing all their training at somebody's farm, the handicapper learns to respect the outfit's chances when it tries a similar maneuver at a later date.

Here are the abbreviations used in *Form* workout reports:

b. For "breezing," which means something faster than a common gallop but done on the horse's own steam under restraint by the exercise rider.

h. "Handily" means mild urging in which the rider's knuckles roll on the horse's neck in the scrubbing motion of a hand ride. A three-furlong workout of .35h is one second faster but no more impressive than an easier jaunt of .36b. At six or seven furlongs, **b** is worth about one and two-fifths seconds more than **h,** and the value increases to as much as three seconds at a mile or beyond.

g.This indication of a workout from the STARTING GATE means that the horse needs to become more comfortably alert there. The symbol is worth a full second of time. That makes .36bg worth .34h. If a workout does not begin from the gate, it begins with a running start, when the horse reaches one of the track's distance-marking poles.

d. For "driving," which usually includes whipping, and is almost never seen in workouts.

(d) For "dogs up," meaning that rubber traffic cones prevented the horse from running close to the rail, and that it traveled farther than it would have otherwise. The dogs protect the strip along the rail during bad weather. A workout of .36bg (d) is therefore worth at least .33h.

• The bullet appears in the past-performance table's workout line when the particular work was the track's fastest of the day at the distance.

tr.t. This signifies that the workout took place on the training track, which invariably is deeper and slower than the main track. At Belmont Park, for example, tr.t. .49h often is at least as impressive as .48b on the main strip.

The official condition of the track during the morning workout period is also supplied by means of the usual f (fast), g (good), sly (sloppy), my (muddy), sl (slow), and hy (heavy). And when the workout distance and time are preceded by "T" for turf course, the handicapper understands that a serious effort is being made to prepare the animal for grass. During periods of bad weather, however, few turf courses are used for workouts or even for racing.

Additional abbreviations not yet used in workout reports might nevertheless contribute to the well-being of horsemen and handicappers. For examples:

45. Meaning that the horse carried 145 pounds of exercise rider and tack. Thus, **52** would mean 152.

5w. The horse ran five widths—or 15 feet—from the rail while rounding the turn. This means that it ran about four extra lengths, taking an extra three- or four-fifths second to finish. Naturally, **2w** would mean two widths and **lw** that the horse hugged the rail. A horse running along the rail loses no ground and no time.

s. For "sweating" or "washy," meaning a state of nerves attributable to track shyness or impaired health.

f. For "fractious," which is frightened or rebellious reluctance to participate, an unpromising sign.

Times. Because workout times are published without elaboration, concealing facts that might give them greater meaning, and because modern trainers increasingly avoid subjecting cheaper horses to stern time trials that might leave them empty on race day, the frequency and length of workouts are usually more significant. Long workouts are essential for better horses preparing to run at a mile or beyond. For these, the four-furlong work is a mere blow out. Among sprinters, especially good, young ones stretching out to six or seven furlongs, a workout at the new distance or longer is a positive indicator, especially if negotiated in something like racing time. Although rules for recognition of superior workout times are abundantly available, none is as effective as personal knowledge of the local track or training strip, and the times reasonably to be expected of various grades of runners. To embrace the usual 12-seconds-per-furlong standard as indicative of respectable morning times is warranted in some places, but is not as useful as study of the daily tabs to see what the fastest times were, what kinds of horses ran them, and whether some lesser animals ran almost as quickly in efforts that might be more impressive than could be divined from the raw times. Beyond reserved alertness to workout time and its meaning, the handicapper is best situated when vigilant about the frequency and distances of works, preparing to like a sprinter that has been on the track four times in the past three weeks, even if the works were all at three or four furlongs. If it is the best sprinter in the race, the frequent works are substantial assurance of readiness to prove it. If a race or two substitutes for works, so much the better. And if no works appear, but nothing is known about the habits of the trainer in that regard, the safest thing to do is pass the race.

GLOSSARY

ACEY DEUCEY—Riding style with right stirrup higher than left for better balance on turns.

ACROSS THE BOARD—Combination bet on a horse to win, place, and show.

ACTION—Horse's manner of running, "way of going"; betting activity craved by gamblers.

ADDED MONEY—Contribution by track to stakes purse otherwise composed of nomination and starting fees paid by owners.

AGED—Of a horse aged seven or older.

AIRING—A workout; a race mainly for conditioning purposes.

ALL-OUT—Maximum effort.

ALSO ELIGIBLE—Horses entered in a race but excluded unless others are scratched.

ALSO RAN—Horse that finishes out of the money.

ALTER—To castrate, geld.

ANKLE BOOT—Leather or rubber protection for fetlock.

ANKLE CUTTER—Horse that cuts fetlock with opposite hoof while running.

APPRENTICE—An inexperienced rider granted weight allowances.

APPRENTICE ALLOWANCE—Weight reduction permitted horses ridden by apprentices in races other than stakes and handicaps.

ARM—Foreleg from elbow to knee; forearm.

ARMCHAIR RIDE—Horse wins easily without rider's urging.

BABY—Two-year-old during first quarter of year.

BABY RACE—Dash of four furlongs or less for green two-year-olds.

BACK—To bet on a horse.

BACK AT THE KNEE—Defective conformation of foreleg bent backward at knee.

BACKSTRETCH—Straight part of track opposite homestretch; stable area.

BACK UP—Slow down relative to others in race.

BAD ACTOR—Fractious horse.

BAD DOER—Horse that eats poorly, indicating illness, discomfort, exhaustion, fear, or loneliness.

BADGER—Horse purchased to obtain track privileges for owner; "badge horse."

BALD—Of a horse with a white face.

BALL—Pill or physic.

BANGTAIL—Tail folded and bound when track is muddy; slang for horse.

BAR PLATE—Horseshoe with rear bar to bolster weak hoof.

BARREL—Horse's torso.

BARRIER—Starting gate.

BASEBALL—In multiple betting, to buy tickets coupling one horse with all the others; "wheeling."

BAT—Writers' (but not jockeys') synonym for whip.

BAY—Brown horse with black mane and tail.

BEAR IN—Race toward rail despite rider's efforts to maintain straight course.

BEAR OUT—Race diagonally away from rail instead of straight.

BEEF—Rider's complaint to stewards about foul tactics of another rider.

BELL—Signal at end of betting period and/or start of race.

BEND—A turn of the track.

BIG APPLE—A major race circuit, especially New York.

BILL DALY—Rider who tries for early lead is "on the Bill Daly," after old-time trainer who favored the tactic.

BLANKET FINISH—Close finish.

BLAZE—Large white patch on horse's face.

BLIND SWITCH—Racing predicament in pocket behind and inside horses.

BLISTER—Treatment of leg with heat or chemical irritant to raise blister that becomes tough scar tissue.

BLOCK HEEL—Shoe with raised heel for horse that tends to scrape heels on track.

BLOODSTOCK AGENT—Professional who buys and sells Thoroughbreds and makes breeding arrangements.

BLOOD TEST—Pre- or post-race analysis of horse's blood in search of illegal drugs.

BLOW OUT—Short workout on the morning of or a day or two before race.

BLUE HEN—Outstanding race mare.

BLUE ROAN—Horse whose black, white, and yellow hairs give its coat a bluish-gray appearance.

BOAT RACE—Fixed race.

BOBBLE—Stumble.

BOG SPAVIN—Puffy swelling on inside of hock.

BOLD EYE—Clear, prominent eye said to signify equine courage.

BOLD FRONT—Long, well-muscled neck.

BOLT—Run off in wrong direction, as when horse heads toward grandstands after completing final turn in race.

BONE SPAVIN—Bony swelling below hock.

BOOK—Jockey's riding schedule; bookmaker's tally of bets and odds; accept a bet as if a bookmaker.

BOOT—Horse's rubber or leather anklet; kick horse when riding.

BOOTS AND SADDLES—Bugle call announcing arrival of horses on track for post parade.

BOTTOM—Thoroughbred stamina; subsurface of racing strip; among starters in race, horse listed last on program.

BOTTOM LINE—Female side of pedigree.

BOW—Racing debut; ruptured flexor-tendon sheath, when tendon protrudes like bow behind cannon bone of foreleg; bowed tendon.

BOX—In exacta or quinella, combination of bets involving three or more horses.

BOY—Male jockey.

BRACE—Horse liniment.

BRACKETS—Maiden victory. When official result charts identified each horse's previous race by index number, a number in brackets meant that horse had won the race.

BREAK—Start of race; teaching young horse to accept saddle, bridle, and rider.

BREAKAGE—Money subtracted from proper mutuel payoffs to leave rounded amounts paid to holders of winning tickets.

BREAK DOWN—Become unable to run because of injury.

BREAK IN THE AIR—Leap upward at start instead of racing forward.

BREAK MAIDEN—Horse or rider wins for the first time.

BREATHER—Rider eases horse slightly to relax it before driving toward finish.

BREEZE—Run easily without encouragement.

BRIDGE-JUMPER—Bettor who makes large show bets on short-priced favorites.

BRISKET—Horse's body between forelegs.

BRITTLE—Of fragile hooves difficult to shoe.

BROKEN KNEE—Skin lesion at knee.

BROKEN WIND—Breathing problems from broken-down, overtaxed lung tissues; "heaves."

BROODMARE—Female horse used for breeding.

BROODMARE DAM—Mare whose female offspring become broodmares.

BROODMARE SIRE—Sire of broodmare.

BROWN—Extremely dark bay, more black than brown.

BRUCE LOWE SYSTEM—Identification of Thoroughbred families by numbers assigned to the original female ancestors.

BRUSH—Horse scrapes fetlock with opposite shoe.

BUCKED SHIN—Painful inflammation from strain, standard in two-year-olds.

BUG RIDER—Apprentice jockey, usually identified by one or more asterisks in published race entries.

BUSHES—Minor-league racing.

BUY THE RACK—Bet on every possible daily double, exacta, quinella, trifecta, or other multiple wagering proposition.

CALK—Horseshoe cleat for better traction in mud or on turf.

CALL—Describe race to audience through public address system; each stage of race at which running positions are recorded for official charts; relate running positions (chart-calling) to person who records them (chart-taker).

CANKER—Foot infection that softens hoof.

CANNON—Principal foreleg bone between knee and ankle. Rear leg bone between hock and ankle.

CANTER—Slow gallop or lope.

CAPPED—Swollen, as of bumped elbow or hock.

CARD—Day's program of races.

CAR FIT—Extreme fright during shipment from one place to another.

CARRY THE TARGET—Run last from start to finish.

CAST—Of horse fallen and unable to rise; of shoe lost or "thrown."

CHALK HORSE—Betting favorite.

CHALK PLAYER—Bettor on favorites.

CHALLENGE—Approach and contend for the lead.

CHART—Result chart.

CHASE—Steeplechase.

CHESTNUT—Brown or tan horse with brown or tan tail and mane; horny growth ("night eye") on inside of horse's legs.

CHOPPY—Of abnormally short stride often signifying soreness.

CHUTE—Extension of stretch to permit straight run from starting gate to first turn.

CIRCUIT—Geographical group of tracks whose race meetings run in sequence.

CLAIM—Buy horse entered in claiming race.

CLAIM BOX—Depository for claims before race.

CLASSIC—Of the year's most important races for three-year-olds, especially Kentucky Derby, Preakness Stakes, and Belmont Stakes.

CLERK OF SCALES—Weighs riders and tack before and after race.

CLEVER—Of a responsive, nimble Thoroughbred.

CLIENT—Purchaser of betting information from tout.

CLIMB—Run with abnormally high action of forelegs.

CLOSE—Gain ground on leader in final stages; of final odds ("closed at 5–1").

CLOSE-COUPLED—Of a horse with a short back.

CLOSE FAST—Finish fast.

CLOTHES—Horse blanket.

CLUBHOUSE TURN—Turn of track nearest clubhouse; first turn of race that begins on homestretch.

COFFIN BONE—Main bone in foot.

COLD—Of horse unready to win because of poor condition or stable maneuvering.

COLD-BLOODED—Of a non-Thoroughbred.

COLT—Unaltered male aged four or less.

COMBINATION—Across-the-board betting ticket.

COME BACK TO—Slow down, probably from fatigue, allowing others to gain ground.

CONDITION—Thoroughbred fitness; train a horse.

CONDITION BOOK—Racing secretary's printed announcement of upcoming programs, including eligibility conditions, purses, weight allowances for each race.

CONNECTIONS—Owner, trainer, other humans involved with horses.

CONSOLATION DOUBLE—When horse is scratched from a daily-double race after betting begins, token payment made to bettors holding tickets coupling that horse with winner of the other race.

COOLER—Covering on horse when it cools out after race or exercise; horse deliberately restrained from running well.

CORN—Callus caused by irritating shoes.

CORONET—Area immediately above hoof; "crown of hoof."

COUPLED—Of horses running as a single betting interest ("entry") in the same race.

COVER—Of a stallion, act of mating with mare.

COW HOCKS—Hocks turned toward each other, like a cow's.

CRESTY—Of a thick-necked horse.

CRIBBER—Horse that gnaws the wood of its stall, swallowing abnormal amounts of air; "crib-biter"; "windsucker."

CROPPER—Fall down in a jump race.

CROUP—Top of hindquarters.

CROWD—Race too close to another horse, causing its rider to take up or change course.

CRYPTORCHID—Male horse with undescended testicle.

CUFF—Horse anklet; credit ("on the cuff").

CULL—Unwanted horse offered for sale.

CUP—A blinker of that shape.

CUP HORSE—Thoroughbred able to race well at long distances.

CUPPY—Of a racing strip that forms compact clods under hooves.

CURB—Sprained hock; a bit with extra strap or chain under horse's chin.

CUSHION—Surface of racing strip.

CUT DOWN—Of a horse injured when struck by shoe of another, or of its own.

DAM—Horse's mother.

DARK—Of a day or track without racing.

DARK HORSE—Underrated animal that wins or has good chance.

DARKEN FORM—Manipulate a horse so that its record conceals its true ability.

DASH—Sprint.

DEAD HEAT—When two horses reach finish wire simultaneously.

DEAD TRACK—A track with less than normal resilience.

DEAD WEIGHT—Lead slabs carried to increase weight on horse.

DECLARE—Scratch horse from race.

DEEP—Of a track with a deep, holding surface.

DERBY—Stakes race for better three-year-olds.

DESTROY—End the life of hopelessly ailing or injured horse.

DISQUALIFY—Officially lower horse's finishing position because it interfered with others during race, carried improper weight, or was drugged.

DISTAFF SIDE—Female ancestry.

DISTANCE OF GROUND—A route race.

DIVISION—Separation of one race into two, because of extra entries; branch of a stable that races concurrently at more than one track.

DO—Of a horse, to eat; good doer; bad doer.

DOGS—Rubber traffic cones placed near rail to prevent horses from kicking up muddy surface during workouts; cheap horses; quitters.

DOPE—Past-performance tables and other information published for handicappers; drugs.

DOSAGE—Breeding theory that attributes high racing quality to horses whose pedigrees contain patterned combinations of certain sire lines.

DRAW AWAY—Win drawing away; draw clear; draw out.

DRENCH—Give liquid medicine to horse.

DRIVE—Full exertion, usually under whipping.

DROP—Give birth to a foal.

DUN—Mousy, grayish brown to gold color, usually with black mane and tail.

DWELL—Of horse that leaves starting gate tardily.

EARLY FOOT—Early speed.

EASE—Spare horse dangerous exertion by slowing it.

EASILY—Of decisive victory without undue effort.

EASY RIDE—When jockey does not try to win.

EIGHTH—Furlong; 220 yards.

EIGHTH POLE—Colored post on inside rail one furlong before finish wire.

EMPTY—Of a horse without sufficient racing energy.

ENTIRE—Of an unaltered male horse.

EWE-NECKED—Of a horse with concave neck, likely to be clumsy.

EXCUSED—Of a horse scratched after official scratch time.

EXERCISE RIDER—Rider in workouts.

EXOTIC WAGERING—Formerly any multiple bet, now any bet requiring that three horses be combined, as in Trifecta.

EXPERIMENTAL FREE HANDICAP—A prominent racing secretary-handicapper's annual ratings of horses by weights, as if all of the particular age were entered in the same handicap race. The Jockey Club handicapper issues one each year.

EXTEND—Force horse to go all out.

FADE—Tire and drop out of contention.

FALSE START—When horse leaves starting gate prematurely.

FALTER—Tire badly.

FAMILY—Horses produced by mares belonging to a female bloodline.

FARRIER—Horseshoer.

FAST TRACK—Dry surface on which horses usually run fast; a track where running times are relatively fast.

FEATHER—Extremely light weight assigned a horse.

FETLOCK—Horse's ankle.

FIELD—The horses competing in a race; in pari-mutuel betting, when more than 12 betting interests are involved in a race, the two or more least highly regarded are grouped as a single betting entry, restoring betting interests to the maximum of 12.

FILLY—Female aged four or less.

FILM PATROL—Crew that records running of each race on television tape or film for review by stewards.

FIRE—Cauterize ailing tissue with hot electric needle or firing iron; produce high speed when needed.

FIT—Of a sharply conditioned horse.

FIVE-EIGHTHS POLE—Colored post on inside rail, five furlongs before finish wire.

FLAG—Small flag held overhead by official posted at actual starting point of race, a few yards from starting gate. When first horse reaches that point, official lowers flag, signaling the start.

FLAG DOWN—Wave at exercise rider to signal that horse is running too fast.

FLASH—Change of odds on tote board.

FLAT—Conventional dirt track, contrasted with steeplechase or turf course; of a horse out of form.

FLAT OUT—All-out exertion.

FLATTENS OUT—Of tired horse that stops trying.

FOAL—Newborn horse; of a mare, to give birth.

FOOT—Speed; soft tissue protected by hoof.

FOREARM—Horse's foreleg between elbow and knee.

FORKED—Of horse's conformation at junctures of forelegs and body.

FORM PLAYER—One who makes selections by handicapping.

FOUL—Infraction of racing rules serious enough to cause disqualification.

FRACTIONS—Clockings at quarter-mile intervals in races and workouts.

FREEMARTIN—Filly twin of a colt.

FRESHENER—Absence from racing to restore horse's energies.

FROG—Fleshy cushion on sole of horse's foot.

FRONT-RUNNER—Horse that prefers to run in front rather than come from behind.

FURLONG—One-eighth of a mile.

FUTURITY—Stakes race in which two-year-olds are entered months in advance, and sometimes before birth.

GAD—Rider's whip.

GAIT—Equine walk, trot, or gallop; action; "way of going."

GALLOP—Fastest gait; workout; easy race or workout.

GARRISON FINISH—Come from behind in the stretch, in manner of old-time rider, Snapper Garrison.

GASKIN—Hind leg from thigh to hock.

GATE—Starting gate; track's daily receipts from admission tickets; entrance to track.

GELDING—Castrated male horse.

GENEROUS—Of a cooperative horse.

GET—Stallion's offspring.

GETAWAY DAY—Last day of race meeting.

GET INTO—Of a rider, to whip horse.

GIMPY—Of a lame horse.

289

GIRTH—Saddle band.

GLIB—Of an especially resilient, fast racing strip.

GO—Of stable or horse, to start in a race; an effort to win.

GOING—Racing surface ("soft going").

GOING AWAY—Winning with an increasing lead.

GO LONG—Of horses racing in route; run long.

GOOD BONE—Impressive equine skeletal structure.

GOOD DOER—Enthusiastic eater.

GO ON—Of horses that run well at increasing distances.

GOOSE-RUMPED—High, sharply sloping hindquarters.

GO SHORT—Of horses running in sprints; run short.

GRAB—Strike foreleg with hind hoof.

GRAB THE BIT—Settle into full stride, pressing against bit.

GRADUATE—Break maiden.

GRANDDAM—Horse's grandmother.

GRANDSIRE—Horse's grandfather.

GRAY—Horse whose black and white hairs combine in a gray coat.

GREEN—Inexperienced.

GROUND—Distance gained or lost during race.

GROUNDED—Of jockey suspended for infractions.

GRUNTER—Horse that breathes noisily during exercise.

GUINEA—Stablehand, after British custom of giving winning groom a guinea.

GUMBO—Heavy mud.

GUN—Effort by jockey to produce burst of speed.

GYPSY—Itinerant horseman; "gyp."

HALF—Half-mile.

HALF BROTHER—Male from same dam but by different sire than another Thoroughbred.

HALF-MILE POLE—Colored pole on inside rail four furlongs from finish wire.

HALF SISTER—Female from same dam but by different sire than another Thoroughbred.

HALTER—Headgear including rope or strap with which horse is led; claim a horse.

HALTER MAN—Trainer who specializes in claims.

HAND—Four inches of equine height, measured from ground to top of withers.

HANDILY—Of relatively easy victory or workout under hand ride without much urging.

HANDLE—Track's receipts at mutuel windows for one race, a single program, or during a longer period.

HAND RIDE—Rider encourages speed by rolling hands rhythmically on horse's neck.

HANDY—Of a nimble horse.

HANGS—Of a horse that shows run on the turn for home or at the top of the stretch but lacks energy to improve position afterward.

HARDBOOT—Kentucky horseman, because of mud caked on old-timers' boots.

HAT TRICK—Of jockey or trainer who wins three races on one program.

HAVE ONE IN THE BOOT—When owner or trainer has bet for the rider, who knows it.

HAYBURNER—Horse that earns less than its feed bill; "oatburner."

HEADED—Beaten by a head, or about one-eighth length.

HEAD OF THE STRETCH—End of final turn; top of the stretch.

HEAT—A race.

HEAVY-FRONTED—Of horse with unusually wide chest, an undesired feature.

HEAVY-HEADED—Of horse that runs with lowered head or fights the reins or responds slowly to guidance.

HEAVY-TOPPED—Of horse whose body seems too large for its legs.

HEAVY TRACK—Racing strip of drying mud, often slow.

HEIGHT—Distance from ground to top of withers, measured in hands.

HERD—Alter direction to force change of direction by other horse or horses.

HERRING-GUTTED—Of horse with slender abdomen, sign of a bad doer.

HIND STICKER—Sharp cleat on outside edge of rear shoe, for traction.

HIP NUMBER—Identification number pasted on horse's hip at auction sale.

HOCK—Hind elbow joint between gaskin and cannon.

HOLE—Stall in starting gate; flaw in temperament or physique of horse.

HOLE CARD—Whatever mysterious problem prevents horse from winning; "I finally found his hole card."

HOMEBRED—Horse bred by its owner; horse foaled in state where it races.

HOMESTRETCH—Straight part of track from final turn to finish.

HONEST—Of a steady, dependable runner.

HOOD—Head covering with blinkers.

HOP—Illegal chemical stimulation of horse.

HORSE—Entire male Thoroughbred aged five or older; of a female, to be in heat.

HORSEMAN—Trainer or, by extension, anyone experienced in upkeep of horses.

HORSES FOR COURSES—Some horses run well at certain tracks, not at others.

HOT—Of a horse expected to win decisively; of a jockey or barn when winning frequently; of a horse overheated by exercise.

HOT-WALKER—Stablehand who walks horse while it cools out.

HURDLE RACE—A jump race over low obstacles.

ICE—Benumb horse's painful feet or legs by standing it in ice.

IMPOST—Weight carried by horse in race.

IN-AND-OUTER—Inconsistent horse.

INDEX—Date of horse's latest race, from era when results charts gave race-index numbers instead of actual dates.

INFIELD—Area within inner perimeter of track.

IN HAND—Of horse running under restraint.

IN LIGHT—Carrying light weight.

INQUIRY—Stewards' post-race investigation of possible infractions.

INSERT—Long nail protruding from shoe for traction.

INSIDE—Anything to horse's left during race or workout; post position or running position relatively close to rail.

INTERFERE—Strike leg with opposite foot; impede another horse during race.

IN THE MONEY—Technically, a finish good enough to earn part of the purse (which may mean a finish as far back as sixth in some races); in betting lingo, a finish in first three.

IN TOUGH—Of a horse racing against better horses.

IRONS—Stirrups.

JAIL—Of a claimed horse's first month in its new barn, when racing rules require it to run at a 25 percent higher claiming price or remain idle.

JAM—Traffic jam during race.

JOCKEY AGENT—Person who books rider's assignments for a percentage of rider's earnings.

JOG—Slow trotting gait.

JOINT—Battery or buzzer.

JOURNEYMAN—Full-fledged jockey.

JUMP—Obstacle over which steeplechasers race.

JUMPER—Horse that runs in steeplechase or hurdle races.

JUMP UP—Of a horse, to win unexpectedly.

JUVENILE—Two-year-old horse.

KEY HORSE—In multiple betting, horse included in combinations because bettor regards it as key to the race.

KIND—Of a tractable horse; Thoroughbred class ("back with its own kind")

KISS THE EIGHTH POLE—Of a horse that finishes far behind.

KNEE SPAVIN—Bony growth behind knee.

LAMINITIS—Serious inflammation of foot.

LAY—Hold a running position deliberately ("I was laying fifth on the backstretch").

LEAD PAD—Saddle accessory in which weights are inserted to raise horse's impost to required level.

LEAKY ROOF CIRCUIT—Minor tracks.

LEATHER—A whip.

LEATHERS—Stirrup straps.

LEG LOCK—When rider hooks legs with another, illegally impeding other's horse.

LEG UP—Build horse's condition; jockey's riding assignment.

LENGTH—Between eight and nine feet.

LIGHT OVER THE KIDNEY—Of a slim-loined horse; wasp-waisted.

LINE—Male or female side of pedigree; morning line.

LOADED SHOULDER—Unusually thick shoulder associated with clumsy gait.

LOAFER—Lazy horse.

LOCK—A certainty.

LOOK FOR A HOLE IN THE FENCE—Of horse that behaves as if it would prefer not to race.

LOOK OF EAGLES—The proud appearance of some good horses, as if they knew their importance.

LOOSE-COUPLED—Of horse with a comparatively long back.

LOOSE HORSE—One that continues in race or workout after losing its rider.

LUG IN—Bear in sharply.

MACHINE—Jockey's illegal battery.

MACHINES—Pari-mutuel equipment and the wagering itself ("You can't buck those machines").

MAKE A RUN—Of a horse that tries to overtake the leader; "make a move"; "make a bid."

MARATHON—Race of more than ten furlongs.

MARE—Female horse aged five or older.

MARTINGALE—Straps from noseband or bit to girth, to keep horse's head down and prevent it from rearing.

MATCH RACE—A race between two horses.

MEANT—Of a horse whose barn will try to win the race; well-meant.

MEAT BALL—Cathartic pill.

MEET—Race meeting.

MIDDLE DISTANCE—Of races at one mile or longer, but less than a mile and a quarter.

MILE POLE—Colored post on infield rail, one mile from finish wire.

MINUS POOL—When so much money is bet on a horse that take and breakage leave insufficient money to pay holders of winning tickets the legal minimum of $2.10. Happens most often in show betting. Track must pay difference from its own funds.

MORNING GLORY—Horse that works impressively but races poorly.

MOVE—Increase speed; workout; bet ("big mover").

MOVE UP—Run in a race of higher class; gain ground.

MUCK OUT—Clean a horse's stall.

MUDDER—Horse that runs well in mud; mudlark ("He can mud").

MUDDY TRACK—Soft and wet.

MUTUEL POOL—Total amount bet to win, place, show, or on one of the multiple-betting propositions.

MUZZLE—Straps that close horse's mouth, preventing it from biting.

NAME—Enter horse in race.

NAVICULAR DISEASE—Crippling ulcer that corrodes navicular bone of foot. Sometimes fatal.

NEAR SIDE—Horse's left side.

NECK—About a quarter of a length.

NERVE—Remove a sensory nerve, eliminating pain but not its cause.

NICK—Nerve a horse; in breeding, a strategic combination of bloodlines.

NIGHTCAP—Last race on the day's program.

NOD—Official gesture permitting jockey to dismount after race.

NOM DE COURSE—Stable name.

NOSE—Smallest possible winning margin.

NUMBER BALL—Numbered pellet drawn from box or rolled from leather bottle to assign post positions, determine which of two or more claiming stables gets the horse, and which of two or more horses is stuck in race despite stable efforts to scratch.

NURSERY RACE—Baby race.

OAKS—Important stakes race for three-year-old fillies.

OATBURNER—Hayburner; a chronic loser.

OBJECTION—Jockey's complaint to stewards about possibly foul riding tactics of another.

ODDS BOARD—Odds display on infield board.

ODDS ON—Odds of less than even money.

OFF—Start of race; difference between track record and time of individual race; difference between speed of horse at distance and what that speed once was or should be ("He's off at least two lengths").

OFF SIDE—Right side of horse, where jockey dismounts.

OFF THE BOARD—Failure to finish in the first four; bet so lightly that odds exceed the 99-1 maximum displayable on odds board.

OFF THE PACE—Run behind the early leaders.

OFF THE TOP—Of deductions from mutuel pool before computation of odds and payoffs.

OFF TRACK—Racing strip other than fast; betting conducted away from the track.

ON EDGE—Sharply conditioned.

ON THE BIT—Of horse eagerly straining against the bit.

ON THE CHIN STRAP—Winning by a large margin.

ON THE GROUND—Of a suspended jockey.

ON THE NOSE—Of a bet that the horse will win.

ON THE RAIL—Running next to inside rail.

ON TOP—In the lead; picked to win.

ONE-RUN HORSE—A type that produces a single burst of speed, usually coming from behind in the homestretch.

OPEN RACE—In which eligibility conditions permit entry by any Thoroughbred of the stated claiming price or allowance category, regardless of sex, place of birth, or previous number of victories. Invariably a race of higher class than one more restricted.

OPTIONAL CLAIMER—A race for horses entered to be claimed but open also to horses that have run in the stated claiming-price range before but are not here entered to be claimed.

OSSELETS—Bony growths on ankle joint.

OUCHY—Sore.

OUT—Out of the money.

OUT OF—A horse is "out of" a dam and "by" a sire.

OUT OF THE MONEY—A loser that fails to earn any part of the purse; in betting, failure to finish third or better.

OUTRIDER—Mounted track employee who escorts horses and their lead ponies to starting gate, pursuing any that bolt away.

OUTSIDE—Away from inside rail; relative to a running horse, anything to its right.

OUTSIDER—Lightly regarded longshot.

OVER AT THE KNEE—Foreleg protrudes forward at the knee.

OVERLAND—Of the course traveled by a horse that races wide around a turn.

OVERLAY—Of horse whose odds exceed its probable chances of winning.

OVERNIGHT RACE—One for which entries close, depending on local rules, a day or two or three before the date of the race.

OVERNIGHTS—The next day's entries, issued in mimeographed form or published in the track program.

OVERREACH—A desirable walking gait in which the hind hoofprints are forward of those left by forefeet, suggesting a long, powerful racing action; when hind shoe strikes foreleg during race or workout.

OVERWEIGHT—Excess poundage carried because rider is too heavy.

PARLAY—Combination bet in which all proceeds of one bet are risked on another.

PASTEBOARD TRACK—Fast racing strip with thin top cushion.

PASTERN—Area between fetlock and coronet.

PEACOCKY—High-headed, nervous horse.

PERIODIC OPHTHALMIA—Periodic loss of vision; moonblindness.

PIGEYE—Small eye, regarded as sign of meanness.

PINCHED BACK—Crowded back during jam in race.

PINK—Uniformed Pinkerton guard at track.

PIPE OPENER—Blow out.

PLATER—Horseshoer, farrier; claiming horse, because owners formerly got silver plates for winning such races.

POCKET—When horse is surrounded

and unable to run freely until opening appears; switch.

POINTS—Features of Thoroughbred conformation; horse's lower legs ("Bay horses always have black points").

POLL—Top of horse's head.

PONY—Any non-racing horse used at a track; lead pony.

POOL—Total amount bet to win, place, show, or in multiple betting.

POST—Starting gate; post position.

POWDER—Light physical contact between racing horses.

PREFERRED—Of horses given priority for entry in a race, such as previous winners or state-bred horses.

PREPOTENT—Of a stallion whose descendants breed true, passing on the ancestor's desired characteristics to their own progeny.

PREP RACE—A comparatively minor race programmed so that nominees to a later stakes can prepare in competition; a race used by barn to sharpen a horse's form.

PROD—Illegal battery.

PRODUCE—Offspring of a broodmare.

PROP—Flat-footed refusal to go from one place to another, including refusal to break from starting gate or go over a jump.

PRUETT GATE—Widely used brand of starting gate.

PUBLIC STABLE—One operated by trainer willing to manage horses for more than one owner.

PULL—Restrain a horse to keep it from winning; stiff.

PULL IN THE WEIGHTS—An advantage in the weights.

PULL UP—Stop a running horse.

PUNTER—Bettor.

PUT DOWN—Destroy a horse.

QUARTER—Quarter-mile; two furlongs; side of hoof.

QUARTER CRACK—Separation of inner and outer hoof walls in quarter area.

QUARTER HORSE—Speedy breed containing Thoroughbred blood, raced at distances of about a quarter mile.

QUARTER POLE—Colored post on infield rail, two furlongs before finish wire.

QUINELLA—Multiple bet in which player tries to pick first two finishers, regardless of order; quiniela; quinela.

RACING BANDAGE—Bandage worn during race; running bandage.

RACING PLATE—Shoe worn for racing.

RACING SECRETARY—Track executive who designs its racing programs and assigns weights to horses in handicap races.

RACING SOUND—Of a horse able to race, though not free of physical problems.

RACK UP—Impede several other horses, forcing them all to break stride, fall, or merely slow down.

RAILBIRD—Racegoer; one who stands at track's outside rail for close observation.

RAIL RUNNER—Horse that prefers to race along inside rail.

RAISED BAR—Bar shoe used to prevent running down.

RANK—Fractious; "running rank"—refusing to be rated early in race.

RATE—Husband a runner's energies for maximum stamina in homestretch.

RECEIVING BARN—Where horses stabled at other tracks wait to go to the local paddock for saddling and racing.

RED BOARD—Practice among authors of selection systems who make selection rules fit previous race results instead of testing rules against future results.

RED ROAN—Horse whose red, yellow, and white hairs form a reddish-gray coat.

REFUSE—Of horse that fails to break or, in jump race, stops in front of a fence.

RIDDEN OUT—Of horse that wins under an energetic hand ride, without whipping.

RIDE SHORT—Ride with short stirrup straps.

RIDGLING—Partly castrated horse, or one with incompletely developed testicles; rigling; risling.

RIM—Shoe with long, horizontal cleat or grab on outer rim, helping horses with tendon problems.

RINGBONE—Disabling bony overgrowth above hoof, sometimes treated by nerving.

RINGER—Horse that races under another's name.

ROAN—Striking grayish or reddish color.

ROAR—Of noisy equine breathing similar to coughing.

ROGUE—Chronically fractious horse.

ROGUE'S BADGE—Blinkers.

ROMP—Easy race.

RUG—Heavy horse blanket.

Rule Off—Expel from racing and bar from admittance to track.

Run Down—Of a horse, scrape heels on track surface; "run down behind."

Run In—Win unexpectedly.

Runner—Messenger who places bets and collects winnings for occupants of private boxes; bookie's door-to-door representative; willing, fast horse.

Running Bandages—Leg wraps worn in races or workouts.

Run Out—Finish out of the money; bear out.

Run-out Bit—Bit with extra leverage on one side, to help rider keep straight course.

Run Wide—Race far from inside rail on turn, losing ground.

Saddlecloth—Fabric between saddle and horse.

Saliva Test—Chemical assay of horse's saliva, usually performed on in-money finishers and favorites, to see if any were drugged illegally.

Salute—When jockey greets stewards by raising whip after race, seeking permission to dismount.

Sand Crack—Vertical crack on hoof from coronet down.

Sanitary Ride—Jockey races wide to avoid flying mud or traffic; horse that does not try in race.

Savage—Of a horse that tries to bite another on track, at paddock, or around barn.

Save Ground—Traveling shortest possible distance, close to inside rail.

Scale of Weights—Officially prescribed weights for each age-sex-distance and time of year; "the scale."

Scale Weights—Weights carried in an official weight-for-age race.

Scenic Route—When horse loses ground by running far from rail on turn; overland.

School—Train horse in new skills, especially at starting gate, in paddock, over jumps, in traffic on track.

Score—Win a race or a bet.

Scratch Sheet—Daily publication printed after scratches, usually with graded handicaps, spot selections.

Season—Duration of year's racing at a track or on a circuit; female period of estrus or "heat."

Seat—Rider's posture on horse.

Second Dam—Horse's maternal grandmother.

Second Sire—Horse's paternal grandfather.

Selling Plater—Claiming racer.

Selling Race—Claimer; obsolete type of race in which winner was auctioned afterward.

Send—Enter horse in race; try to win with a horse.

Send Away—Open starting gate to begin race.

Send It In—Bet heavily.

Sesamoiditis—Bone inflammation above and behind fetlock.

Set Down—Suspend someone from racing; ask horse for speed in race or work.

Sex Allowance—Weight concession to females in race against males.

Shadow Roll—Sheepskin or cloth

cylinder across horse's nose, blocking view of ground and preventing it from shying at objects on ground.

SHAKE UP—Vigorous use of reins or whip to make horse run faster.

SHANK—Rope or strap attached to halter for leading horse by hand.

SHED ROW—Barn area; the backstretch community.

SHIPPING FEVER—Respiratory ailment associated with shipment from one climate to another.

SHOE BOARD—Track display describing race entrants' footgear.

SHOO-IN—Supposedly sure winner.

SHORT—Of horse that tires in stretch, needing more work; short of condition.

SHORT PRICE—Low odds.

SHOW WEAR—Fetlocks swollen by overwork.

SHUFFLE—Of active hand ride by jockey rolling hands and moving feet.

SHUFFLED BACK—Of horse crowded backward in race.

SHUT OFF—Cross in front of another horse, forcing it to take up or go around.

SICKLE HOCKS—Hocks that point away from each other.

SILKS—Rider's racing shirt.

SIRE—Horse's male parent.

SIT-STILL—Riding style in which jockey defers whipping as long as possible; of ride by jockey who loses race without apparent exertion; "sit chilly."

SIXTEENTH POLE—Colored post on infield rail one-half furlong before finish wire.

SKIN—Increase track speed by rolling and hardening the cushion.

SKINNED TRACK—Dirt track, contrasted to grass.

SKITTISH—Of a nervous, flighty horse.

SLAB-SIDED—Of horse whose last rib is not close to hip, suggesting a long, weak back.

SLEEPER—Underestimated horse that surprises, or could.

SLOPPY—Of racing strip covered with puddles but not muddy, base of track not yet softened by moisture.

SLOT—Post position.

SLOW—Of track wetter than good, but not muddy.

SLOW PILL—Sedative to dull horse's nervous system, preventing it from performing well.

SMART MONEY—Bets by insiders or sharp handicappers; insiders.

SNATCH—Sudden violent action with reins, halter or shank; "snatch up," "snatch around."

SNIP—Small white or flesh-colored patch on horse's nose.

SNUG—Keep horse under tight rein during race or work; "snug back," "snug hold."

SOCKS—White ankles.

SOLID—Of a fit horse in a suitable race.

SOPHOMORE—Three-year-old.

SPANISH BIT—Painful bit used in schooling fractious horses.

SPARK—Use a battery in race.

SPAVIN—Bony outcropping of inflamed joints.

SPECIAL WEIGHTS—Even weights prescribed mainly in non-claiming maiden races and modified only by age, sex, or apprentice allowances.

SPEEDY CUT—Leg injury from contact with opposite hoof while racing or working.

SPIT OUT THE BIT—When tired horse slows, easing its pressure on the bit.

SPLINT—Bony growth on horse's shin.

SPLIT RACE—Of a large field divided in two.

SPLITS—Fractional running times stated not cumulatively but according to the separate clocking of each quarter-mile fraction.

SPONGE—Insert sponge or other foreign object in horse's nostrils, impairing respiration and preventing true performance.

SPOT—Concede weight to another horse; opportunity for winning race or bet.

SPOT PLAY—When bettor risks money only on exceptionally playable race, outstanding horse, or at attractive odds.

SPRING HALT—Nerve-muscle affliction causing spasms in hind legs.

STALE—Of an overworked horse; of a horse, to urinate.

STALL GATE—Starting gate.

STALLION—Entire male horse.

STALL WALKER—Restless horse that paces stall.

STAND—Of a stallion, to be a stud.

STAR—White marking on horse's forehead.

START—Compete in race; leave starting gate.

STARTER'S LIST—Horses suspended from racing for poor behavior at starting gate.

STAYER—A dependable router.

STEADY—Restrain horse to prevent it from running into others or help it recover after stumbling.

STICK—Whip.

STICKER—Horseshoe cleat.

STICK HORSE—One that performs better when whipped.

STIFF—Deliberately prevent horse from winning; unfit or outclassed horse or one being stiffed.

STIFLE—Front of horse's thigh.

STING—Use battery in race.

STIRRUPS—Where mounted rider supports feet; irons.

STOCKINGS—White color from ankle toward knee. Longer than socks.

STOOPER—Person who prowls tracks in search of cashable mutuel tickets lost or mistakenly discarded by others.

STRAIGHT—Win bet; "straight, place, and show."

STRAIGHT AS A STRING—Of horse all-out to win; "strung out."

STRAIGHTAWAY—Straight part of track; stretch.

STRETCH CALL—Position in homestretch when call is taken for results charts, usually a furlong from finish wire.

STRETCH TURN—The bend that leads into homestretch.

STRIDE—Horse's way of going or amount of ground it covers after each foot has landed on ground once.

STRING—Horses owned by one stable or trained by one person.

STRIP—Racing strip; narrow white marking on horse's face.

STRIPE—Marking similar to strip, but longer.

STUD—Stallion; breeding farm.

STUDBOOK—Official Thoroughbred registry; a stallion's mating schedule.

STUDDISH—Of young colt aggressively hard to handle.

STUD FEE—Payment by breeder to owner of stallion for its stud services.

SUBSCRIPTION—Fee paid to enter horse in stakes.

SULK—Of horse that refuses to run or fails to respond to rider's guidance.

SURCINGLE—Strap that holds blanket on horse.

SURE THING—Of a horse regarded as a sure winner.

SUSPENSION—Punishment that makes person temporarily ineligible to ride or work at track.

SWAMP FEVER—Infectious equine anemia, a major medical problem among horses.

SWEAT THE BRASS—Overwork a horse.

SWEEPSTAKES—A stakes race.

TACK—Horse's reins and other equipment; jockey's gear.

TAG—Claiming price.

TAIL FEMALE—Horse's female ancestry from dam backward.

TAIL MALE—Horse's male ancestry from sire backward.

TAKE—Money deducted from each mutuel pool for track and government revenue; takeout.

TAKE BACK—Restrain a horse to give it a breather during race or to avoid trouble.

TAKE CARE OF—Of jockeys who violently prevent others from winning, either to win themselves or for revenge.

TAKE DOWN—Disqualify a horse that finishes in money, signified by removing or lowering its number on the list of leading finishers posted on the infield board.

TAKEOUT—Take.

TAKE UP—Slow suddenly to avoid collision or other trouble.

TAP-ROOT MARE—Founding ancestress of a Thoroughbred family.

TEASER—Cheap stallion that tests mare's readiness for mating.

TELETIMER—Electronic equipment that times races, flashes fractional and final times on tote board.

TENDERFOOT—Sore-footed horse.

THIEF—Unreliable, "dishonest" horse that runs worst when expected to perform well.

THIRD SIRE—Horse's paternal great-grandfather.

THOROUGHPIN—A large bog spavin that may go entirely through upper hock.

THREE-EIGHTHS POLE—Colored post on infield rail three furlongs before finish wire.

THREE-QUARTER POLE—Colored post on infield rail six furlongs before finish wire.

THROAT LATCH—Area outside upper section of horse's throat.

THRUSH—Inflammation of frog.

TICK—One-fifth of a second.

TIED ON—Reins knotted and crossed, for stout hold.

TIGHT—Fit and ready.

TIGHTENER—Race or work intended to bring horse to peak form.

TIMBER—Hurdle or other obstacle in jump race.

TIMBER RIDER—Steeplechase jockey.

TIMBER TOPPER—Horse that races over jumps.

TOE PLATE—Shoe with front cleat to prevent slipping.

TONGUE STRAP—Band that ties horse's tongue down to prevent animal from swallowing it during race or workout or to prevent interference with bit.

TOP HORSE—One listed first in program of race.

TOP LINE—Male side of pedigree.

TOP WEIGHT—Heaviest impost in field.

TOTALISATOR—Automatic pari-mutuel machinery that records bets as they are made and calculates odds.

TOW ROPE—Win from wire to wire as if hauling others on a rope.

TRACK KITCHEN—Backstretch mess hall.

TRACKMASTER—Executive in charge of maintaining racing strip.

TRAINING TRACK—Auxiliary track for workouts.

TRAPPY—Of a nimble, kind horse.

TRAVEL IN STRAW—Ship with the horses, like stablehands.

TRIAL—A preparatory race; a workout in which horse is asked for top speed.

TRIPLE CROWN—Mythical award to three-year-old that wins Kentucky Derby, Preakness Stakes, and Belmont Stakes.

TROUBLE LINE—Brief comment at end of each past-performance line in Eastern editions of *Daily Racing Form*.

TUCKED UP—Sudden abdominal slenderness associated with overwork.

TURF COURSE—Grass track.

TURN OUT—Send horse to farm for pasturage and rest.

TWITCH—Noose around horse's nose and upper lip. When tightened, inflicts pain to keep horse tractable in starting gate or saddling enclosure.

UNDERLAY—Of a horse going at odds lower than its real chances warrant.

UNDER WRAPS—Of horse prevented from extending itself in workout or race.

UNWIND—Taper off horse's training before resting it or sending it to stud.

UP—Of the rider assigned to a horse; the pre-race order to jockeys, "Riders up!"

URINE TEST—Chemical analysis of horse's urine in search of illegal drugs.

USED UP—Of an exhausted horse.

VALET—One who carries tack and takes care of jockey's clothing.

VAN—Motor truck for shipping horses; to ship in that way.

VARIANT—Difference between official and normal racing times caused by weather or track texture; speed variant; track variant.

VEER—Swerve.

VET'S LIST—Ill or injured horses declared ineligible for racing by track veterinarian.

VICE—Undesirable habit of horse.

WAKE-UP—Horse that wins unexpectedly after showing poor form.

WALKING RING—Oval near saddling enclosure, where horses walk and jockeys mount before leaving for pre-race post parade.

WALKOVER—Race from which all but one horse have been scratched, permitting horse to win by walking the distance.

WARM-UP—Pre-race gallop.

WASHY—Of a heavily sweating horse.

WAY OF GOING—Horse's manner of running at full stride.

WEANLING—Newly weaned horse.

WEAVE—Move with swaying, rocking motion in stall; follow erratic course during race or work.

WEBFOOT—Mudder.

WEIGH IN—Of jockeys weighed with tack after race.

WEIGH OUT—Of jockeys weighed with tack before race.

WEIGHT-FOR-AGE RACE—When horses carry weights prescribed by the scale of weights.

WELL LET DOWN—Of horse with long, arched ribs, long forearms, and short cannon bones for good lung capacity and lengthy stride.

WELL RIBBED UP—Of horse that is short-coupled, with a strong back.

WELL-SPRUNG RIBS—Full, arched ribs for lung capacity.

WELTERWEIGHTS—Imposts 28 pounds over those of the official scale of weights.

WHEEL—Turn sharply, like a pinwheel; in multiple betting, combinations of tickets involving bettor's prime selection with every other horse.

WHISTLE—Noisy equine breathing, caused by swollen respiratory tissues.

WHOOP-DE-DOO—Riding style dependent on early speed and much whipping.

WIND—Horse's lung capacity.

WIND SUCKER—Horse that swallows air.

WINTER—Spend that season out of competition.

WITHERS—High point of horse's back, forward of saddle.

WOUND UP—Of a fit, ready horse.

YEARLING—A horse on the January 1 following its birth, and for the year thereafter.

YOUNGSTER—Two-year-old.

INDEX

Page numbers in bold type refer to Encyclopedia articles.